The Talmud
of the
Land of Israel

Chicago Studies in the History of Judaism
Edited by Jacob Neusner

The University of Chicago Press
Chicago and London

The Talmud of the Land of Israel

*A Preliminary
Translation and
Explanation*

Volume 27   Sotah

Translated by   Jacob Neusner

JACOB NEUSNER is University Professor and the Ungerleider Distinguished Scholar of Judaic Studies at Brown University. In addition to
editing and translating *The Talmud of the Land of Israel*, he is the au-
thor of many books, including *Judaism: The Evidence of the Mishnah*
and *Judaism in Society: The Evidence of the Yerushalmi*.

The University of Chicago Press, Chicago 60637
The University of Chicago Press, Ltd., London

© 1984 by The University of Chicago
All rights reserved. Published 1984
Printed in the United States of America

93 92 91 90 89 88 87 86 85 84   5 4 3 2 1

Library of Congress Cataloging in Publication Data
Main entry under title:

Sotah.

  (The Talmud of the land of Israel ; v. 27) (Chicago
studies in the history of Judaism)
    Bibliography: p.
    Includes index.
    1. Talmud Yerushalmi. Sotah—Commentaries.
I. Neusner, Jacob, 1932–   . II. Title. III. Series:
Talmud Yerushalmi. English. 1982 ; v. 27. IV. Series:
Chicago studies in the history of Judaism.
BM498.5.E5   1982   vol. 27   296.1'2407s   84-14
[BM506.S7]   [296.1'2407]
ISBN 0-226-57687-6

For Eugene Borowitz, who has made
theology of Judaism accessible and important to
a whole new age

Contents

Foreword

This translation into English of the Talmud of the Land of Israel ("Palestinian Talmud," "Talmud Yerushalmi") is preliminary and provisional, even though it is not apt to be replaced for some time. It is preliminary, first, because a firm and final text for translation is not in hand; second, because a modern commentary of a philological and *halakhic* character is not yet available; and third, because even the lower criticism of the text has yet to be undertaken. Consequently, the meanings imputed to the Hebrew and Aramaic words and the sense ascribed to them in this translation at best are merely a first step. When a systematic effort at the lower criticism of the extant text has been completed, a complete philological study and modern dictionary along comparative lines made available, and a commentary based on both accomplished, then the present work will fall away, having served for the interim. Unhappily, as I said, that interim is apt to be protracted. Text critics, lexicographers, and exegetes are not apt to complete their work on the Yerushalmi within this century.

The purpose of this preliminary translation is to make possible a set of historical and religions-historical studies on the formation of Judaism in the land of Israel from the closure of the Mishnah to the completion of the Talmud of the land of Israel and the time of the composition of the first *midrashic* compilations. Clearly, no historical, let alone religions-historical, work can be contemplated without a theory of the principal document and source for the study, the Palestinian Talmud. No theory can be attempted, however tentative and provisional, without a complete, prior statement of what the document appears to wish to say and how its materials seem to have come to closure. It follows that the natural next steps, beyond my now-finished history of Mishnaic law and account of the Judaism revealed in that history, carry us to the present project. Even those steps, when they are taken, will have to be charted with all due regard to the pitfalls of a translation that is preliminary, based upon a text that as yet has not been subjected even to the clarifying exercises of lower criticism. Questions will have to be shaped appropriate to the parlous state of the evidence. But even if the historical and religions-historical program were to be undertaken in the Hebrew language, instead of in English, those who might wish to carry on inquiries into the history of the Jews and of Judaism in the land of Israel in the third and fourth centuries would face precisely the same task we do. No one can proceed without a systematic account of the evidence and a theory of how the evidence may, and may not, be utilized. Further explanation of the plan and execution of this work will be found in volume 34, pages x–xiv. The glossary, abbreviations, and bibliography for the whole series are in volume 34, pp. 225–31.

It remains only to thank those who helped with this volume.

My student, Mr. Louis Newman, checked my translation against the Leiden Manuscript and the *editio princeps*, and saved me a great deal of tedious work in so doing. He also uncovered more than a few points requiring attention and correction. I am grateful for his hard and careful work. Professor Alan J. Avery-Peck of Tulane University served as the critical reader for this volume. I am thankful for the many corrections and observations supplied by him, and still more, for his willingness to take time out to study this tractate and so improve my work on it. I retain full responsibility for whatever unsolved problems and deficiencies may remain.

Introduction to Sotah

The tractate before us deals with the ordeal to which the accused wife is forced to submit if her husband expresses jealousy concerning her behavior and if she then ignores him. A fair proportion of the Mishnah's consideration of the theme of the ordeal consists of the story of what happens to such a woman. This topic covers the first six chapters. The tractate proceeds in the next three to consider two further matters, the laws of draft exemption in time of war, and the neglected corpse, Deut. 20:1–9 and Deut. 21:1–9, respectively. The link between the materials on the accused wife, chapters one through six, and the materials on draft exemptions and the neglected corpse, chapters eight and nine, is a list of rites conducted only in the Hebrew language, chapter seven. These include the ordeal of the accused wife, the speech of the anointed for battle, and the declaration of the elders of the town nearest the neglected corpse.

The biblical passage on the accused wife is at Num. 5:1–31 and reads as follows:

The Lord said to Moses, "Command the people of Israel that they put out of the camp every leper, and every one having a discharge, and every one that is unclean through contact with the dead; you shall put out both male and female, putting them outside the camp, that they may not defile their camp, in the midst of which I dwell." And the people of Israel did so, and drove them outside of the camp; as the Lord said to Moses, so the people of Israel did.

And the Lord said to Moses, "Say to the people of Israel, When a man or a woman commits any of the sins that men commit by breaking faith with the Lord, and that person is guilty, he shall confess his sin which he has committed; and he shall make full restitution for his wrong, adding a fifth to it, and giving it to him to whom he did the wrong. But if the man has no kinsman to whom restitution may be made for the wrong, the restitution for wrong shall go to the Lord for the priest, in addition to the ram of atonement with which atonement is made for him. And every offering, all the holy things of the people of Israel, which they bring to the priest, shall be his; and every man's holy things shall be his; whatever any man gives to the priest shall be his."

And the Lord said to Moses, "Say to the people of Israel, If any man's wife goes astray and acts unfaithfully against him, if a man lies with her carnally, and it is hidden from the eyes of her husband, and she is undetected though she has defiled herself, and there is no witness against her, since she was not taken in the act; and if the spirit of jealousy comes upon him, and he is jealous of his wife who has defiled herself; or if the spirit of jealousy comes upon him, and he is jealous of his wife, though she has not defiled herself; then the man shall bring his wife to the priest, and bring the offering required of her, a tenth of an *ephah* of barley meal; he shall pour no oil upon it and put no frankincense on it, for it is a cereal offering of jealousy, a cereal offering of remembrance, bringing iniquity to remembrance.

"And the priest shall bring her near, and set her before the Lord; and the priest shall take holy water in an earthen vessel, and take some of the dust that is on the floor of the tabernacle and put it into the water.

"And the priest shall set the woman before the Lord, and unbind the hair of the woman's head, and place in her hands the cereal offering of remembrance, which is the cereal offering of jealousy. And in his hand the priest shall have the water of bitterness that brings the curse. Then the priest shall make her take an oath, saying, 'If no man has lain with you, and if you have not turned aside to uncleanness, while you were under your husband's authority, be free from this water of bitterness that brings the curse. But if you have gone astray, though you are under your husband's authority, and if you have defiled yourself, and some man other than your husband has lain with you, then' (let the priest make the woman take the oath of the curse, and say to the woman) 'the Lord make you an execration and an oath among your people, when the Lord makes your thigh fall away and your body swell; may this water that brings the curse pass into your bowels and make your body swell and your thigh fall away.' And the woman shall say, 'Amen, Amen.'

"Then the priest shall write these curses in a book, and wash them off into the water of bitterness; and he shall make the woman drink the water of bitterness that brings the curse, and the water that brings the curse shall enter into her and cause bitter pain. And the priest shall take the cereal offering of jealousy out of the woman's hand, and shall wave the cereal offering before the Lord and bring it to the altar; and the priest shall take a handful of the cereal offering, as its memorial portion, and burn it upon the altar, and afterward shall make the woman drink the water. And when he has made her drink the water, then, if she has defiled herself and has acted unfaithfully against her husband, the water that brings the curse shall enter into her and cause bitter pain, and her body shall swell, and her thigh shall fall away, and the woman shall become an execration among her people. But if the woman has not defiled herself and is clean, then she shall be free and shall conceive children.

"This is the law in cases of jealousy, when a wife, though under her husband's authority, goes astray and defiles herself, or when the spirit of jealousy comes upon a man and he is jealous of his wife; then he shall set the woman before the Lord, and the priest shall execute upon her all this law. The man shall be free from iniquity, but the woman shall bear her iniquity."

The first six chapters of the tractate fall into two main parts, the narrative center and some miscellaneous materials before and after it. The narrative runs through the first three chapters, as indicated in the following outline. Then we have a miscellany of materials on women who do not have to undergo the ordeal, with special attention to the matter of conflicting testimony and other sorts of evidence that the women should undergo the rite or should be exempted from doing so. This final unit ends where the treatment of the accused wife's ordeal began. The exposition of the topic through narrative, on the one side, and an exercise in some obvious formalities, on the other, complete the treatment of the topic.

I. Invoking the ordeal (1:1–3)

1:1   He who expresses jealousy to his wife [concerning her relations with another man]—Eliezer says, "He does so before two witnesses and imposes on her the requirement of drinking the bitter water on the testimony of a single witness or even on his own testimony." Joshua: Two required at both stages.

1:2   How does he express jealousy to her.

1:3   And these women are prohibited from eating heave offering and five other prohibitions. Including she whose husband has sexual relations with her on route to Jerusalem for the ordeal. Two disciples of sages accompany the couple.

Narrative of the ordeal (1:4–3:5, 6–8)

1:4–6   They would bring her up to the high court in Jerusalem and admonish her. Narrative.

1:7–9   By that same measure by which a man metes out, they mete out to him. Extensive aggadic interlude.

2:1   The husband would bring her meal offering in a basket of palm twigs. Triplet: Comparison of this meal offering to all others.

2:2–3   The husband would bring a new clay bowl, etc. The narrative continues.

2:4   The writing of the scroll.

2:5–6   To what does she say, 'Amen, Amen.' Six-part construction.

3:1–2   He would take her meal offering. . . . He waved it. The narrative continues.

3:3   Triplet: If before the scroll is blotted out, she said, "I am not going to drink the water," her scroll is put away. Two further situations.

3:4–5   She hardly has sufficed to drink it before her face turns yellow, her eyes bulge out, and her veins swell, etc. Narrative continues.

3:6–8   If her meal offering was made unclean before it was sanctified in a utensil, it is redeemed. If afterward, it is burned. These are the ones whose meal offerings are to be burned and six other categories. Difference between priest and priest girl, difference between man and woman, twelve entries in all.

Rules of the ordeal (4:1–6:4)

A. *Exemptions and applicability.* 4:1–5:1, 2–5

4:1   A betrothed girl, a childless brother's widow awaiting levirate marriage—neither undergo the ordeal of drinking the water nor receive a marriage contract. Widow married to a high priest, etc., likewise.

4:2   And these do not undergo the ordeal of drinking the bitter water or receive a marriage contract.

4:3   A woman pregnant by another husband and one giving suck to a child by another husband do not undergo the ordeal of drinking the water and do not receive the marriage contract, so Meir. Sages.

4:4   The wife of a priest drinks the water and if proved innocent can go back to her husband.

4:5   And these are women whom a court subjects to warning in behalf of a husband who cannot do so.

5:1   Just as the water puts her to the proof, so it puts the suspected adulterer to the proof, so Aqiba.

5:2–5   On that day did Aqiba expound—construction of three items, all of them irrelevant to this tractate, and an appendix.

B. *Testimony and exemptions from the ordeal.* 6:1–4

6:1   He who expressed jealousy to his wife, but she went aside in secret, "even if he heard from a bird, he puts her away, but pays off her marriage contract," so Eliezer. Joshua.

6:2–3   If one witness said, "I saw that she was made unclean," she would not undergo the ordeal.

6:4   If one witness says, "She was made unclean," and one says, "She was not," if one says, "She was unclean," and two say, "She was not," she would undergo the ordeal. If two say, "She was made unclean," and one says, "She was not," she would not undergo the ordeal.

The second part of the tractate begins with a catalogue of rites said in any language and those said only in Hebrew. It is the latter set of rites that is worked out. Chapter seven, which follows, contains the catalogue.

IV. **Rites conducted in Hebrew** (7:1–9:15)

A. *A catalogue.* 7:1–8

7:1–2 These are said in any language—and these are said only in Hebrew. The pericope of the accused wife heads the list, explaining the connection between chapters one through six and chapters seven through nine. 7:2: These are said only in Hebrew along with first fruits, *halisah*, blessings and curses, blessing of priests, blessing of high priest, pericope of the king, pericope of the heifer whose neck is to be broken, and of the anointed for battle.

7:3   Verses of the first fruits—how so?

7:4   *Halisah*—how so?

7:5   Blessings and curses—how so?

7:6   Blessings of the priests—how so?

7:7   Blessing of the high priest—how so?

7:8   The pericope of the king—how so?

B. *The anointed for battle and the draft exemptions.* 8:1–7
The Scriptural passage on the draft exemptions is at Deut. 20:1–9:

When you go forth to war against your enemies, and see horses and chariots and an army larger than your own, you shall not be afraid of them; for the Lord your God is with you, who brought you up out of the land of Egypt. And when you draw near to the battle, the priest shall come forward and speak to the people, and shall say to them, "Hear, O Israel, you draw near this day to battle against your enemies: let not your heart faint; do not fear, or tremble, or be in dread of them; for the Lord your God is he that goes with you, to fight for you against your enemies, to give you the victory." Then the officers shall speak to the people, saying, "What man is there that has built a new house and has not dedicated it? Let him go back to his house, lest he die in the battle and another man dedicate it. And what man is there that has planted a vineyard and has not enjoyed its fruit? Let him go back to his house, lest he die in the battle and another man enjoy its fruit. And what man is there that has betrothed a wife and has not taken her? Let him go back to his house, lest he die in the battle and another man take her." And the officers shall speak further to the people, and say, "What man is there that is fearful and fainthearted? Let him go back to his house, lest the heart of his fellows melt as his heart." And when the officers have made an end of speaking to the people, then commanders shall be appointed at the head of the people.

8:1   The anointed for battle speaks in Hebrew. Exegesis of Deut. 20:1–4.
8:2   Exegesis of Deut. 20:5–6.
8:3   Continuation of foregoing on draft exemptions.
8:4   These are the ones who do not move from their place: continuation of foregoing. Exegesis of Deut. 24:5.
8:5   Exegesis of Deut. 20:8.
8:6   Exegesis of Deut. 20:9.
8:7   Completion of foregoing construction.

The concluding subdivision of the unit turns to the rite of the heifer offered when a neglected corpse turns up.

C. *The rite of the heifer.* 9:1–9, 10–15
   The law of the neglected corpse is at Deut. 21:1–9:

If in the land which the Lord your God gives you to possess, any one is found slain, lying in the open country, and it is not known who killed him, then your elders and your judges shall come forth, and they shall measure the distance to the cities which are around him that is slain; and the elders of the city which is nearest to the slain man shall take a heifer which has never been worked and which has not pulled in the yoke. And the elders of that city shall bring the heifer down to a valley with running water, which is neither plowed nor sown, and shall break the heifer's neck there in the valley. And the priests the sons of Levi shall come forward, for the Lord your God has chosen them to minister to him and to bless in the name of the Lord, and by their word every dispute and every assault shall be settled. And all the elders of that city nearest to the slain man shall wash their hands over the heifer whose neck was broken in the valley; and they shall testify, "Our hands did not shed this blood, neither did our eyes see it shed. Forgive, O Lord, thy people Israel, whom thou hast redeemed, and set not the guilt of innocent blood in the midst of thy people Israel; but let the guilt of blood be forgiven them." So you shall purge the guilt of innocent blood from your midst, when you do what is right in the sight of the Lord.

9:1   The rite of the heifer is said in Hebrew.

9:2–4   Exegesis of Deut. 21:1. Measuring the distance from the neglected corpse to the nearby town. Triplet.

9:5   Narrative of rite.

9:6   The narrative continued. Exegesis of Deut. 21:8.

9:7   Triplet: If the murderer was found before the neck was broken, the heifer goes forth to the herd. If afterward, the heifer is buried. If later on the murderer is found, he is tried.

9:8   Triplet: If one witness says, "I saw the murderer," and one says, "You did not see him," etc. It must be in a case of doubt (parallel: M. 6:4).

9:9   Aggadic conclusion to the whole: When murderers became many, the rite of breaking the neck was cancelled; when adulterers became many, the ordeal of the bitter water was cancelled.

9:10   Appendix: The cessation of ancient practices. Yohanan did away with confession.

9:11–13   Appendix continued: Cancellation of Sanhedrin led to end of singing at wedding feasts, etc.

9:14   Triplet: In the war against Vespasian, they decreed against wearing of wreaths by bridegrooms, etc.

9:15   Cessation of virtues with the death of great sages, parallel to cessation of various celebration rites at the destruction of the Temple.

1 Yerushalmi Sotah
Chapter One

1:1

[166/A]   *He who expresses jealousy to his wife [concerning her relations with another man (Num. 5:14)]—*

[B]   *R. Eliezer says, "He expresses jealousy before two witnesses, and he imposes on her the requirement of drinking the bitter water on the testimony of a single witness or [even] on his own evidence [that she has been alone with the named man]."*

[C]   *R. Joshua says, "He expresses jealousy before two witnesses, and he requires her to drink the bitter water before two witnesses."*

[I.A]   It is written, "If the spirit of jealousy comes upon him, and he is jealous of his wife who has defiled herself" (Num. 5:14).

[B]   [The meaning is] that he should not express a spirit of jealousy toward her in a moment of levity or idle chatter, or in a setting of light-headedness or harsh argument, but in a spirit of patience [reversing the order of the penultimate and ultimate items].

[C]   If he transgressed and expressed his jealousy to her in one of these ways, what is the law?

[D]   Have these matters been expressed [merely] as a matter of what is religious duty, [or does the violation of these conditions constitute] an invalidating fact [so that the act of jealousy has not been properly carried out]?

[E]   If you say that [they have been listed merely] as a matter of what is religious duty, then his act of declaring jealousy is valid.

9

[F]   If you say [that violation of these conditions constitutes] an in-
       validating fact, then the act of declaring jealousy has not been
       properly carried out.

[G]   The answer is as follows: At any point [in the cited passage
       (Num. 5:11–13)] in which the language "ordinance" [or] "To-
       rah" is used, [then what is specified is essential to the perfor-
       mance of the rite, with the result that failure to carry out the
       law as specified] constitutes an invalidating fact.

[II.A] R. Joshua said in the name of R. Eliezer, "It is a firm obliga-
       tion [for a husband to express his jealousy to the wife, should
       occasion warrant it]. [He has no choice.]"

[B]   R. Joshua said, "It is a matter of choice."

[C]   Said R. Eleazar b. R. Yosé before R. Yosa, "The opinion of R.
       Eliezer [that it is a firm obligation] accords with the position of
       the House of Shammai [which is cited presently].

[D]   "And the opinion of R. Joshua accords with the position of the
       House of Hillel."

[E]   That the opinion of R. Eliezer accords with the position of the
       House of Shammai is in the following context:

[F]   The House of Shammai say, "A man should divorce his wife
       only if he discovered in her a matter of adultery."

[G]   If then he discovered in her ugly things, as to divorcing her, he
       has no right, for he has not found in her a matter of adultery.

[H]   But to keep her as his wife, he has no right, for, [after all], he
       did discover ugly things about her.

[I]   On that account, [Eliezer] says, "It is an obligation [to go
       through with the rite of finding out whether or not the wife has
       committed adultery, since he has no alternative]."

[J]   For lo, it has been taught on the authority of the House of
       Shammai, "I know [as grounds for divorce] only the case of the
       woman who goes forth [from marriage] by reason of having
       committed adultery.

[K]   "How do I know [the law pertaining to] her who goes forth [in
       public] with her hair disheveled, her clothing in shambles [so
       that her skin shows], and her arms uncovered?

[L] "Scripture says, '. . . because he has found some indecency in her' " (Deut. 24:1). [The term "some" is understood to encompass the offenses listed at K.]

[M] [A further point:] R. Mana said, "[The husband has the right to divorce the wife on account of ugly matters, short of proof of adultery, only] it is when the matter is confirmed through witnesses.

[N] "But in the present context [the husband has the right to administer the rite] without witnesses [confirming what she has done]."

[O] And the opinion of R. Joshua accords with the position of the House of Hillel.

[P] For the House of Hillel say, "[Appropriate grounds for divorce include] even a case in which she burned his soup."

[Q] On that account, [Joshua] says, "It is a matter of choice [and not an obligation, to impose the rite of the bitter water.]"

[R] If he wants to express jealousy, he expresses jealousy.

[S] If he wants to divorce her, he divorces her.

[III.A] And what is the Scriptural basis for the position of R. Eliezer [at M. 1:1B]?

[B] "For he has found a matter of indecency in her" (Deut. 24:1).

[C] "Indecency" refers to her going in secret with another man.

[D] "Matter" refers to the rite of expressing jealousy.

[E] [As to the word "matter":] Matter [is stated here, and] matter [is stated later on; "On the evidence of two witnesses shall a matter be sustained" (Deut. 19:15)].

[F] Just as, in that other context, two witnesses are required, so, in the present matter, two witnesses are required.

[G] *And he imposes on her the requirement of drinking the bitter water on the testimony of a single witness or even on his own evidence [M. 1:1B].*

[H] "If she acts unfaithfully against him" (Num. 5:12)—[this is confirmed, even if there are no further witnesses], in accord with the stipulations which [the husband] made with her in the presence of others. [That is, if in the presence of others he has made certain stipulations, then his own evidence suffices that these known stipulations have been violated.]

[**IV**.A]   It was taught: **R. Yosé b. R. Judah says in the name of R. Eliezer, "He expresses jealousy on the testimony of a single witness or even on his own evidence.**

[B]   **"And he imposes the requirement of drinking the bitter water on the testimony of two witnesses [that she has been alone with the named man] [vs. M. 1:1B] [T. Sot. 1:1].**

[C]   "Here it is stated, 'For he has found a matter of indecency in her'—

[D]   "and 'finding' in all contexts means in the presence of [two] witnesses.

[E]   "How does R. Eliezer interpret the word 'matter'?

[F]   "It refers to any sort of thing which is apt to result in an act of adultery."

[**V**.A]   [In accord with Eliezer's position at M. 1:1B,] as to imposing the requirement of drinking the bitter water on the testimony of a single witness, what [is the basis for that position]?

[B]   Now if what he himself says, which prevents the imposition upon him of the requirement of taking an oath governing monetary matters, suffices to require the wife to undergo the ordeal of drinking the bitter water,

[C]   the evidence of a single witness, which does have the power to require him to take an oath covering monetary matters—is it not an argument a fortiori [that that evidence should suffice to require the wife to undergo the rite!]

[D]   As to a relative, what is the law as to his having the power to testify and so require the wife to undergo the rite?

[E]   Who is closer and more closely related than her husband!

[F]   A witness who reports only what he has heard—what is the law as to his having the power to impose upon her the requirement to undergo the ordeal?

[G]   What is the difference between such a witness and a relative?

[H]   As to a relative, even though at this moment he is not valid to give testimony, he may become valid in the future.

[I]   But a witness who testifies what he has heard from another party will never be valid, neither now nor in the future. [Accordingly, hearsay evidence is excluded.]

[VI.A]   What is the Scriptural basis for the position of R. Joshua?

[B]   "For he has found a matter of indecency in her" (Deut. 24:1)—

[C]   "Matter" refers to expressing jealousy.

[D]   "For he has found"—and there is no finding except before witnesses [hence, two witnesses are required for the expression of jealousy and the warning not to associate with a given man]. [Omitted following Pené Moshe: And he expresses jealousy before a single witness or on his own evidence, etc.]

[E]   How does R. Joshua interpret Scripture's reference to indecency?

[F]   It is indecency which comes about on account of the matter [concerning which he had warned her to begin with].

[VII.A]   [Reverting to III.A–B:] [Sages] replied to the position of R. Yosé b. R. Judah, "[If the husband claims to have warned the wife on the basis of his own evidence, or on the basis of a single witness, and that suffices,] then there is no end to the matter [since the husband can always claim, without corroborating evidence, to have warned the wife about thus-and-so] [T. Sot. 1:1].

[B]   "Does he have the power to express jealousy to her in private, and then to bring witnesses that she indeed went in secret with the named man, so as to invalidate her right to collect her marriage settlement? [Surely not.]"

[C]   Said R. Yosé, "What business did she have to go in private [with another man anyhow, whether warned or not]? [In any event by the law of the Torah, she may then lose her rights to her marriage settlement.]

[D]   "But [the question raised at A] concerns [the Eliezer] of our Mishnah passage: '[Eliezer wants the jealousy expressed before two witnesses, but the requirement to drink the water may be on the husband's own testimony or that of a single witness, M. 1:1B].'

[E]   "Does he have the power to express jealousy to her [Pené Moshe: before two witnesses and then] to state that she had gone in private with the named man and so to invalidate her right to collect her marriage settlement on the basis of his own testimony? [Surely not.]"

[F]   Said R. Mana, "Even in accord with that Tanna [namely, Yosé b. R. Judah], the question remains a valid one [and must be dealt with, contrary to C–E].

[G]   "It is in accord with the one who has said that the husband has a right to express jealousy to her [and warn her from going in private] even with her father or her son.

[H]   "Does he have the power to express jealousy to her in regard to her father or her son and to bring witnesses that she has gone in private with them so as to invalidate her right to collect her marriage contract? [Surely not!]

[I]   "If now you say, 'What business did she have to go in private with them,' the Torah indeed has permitted her to go in private [with her father or her son]. [So, in accord with the present context, she had every right to do what she did, and, accordingly, we may now say, 'There is no end to the matter!' "]

[J]   [The position that the law is as just now stated is explained next.] For R. Yohanan has said in the name of R. Simeon b. Yohai, "It is written, 'If your brother, the son of your mother, or your son, or your daughter, or the wife of your bosom, . . . entices you in secret . . . (Deut. 13:6).

[K]   " 'Your daughter in secret, and your mother in secret . . .'— [this indicates that] a man may go in private with his mother and live with her, with his daughter and live with her, with his sister, but he may not live with her."

[VIII.A]   Witnesses who testify that the husband has expressed jealousy [concerning a particular man] who are proved to be perjurers are flogged [on account of committing perjury].

[B]   Witnesses to her going in private with the named man, who turn out to be perjurers, you will certainly say are flogged.

[C]   But what is the law as to their having to pay [the value of her marriage settlement, of which they have conspired to deprive her]?

[D]   [Do we say that] it is not by reason of the strength of their testimony that she lost her marriage settlement, [but, rather, that she would have lost it anyway]?

[E]   Or do we say that the law is in accord with that which R. Ba, R. Judah in the name of Samuel stated: "In the rules governing perjured witnesses, they do not derive one matter [16c] from some other? [That is, in the present case, we do not invoke the reason given at D, because the punishment of perjurers is a distinct legal matter, governed by its own logic and rules, and we do indeed do to the perjurers what they conspired to do, even if they did not really have the power to effect their conspiracy.] And here, they do pay." [This question is not answered.]

[**IX**.A]   If the wife was accused by one witness of having gone in the morning in private [with the named man], and if she then was accused by another witness of having gone in the evening in private with the named man, [what is the law]? [Does this constitute testimony which is joined together, so that, in Joshua's view, that case is now complete?]

[B]   The answer to that question is in accord with the following:

[C]   **If two people saw her continue alone with the husband [after she had gotten her writ of divorce from him], she does require a second writ of divorce from him. If only one person saw it, she does not require a second writ of divorce from him. If one saw it in the morning and one at twilight—this was an actual case, and R. Eleazar b. Tadai came and asked sages, who ruled, "It is only a single witness [at a time], and she does not require a second writ of divorce from him" [T. Git. 5:40–S] [So also at A the witnesses do not join together.]**

[**X**.A]   If the husband expressed jealousy to her in the presence of a single witness in the morning, and in the presence of another witness at the eventide, since this is a single person [who has expressed the jealousy, namely the husband], and she is a single person [to whom the jealousy was expressed], do we say that this is a valid act of expressing jealousy or not?

[B]   Let us derive the answer from the following:

[C]   The evidence of witnesses is not combined [so that we have the testimony of two witnesses] unless the two of them saw the incident simultaneously.

[D]   R. Joshua b. Qorha says, "Even if they saw it sequentially [it is combined]."

[E]   R. Jeremiah, R. Samuel bar Isaac in the name of Rab: "Sages [= C] concede to R. Joshua b. Qorha in the matter of witnesses to the claim of one to be the first-born and in the case of witnesses to the claim of one to have established rights of ownership through usucaption, [that successive, not only simultaneous, witness, is acceptable]."

[F]   Rabba in the name of R. Jeremiah: "Also in the case of testimony as to the presence of the signs of puberty, the fact is the same, [that successive witnesses join together]."

[G]   This is indeed self-evident. If one says, "I saw two hairs in his privy parts," and the other said, "I saw two hairs on his body," [the two statements are acceptable as joined testimony that the person is now mature].

[H]   [If] one says, "I saw a single hair on his privy parts," and one says, "I saw a single hair on his belly and nothing more,"—all the more so do we deem a hair on his privy parts and one on his body [to constitute the required two pubic hairs, so that the person is now deemed mature].

[I]   If two say [editio princeps: If one says], "We saw a single hair on his privy parts," and two say [editio princeps: one says], "We saw a single hair on his belly"—

[J]   R. Yosé b. R. Bun and R. Hoshaiah, son of R. Shimi—

[K]   one said, "He is unfit [not yet mature]," and the other said, "He is fit."

[L]   The one who said that he is unfit [deems the testimony to be equivalent to that of one who testifies concerning the appearance] of only part of the required sign of [maturity].

[M]   The one who said that it is valid [maintains], "I say [that there were two], but one of them may have fallen out."

[N]   If one party says [editio princeps: two parties say], "I saw two hairs on his privy parts," and one says [editio princeps: two say], "I saw two hairs on his belly"—

[O]   R. Ba said, "In the opinion of all parties, he is now valid [mature], [since there is sure evidence that there are the requisite pubic hairs]."

[P]   Said R. Haggai, "In the opinion of all parties, he is invalid."

[Q]   R. Yudan said, "It is yet subject to dispute."

[R]   R. Yosé said, "It is still subject to dispute."

[S]   Said R. Yosé to R. Haggai, "Lo, R. Yudan, [my teacher], ruled in accord with my view of the matter."

[T]   He said to him, "Now since I differ from his [your] master, all the more so do I disagree with him [you]!"

[U]   Said R. Mana, "R. Haggai's ruling is quite sound. For if we have a bond which bears four seals, and one party gives testimony concerning two of them, while another gives testimony concerning two of them, and someone cavils at the value of the bond, is the bond of any value whatsoever? [Hardly!] For does not each seal require the validation of two witnesses? Here, too, each sign of puberty requires the validation of two witnesses."

[V]   R. Hinena derived the same fact from the case of [attesting to full use and enjoyment of a property] throughout the years of usucaption [to which testimony must be brought]. [That is, if one wishes to establish the claim of title through usucaption, he must bring evidence that he has held and used the property for a given number of years.] Now if one witness testified that he had enjoyed usucaption for the first, second, and third years, and one witness testified that he had enjoyed usucaption for the fourth, fifth, and sixth years, it is possible that such [joined testimony is worth a thing? [Hardly!] Is it not so that each year of usucaption must be attested by two witnesses? Here too, each sign of maturity requires the validation of two witnesses. [Cf. Y. San. 3:9 **IV**.]

The positions of Eliezer and Joshua are subjected to full and thoughtful analysis, with attention both to the Scriptural foundations for the view of each (both, unit **II**; Eliezer, units **III–V**, **VII**; Joshua, unit **VI**). Units **VIII** and **IX** then expand the range of discourse within the framework of Joshua's theory that two witnesses are required. But the real issue is disjoined testimony, which can be raised in diverse contexts. There are some unsolved textual problems, particularly at units **IV** and **VII**; in general I have followed the views of Pené Moshe, as against Qorban Ha'edah. The bulk of unit **X** is at Y. San. 3:9 **IV**, with only minor differences.

1:2

[A] *How does he express jealousy to her?*

[B] *[If] he stated to her before two witnesses, "Do not speak with Mr. So-and-so," and she indeed spoke with him,*

[C] *she still is permitted to have sexual relations with her husband and [if married to a priest] is permitted to eat heave offering.*

[D] *[If] she went with him to some private place and remained with him sufficient time to become unclean,*

[E] *she is prohibited from having sexual relations with her husband and is prohibited from eating heave offering.*

[F] *And if he [her husband] should die, she performs the rite of halisah but is not taken into levirate marriage.*

[I.A] The operative criterion, therefore, appears to be that she actually talk with the named man, [since M. 1:2B refers to speaking with the man].

[B] Then if she should go to some secluded place with him, but did not say a thing to him, is her being in private with him nothing?

[C] Reference to her speaking with him serves the purpose of indicating to you that even if she spoke with him but was not in private with him, [it adds up to nothing]. [In fact, the operative criterion is going into a secluded place with the named man. That is why, if she did not do so,] she is still *permitted to have sexual relations with her husband and is permitted to eat heave offering.*

[D] The Mishnah pericope employs chaste language. [What it means when it refers to speaking is], "Do not go in private with Mr. So-and-so."

[II.A] What is the law as to the husband's expressing jealousy to her about two different men simultaneously?

[B]   R. Yudan says, "It is subject to dispute."

[C]   "He who says, 'He expresses jealousy to her even in regard to her father and her son,' maintains that he expresses jealousy to her in regard to two men at once."

[D]   R. Yosé raised the question: "May the husband express jealousy to her about [going in private at one time with] as many as a hundred men?"

[E]   [Answering this question in the negative,] said R. Yosé b. R. Bun, "If he said to her, 'Do not enter the synagogue,' [that is null]. [Likewise it is legitimate for a woman to be alone with many men at one time, and hence the answer to D is negative.]"

[III.A]   *If she went with him [to some private place, M. 1:2D]—*

[B]   Said R. Mana, "The language in use is, 'With him.' Lo, if they walked single file, there is no objection."

[C]   R. Abin said, "Even if they walked single file, in any event there is reason to suspect [that] something [is going on]."

[D]   [If they went into] the public plaza by night, a ruined house by day, or dark alleys by day [this constitutes going into a secluded place].

[IV.A]   **They asked Ben Zoma, "Why is a doubt in private domain deemed unclean?"**

[B]   **He said to them, "What is the status of the accused wife in respect to her husband?**

[C]   **"Has she certainly committed adultery, or has she only possibly committed adultery?"**

[D]   **They said to him, "[She has only] possibly [committed adultery]."**

[E]   **He said to them, "Nonetheless, we find that she is prohibited to her husband.**

[F]   **"On this basis you may also reason on a matter of doubt involving a creeping thing: Just as, in this case, in private domain, we deem a matter of doubt to be unclean, so in the other case, in private domain, we deem a matter of doubt to be unclean.**

[G]   "If you argue: Just as here, that is the case where there is
intelligence for interrogation involving private domain, so a
matter of doubt is deemed unclean while in the public domain, a matter of doubt is deemed clean" [T. Toh. 6:1D–J].

[H]   The opinions attributed to the rabbis are at variance.

[I]   For R. Zeira, R. Yosa in the name of R. Yohanan: "A minor
who committed adultery—she does not thereby intend to be
prohibited to her husband. [She is treated as one who has been
raped, and is permitted to have sexual relations with her
husband.]

[J]   "And yet we have learned: *Whoever lacks understanding to be
interrogated—a matter of doubt concerning him is resolved in
favor of cleanness* [*M. Toh. 3:6C–D*].

[K]   "Lo, if he has sufficient intelligence to be interrogated, a matter of doubt affecting him is resolved as unclean.

[L]   "And yet in the present case, even though the girl has sufficient intelligence so that she may be interrogated, a matter of
doubt concerning her is deemed resolved as clean."

[M]   "And why is a matter of doubt in the public domain deemed
clean?" [the students asked Ben Zoma].

[N]   He said to them, "We find that the community prepares the
Passover offering in a state of uncleanness when the majority
of the community is unclean.

[O]   "And if in a matter of certain uncleanness, the community is
permitted [to violate the rules of cleanness], all the more so
in a matter of doubtful uncleanness [do we extend a lenient
ruling to the community]" [T. Toh. 6:16K–M].

[V.A]   There we have learned: *In respect to all other forbidden sexual
relations, Scripture has treated him who begins the sexual act
as culpable just as is he who completes it, and such a one is
liable for each and every act of sexual relations. But this strict
rule does the law impose even more stringently in the case of
the bondwoman: it treats in her regard the man who does the
act intentionally as equivalent to the one who does it inadvertently* [*M. Ker. 2:4K–M*].

[B]   R. Jeremiah, R. Ba bar Mamel in the name of Rab, "The sexual relations [referred to in connection with the slave woman,
'If a man lies carnally with a woman who is a slave, betrothed

to another man . . .' (Lev. 19:20)], refers to an actual emission of semen.

[C] "Now here, [with regard to the betrothed slave woman], sexual relations are mentioned, and there, [with regard to the accused wife], sexual relations are at issue [Num. 5:13, cited at H].

[D] "In the present case, the law holds that sexual relations mean an actual emission of semen, while in regard to the accused wife, you say [that merely if the woman remains with the named man for sufficient time to become unclean, even if sexual relations do not actually take place, she is subject to the ordeal]."

[E] Said R. Yosé, "The case of the accused wife is different, for in the present case it is written, '. . . and it is hidden from the eyes of her husband, and she is undetected though she has defiled herself' (Num. 5:13).

[F] "Once she goes into private, the Torah calls her unclean. [And that is without regard to whether or not she has actually engaged in sexual relations.]

[G] "But here [in the case of the betrothed slave woman], violation of the law occurs only if there is an actual emission of semen."

[H] If so, then with what regard is the language ". . . if a man lies carnally with her . . ." (Num. 5:13) used?

[I] It serves to indicate that a given measure of time [of going in private is what is involved in declaring the woman to have violated her obligations to her husband, even though she does not actually have sexual relations].

[J] This is in line with that which is taught:

[K] ". . . and it is hidden from the eyes of her husband . . . and she has defiled herself" (Num. 5:13).

[VI.A] **And how long is "the time required for becoming unclean" [M. 1:2D].**

[B] **Sufficient time to have sexual relations.**

[C] **And how much is sufficient time for having sexual relations?**

[D] **Sufficient time for sexual contact.**

[E] **And how much is sufficient time for sexual contact?**

[F]   **Sufficient time to uncover [the sexual organs].**

[G]   **R. Eliezer says, "Sufficient to walk around the date palm."**

[H]   **R. Joshua says, "Sufficient to mix the cup."**

[I]   **Ben Azzai says, "Sufficient to drink it."**

[J]   **R. Aqiba says, "Sufficient to roast an egg."**

[K]   **R. Judah b. Paterah says, "Sufficient to swallow three eggs in succession."**

[L]   **R. Eleazar b. Jeremiah says, "Sufficient for a weaver to tie a knot."**

[M]   **Hanan b. Pinhas says, "Sufficient for her to put her finger into her mouth."**

[N]   **Pelimo [Yerushalmi: Minyamin] says, "Sufficient to put out her hand and take a loaf of bread from a basket."**

[O]   **Even though there is no clear proof for the proposition, there is at least a hint as to the proposition, since it says, "For on account of a harlot, to a loaf of bread" (Prov. 6:26) [T. Sot. 1:2E–R].**

[P]   Said R. Yosé, "All of the foregoing specifications of time apply once he has completed untying the petticoat. [That is, this additional amount of time is added to the specified intervals just now given.]"

[Q]   Said R. Yohanan, "Each one of the cited authorities specified the measure which applied to him [in his own sexual life]."

[R]   Now did Ben Azzai ever get married?

[S]   There are some who wish to propose that he [took the measure] based on his own [unfulfilled] passion.

[T]   And there are those who wish to say that once he actually did have sexual contact at one point but that he withdrew [prior to orgasm].

[U]   And there are those who wish to propose [that he knew by divine revelation, in line with the following verse of Scripture:] "The mysteries of the Lord are for those who fear him, and he makes known to them his covenant" (Ps. 25:14).

[**VII**.A]   [It was taught: Rabbi says, "There are three references to uncleanness stated in [the commencement of] the pericope [on the
accused wife, each one prohibiting the woman in some aspect].

[B]   "One refers to [prohibiting return to] the husband, one [pro-
hibiting marriage to] the lover, and one to [her eating] heave
offering." [The references to uncleanness or defilement are as
follows: "If a man lies with her carnally . . . and she is undetected though she has defiled herself" (Num. 5:13); "and he is
jealous of his wife, who has defiled herself" (Num. 5:14); "and
he is jealous of his wife, though she has not defiled herself"
(Num. 5:14).]

[C]   Now as to heave offering, do we find a case in which a woman
is permitted to have sexual relations with her husband and prohibited to eat food in the status of heave offering [should she
be married to a priest]? (Pené Moshe and Yerushalmi: prohibited from sexual relations . . . and permitted to eat . . .) [Who
needs a verse to make such an obvious point!]

[D]   Indeed, why not? There is, after all, the case of the daughter of
a priest who is married to an Israelite [and hence prohibited
from eating food in the status of heave offering]. Now if she is
raped, is she not [still] permitted to have sexual relations with
her husband, while forbidden to eat food in the status of heave
offering?

[E]   Then we do not find the case of a woman who is prohibited to
have sexual relations with her husband and yet permitted to eat
food in the status of heave offering [and it is surely not to such
a case that reference is made at B].

[F]   [The exegetical remark at B then must be assigned to some
other purpose.] Said R. Abin, "It is stated [differently,
namely], one refers to the husband, one to the lover, and one
to the levirate brother-in-law."

[G]   Said R. Yosé b. R. Bun, "The Mishnah pericope itself has
made the same point: *And if her husband should die, she performs the rite of halisah but is not taken into levirate marriage*"
[*M. 1:2F*].

[H]   [Relevant to B,] R. Jacob bar Idi taught before R. Jonathan:
" 'But if you have gone astray, though you are under your husband's authority, and if you have defiled yourself, and some

man other than your husband has lain with you . . .' (Num. 5:20)—

[I]   "This then excludes a case of rape."

[J]   What do you derive from the reference [to ". . . under your husband's authority . . .]"?

[K]   He said to him, "Just as '. . . under your husband's authority . . .' is of her own free will, so in the present case, [the prohibited act of sexual relations must be] of her own free will [just excluding cases of rape]."

[VIII.A]   [What follows is at Y. Yeb. 10:1 and follows Pené Moshe: As to the accused wife, just as she is prohibited from returning to her husband [M. 1:2E], so she is prohibited from marrying her lover.

[B]   Just as she is prohibited from marrying the brother of her husband, so she is forbidden from marrying the brother of her lover [M. 1:2F].

[C]   Is it then possible to argue: Just as the co-wife of the accused wife is forbidden to marry the brother of her husband, so [if the lover marries her and dies childless] she would be forbidden to marry the brother [16d] of her lover?

[D]   Let us derive the answer to that question from the following rule:

[E]   **The woman whose husband goes overseas, and whom they come and tell, "Your husband has died,"—**

[F]   **and he has a brother, who enters into levirate marriage with her, and the levir dies,**

[G]   **and afterward her husband returns home—**

[H]   **The husband is prohibited from marrying her [in line with M. Yeb. 10:1], but permitted to marry her co-wife,**

[I]   **he is prohibited from marrying her, but permitted to marry the wife of his brother [T. Yeb. 14:3A–F].**

[J]   Now is not the wife of his brother equivalent to the co-wife of an accused wife [since the hapless woman is equivalent to an adulteress]?

[K]   That then implies that the co-wife of a woman accused of adultery is permitted to marry the brother of [the accused woman's
suspected] lover.

[L]   [This is no proof, for the authority for this rule is null. For,]
Said R. Yudan, "The law follows the view of rabbis of that
place [Babylonia].

[M]   "For R. Hila said, 'They teach there: All those women who are
prohibited to marry a man and have sexual relations do not require a writ of divorce from him, except in the case of a married woman alone.' [There is no parallel, then, between the co-
wife of the brother and the co-wife of the accused wife.]

[N]   "R. Aqiba says, 'Also in the case of the sister of his wife and
the sister of his brother [a writ of divorce is required]. [That is,
if he thought the prohibited party had died and married his
wife's sister or his brother's sister, and then learned that the
wife or brother was yet alive, he must issue a writ of divorce.
Now if Aqiba requires a writ of divorce in the case of the
brother's wife, then the brother's wife should also be forbidden, and, in line with J, the wife of the brother is equivalent to
the co-wife of an accused wife, so there too, the co-wife of a
woman accused of adultery should be forbidden to marry the
brother of the lover, K.]'

[O]   "But in accord with the view of the rabbis of our locale [the
land of Israel, as we shall see now in Yohanan's name, who can
concur with the cited passage above]? [For all parties here concur that a writ of divorce is required. So it is not Aqiba alone.
Hence the problem is to determine who will concur with the
law of I–K.]"

[P]   R. Hiyya in the name of R. Yohanan: "All concur in the case
of the wife of his brother [married in error, as explained] that
she requires a writ of divorce from him, because, in accord
with the laws governing a man's wife, he has acquired her [as
his wife]. [That is, when he married her, it was assumed to be
a legal marriage. She is treated as his legal wife and hence requires a writ of divorce.]

[Q]   "[If she is deemed validly married so as to require a writ of
divorce,] she is a prohibited connection. [Accordingly, it is as if
his brother has married a woman who is prohibited to him.]
And a woman who is prohibited for marriage serves to exempt

her co-wife [from the requirement of levirate marriage]. [Thus the rabbis of the Holy Land cannot concur with I.]"

[R]   Said R. Hinena, "Even in accord with the rabbis of our locale, the passage is in full accord.

[S]   "They have imposed an extralegal penalty on her [the accused wife], and they did not impose that penalty on her heirs [in the present context: the wife of his brother so far as the levirate requirement is concerned]."

[T]   Said R. Hananiah, son of R. Hillel, "If the ruling accords with the rabbis of that other place, then he should be permitted to marry her. [Since they hold that she requires no writ of divorce either, he should be permitted to marry her as well, for she is deemed to have acted under constraint. Hence the cited passage surely conforms to the theory of the authorities of the Holy Land.]"

[IX.A]   R. Zeira in the name of R. Yohanan: "The co-wife of an accused wife is forbidden [to enter into a levirate marriage],

[B]   and the co-wife of a divorcée [whom the husband remarried] is permitted to enter levirate marriage."

[C]   R. Jacob in the name of R. Yohanan: "All co-wives are permitted [to enter levirate marriage] except for the co-wife of an accused wife."

[D]   Samuel said, "The divorced wife herself is permitted to enter levirate marriage [Pené Moshe]."

[E]   Does he dispute [with A–C]?

[F]   [No, he does not differ.] Since the discussion concerned co-wives, they did not mention divorced wives.

[G]   As to the co-wife of an accused wife, why is she forbidden [to enter levirate marriage if the cuckolded husband dies without children]?

[H]   R. Yohanan said, "It is because it is because of the stench of licentiousness which has affected her [willy-nilly]."

[I]   Rab said, "It is because in her regard uncleanness is written in the list of prohibited connections."

The clarification of the Mishnah's rule, essentially through exegesis of its language, is accomplished at units **I–III**. Unit **IV** is inserted whole, with some interpretative material, from Tosefta Tohorot as indicated. Unit **V**, along these same lines, compares the present law to that of another context. Unit **VI** introduces a relevant complement of the Tosefta and provides an exegesis thereof. Units **VII, VIII**, and **IX**, borrowed from Y. Yeb. 10:1, then expand the range of discourse by bringing up a problem which touches at best tangentially the Mishnah's present interests. A better understanding of the analogies introduced for discussion is to be gained by consulting the passage in its appropriate context.

1:3

[A] *And these women are prohibited from eating heave offering:*

[B] *She who says, "I am unclean to you," and she against whom witnesses testified that she is unclean;*

[C] *and she who says, "I shall not drink the bitter water," and she whose husband will not force her to drink it;*

[D] *and she whose husband has sexual relations with her on the way [up to Jerusalem for the rite of drinking the water].*

[E] *What should he do in respect to her?*

[F] *He brings her to the court in that place [in which they live], and [the judges] hand over to him two disciples of sages, lest he have sexual relations with her on the way.*

[G] *R. Judah says, "Her husband is trustworthy in regard to her [not to have sexual relations in this circumstance]."*

[I.A] The Mishnah pericope before us does not accord with the view expressed in the first Mishnah, in which we have learned:

[B] *Aforetimes they did rule: Three sorts of women go forth and collect their marriage contract:*

[C] *She who says, "I am unclean for you."*

[D] *"Heaven [knows] what is between you and me [namely, your impotence]."*

[E]   "I am removed from [having sexual relations with all] Jews.
       [They reverted to rule: So that a woman should not covet some-
       one else and spoil her relationship with her present husband,
       she who says, "I am unclean for you," must bring proof of her
       claim] [M. Ned. 11:12]. [Now the present pericope accepts the
       woman's testimony without her bringing corroborating evi-
       dence, thus in accord with the position of the first Mishnah,
       while the later version, that she has to bring evidence, contra-
       dicts the present rule.]

[F]   Said R. Abin, "And even if you say that the rule before us ac-
       cords with the later version of the Mishnah, in any event there
       are grounds for [thinking that] the matter [is as the woman
       states, for she was warned and went in private with the named
       man]."

[II.A] It was taught: "And some man other than your husband has
       lain with you" (Num. 5:20)—thus excluding a case in which
       the sexual relations with another man came before those with
       your husband [that is, excluding a case in which the woman
       has sexual relations with the named man prior to marriage to
       her husband]. [The curse will then not apply.]

[B]   Said R. Ila, "This is in line with that which is said: '. . . be-
       sides the burnt offering of the morning . . .' (Num. 28:23)
       [meaning, afterward]."

[C]   Have we not learned: Just as the water puts her to the proof, so
       the water puts [the lover] to the proof. . . . Just as she is pro-
       hibited to her husband, so she is prohibited to her lover . . .
       [M. 5:1A, C]?

[D]   "Just as she is prohibited to the brother of her husband, so she
       is prohibited to the brother of the lover.

[E]   "Just as the water tests her—for each and every act of sexual
       relations which she has with her husband after her lover,

[F]   "so the water tests him." [Now this indicates that if the hus-
       band has sexual relations after the lover does, the woman still
       has to undergo the ordeal, contrary to the view of A.]

[G]   R. Abin in the name of R. Hila, "Here [at M. 1:3D], we deal
       with a case in which he acts knowingly,

[H]   "while there, [at C, when the water affects her even after the husband has sexual relations in the aftermath of her relations with the lover,] it is when he did so unknowingly."

[III.A]   [With reference to M. 1:3H,] R. Hiyya bar Joseph sent after his wife and gave orders for three disciples to go with her, so that, if one of them would have to turn aside [to heed a call of nature], she would be left alone with two others.

[B]   Now have we not learned, *They hand over to him two disciples of sages lest he have sexual relations with her on the way*? [Why did Hiyya send three?]

[C]   Said R. Abin, "With her husband, lo, there are three."

[IV.A]   [With regard to Judah's position, that the husband is believed, the following alludes to and then carries forward M. Ket. 2:9F–H: *A person is not believed to testify in his own behalf. Said R. Zekhariah b. Haqqassab, "By this sanctuary! Her hand did not move from mine from the time that the gentiles entered Jerusalem until they left it." They said to him, "A person cannot give testimony in his own behalf."*] **But even so, he set aside a house for her by herself. She was supported by his property.**

[B]   **But he never was alone with her, except in the presence of her children [T. Ket. 3:2E].**

[C]   And he cited in his own regard of the following verse of Scripture: "I am weary with my groaning, and I find no rest" (Jer. 45:3).

[V.A]   It was taught [following the Tosefta's version]:

[B]   *R. Judah says, "Her husband is trustworthy in regard to her [not to have sexual relations in this circumstance]" [M. Sot. 1:3G]—*

[C]   **"on the basis of an argument a fortiori:**

[D]   **"Now if in the case of a menstruating woman, on account of sexual relations with whom one incurs the penalty of extirpation, her husband is trustworthy in regard to her, in the case of an accused wife, on account of which the husband does not incur the penalty of extirpation, is it not logical that her husband should be deemed trustworthy in regard to her?"**

[E]   They said to him, "Now all the more so: Since one does not incur the penalty of extirpation for having sexual relations with her, her husband really should not be deemed trustworthy in regard to her.

[F]   "Another matter: No. If you have said the rule in the case of the menstruating woman, who becomes permitted after she is prohibited, will you state the same rule in regard to the accused wife, who will never be permitted once she is prohibited?

[G]   "And so Scripture says, 'Stolen water is sweeter' " (Prov. 9:17) [T. Sot. 1:2S–X].

[H]   R. Yosé says, "Scripture has expressed its trust in him with regard to her, since it says, 'And the husband shall bring his wife to the priest' " (Num. 5:15) [T. Sot. 1:3A].

[I]   They said to him, "It is only on condition that there are witnesses."

The Talmud's discussion begins with a comparison of the present rule to one presented elsewhere. Units **II** and **III** are relevant only in theme. Unit **IV** provides a position contrary to Judah's, though, in Judah's behalf, it would be easy to distinguish that case from the present context. Unit **V** presents an expanded argument between Judah and sages.

1:4

[A]   *They would bring her up to the high court which is in Jerusalem and admonish her as they admonish witnesses in a capital crime.*

[B]   *They say to her, "My daughter, much is done by wine, much is done by joking around, much is done by kidding, much is done by bad friends. For the sake of the great Name which is written in holiness, so act [by confessing] that it will not be blotted out by water" (Num. 5:23).*

[C]   *And they tell her things which neither she nor the family of her father's house should be hearing.*

[I.A]   [And just as the court admonishes her to repent, so they admonish her not to repent.

[B]   Therefore they say to her, "Now my daughter, if it is perfectly clear to you that you are clean, stand your ground and drink.

[C]   "For these waters are like a dry salve which is put on living flesh and does no harm.

[D]   "If there is a wound, it penetrates and goes through [the skin; if there is no wound, it has no effect]" [T. Sot. 1:6].

[II.A]   R. Zabedeh, son-in-law of R. Levi, would tell the following story.

[B]   R. Meir would teach a lesson in the synagogue of Hammata every Sabbath night. There was a woman who would come regularly to hear him. One time the lesson lasted a longer time than usual.

[C]   She went home and found that the light had gone out. Her husband said to her, "Where have you been?"

[D]   She replied to him, "I was listening to the lesson."

[E]   He said to her, "May God do such-and-so and even more, if this woman enters my house before she goes and spits in the face of that sage who gave the lesson."

[F]   R. Meir perceived with the help of the Holy Spirit [what had happened] and he pretended to have a pain in his eye.

[G]   He said, "Any woman who knows how to recite a charm over an eye—let her come and heal mine."

[H]   The woman's neighbors said to her, "Lo, your time to go back home has come. Pretend to be a charmer and go and spit in R. Meir's eye."

[I]   She came to him. He said to her, "Do you know how to heal a sore eye through making a charm?"

[J]   She became frightened and said to him, "No."

[K]   He said to her, "Do they not spit into it seven times, and it is good for it?"

[L]   After she had spit in his eye, he said to her, "Go and tell your husband that you did it one time."

[M]   She said to him, "And lo, I spit seven times?"

[N]   R. Meir's disciples said to him, "Rabbi, in such a way do they disgracefully treat the Torah [which is yours]? If you had told us about the incident with the husband, would we not have brought him and flogged him at the stock, until he was reconciled with his wife?"

[O]   He said to them, "And should the honor owing to Meir be tantamount to the honor owing to Meir's creator?

[P]   "Now if the Holy Name, which is written in a state of sanctification, the Scripture has said is to be blotted out with water so as to bring peace between a man and his wife, should not the honor owing to Meir be dealt with in the same way!"

[III.A]   *And they tell her things which neither she nor the family of her father's house should be hearing [M. 1:4C].*

[B]   For example: the story of Reuben and Bilhah, the story of Judah and Tamar.

[C]   "What wise men have told" (Job 15:18)—this refers to Reuben and Judah.

[D]   "And their fathers have not hidden" (Job 15:18)—

[E]   And what reward did they get for this?

[F]   "To whom alone the land was given, and no stranger passed among them" (Job 15:19).

[G]   When Moses came to bless them: "Let Reuben live and not die, nor let his men be few" (Deut. 33:6).

[H]   "And this be said of Judah . . ." (Deut. 33:7).

[I]   R. Hezekiah in the name of R. Aha, R. Hiyya, interpreted the following three verses as praise:

[J]   "She sat at the entrance of Enaim ['eyes']" (Gen. 38:14). Is it possible that this is so?

[K]   Even the most reprobate of whores does not do it that way!

[L]   But: She set her eyes at that Gate to which all eyes look, saying before Him, "Lord of all ages! Let me not go forth empty-handed from this household."

[M]   Another matter: "At the entrance to Enaim"—She opened his eyes, saying to him, "I am available! I am in a state of cleanness [not in my menstrual period]!"

[N]   Now Eli was very old, and he heard all that his sons were doing to all Israel, and how they lay with the women who served at the entrance to the tent of meeting" (1 Sam. 2:22).

[O]   "They had sexual relations" is what is written.

[P]   For the women would bring their bird offerings to complete the rite of purification [after having produced babies], and they would keep them back [and not offer them up].

[Q]   The Holy One, blessed be he, imputed it to them [for not offering up their bird offerings] as if they had had sexual relations with those women.

[R]   Said R. Tanhuma, "Lo, he admonished them: 'Why then look with greedy eye at my sacrifices and my offerings . . .' (1 Sam. 2:29)."

[S]   Now if you say that here was a most serious transgression, why should he exempt them from admonition on account of the most severe sort of transgression [having sexual relations with the women] and admonish him only for the lesser transgression?

[T]   "Yet his sons did not walk in his ways, but turned aside after gain; they took bribes and perverted justice" (1 Sam. 8:3).

[U]   For they took tithes and then made decisions.

[V]   Said [17a] R. Berekhiah, "When a caravan would go by, they would neglect their public duties to Israel and would go and transact business with the caravan."

After unit **I**, the Talmud presents an anthology of stories and biblical exegesis relevant in only a general way to the theme of the Mishnah.

1:5

[A]   *[Now] if she said, "I am unclean" she gives a quittance for her marriage contract [which is not paid over to her], and goes forth [with a writ of divorce].*

[B]   *And if she said, "I am clean," they bring her up to the eastern gate, which is at the entrance of Nicanor's Gate.*

[C]   *There it is that they force accused wives to drink the bitter water,*

[D]   *purify women after childbirth, and purify lepers.*

[E]   *And a priest grabs her clothes—if they tear, they tear, and if they are ripped up, they are ripped up—until he bares her breast.*

[F]   *And he tears her hair apart [Num. 5:18].*

[G]   *R. Judah says, "If she had pretty breasts, he did not let them show. And if she had pretty hair, he did not pull it apart."*

[I.A]   It is written, "And the priest shall bring her near, and set her before the Lord . . ." (Num. 5:16).

[B]   This refers to Nicanor's Gate.

[C]   At every place at which "before the Lord" is mentioned, the reference is to Nicanor's Gate.

[II.A]   It is written, "If a man sins against a man, God will mediate for him; but if a man sins against the Lord, who can intercede for him?" (1 Sam. 2:25).

[B]   R. Hiyya bar Ba and R. Joshua b. Levi:

[C]   R. Hiyya bar Ba interpreted the passage to apply to the lover.

[D]   And R. Joshua b. Levi interpreted the passage to apply to the [faithless] wife.

[E]   R. Hiyya bar Ba interpreted the passage to speak of the lover: "This one supports and maintains the woman, and you come and take over what is available ('TD) [to her]!"

[F]   R. Joshua b. Levi interpreted the passage to apply to the woman: "This one supports and maintains you, and you set your eyes on someone else?!"

[III.A]   Now do they humiliate the woman merely by reason of doubt [in the procedures specified at M. 1:5E–G]?

[B]   Said R. Simlai, "In every place in which you find fornication, you find that an indiscriminate slaughter overspreads the world."

[**IV**.A]   The Scripture states that they recite the formula to the woman, and then they humiliate her [Num. 5:19–22, 23–27).

[B]   The Mishnah, [by contrast], states that they humiliate her and afterward they read the curse to her.

[C]   Said R. Ili, "Since it is written, 'And he shall set the woman up . . .' (Num. 5:16)—and was she sitting down before?

[D]   "But because of the first time he stood her up, her hair already was disheveled."

[**V**.A]   The opinions assigned to R. Judah are at variance with one another.

[B]   There he has said: *"A man is covered in front, and a woman is covered front and back," the words of R. Judah. [But sages say, "A man is stoned naked, but a woman is not stoned naked"] (M. San. 6:3).*

[C]   And here he has said this [that we take precautions not to show off her private parts].

[D]   There [in connection with the execution,] in any event the woman is being prepared for death.

[E]   But here, perhaps she may turn out to be pure, and the youthful priests may compete [for her charms].

[F]   The opinions assigned to sages are at variance.

[G]   There they say, *A man is stoned naked, but a woman is not stoned naked.*

[H]   And here they say this [that the woman's clothing is ripped and her hair messed up]!

[I]   [The difference is based on the instructions given by Scripture for the two different situations, one the death penalty, the other the humiliation of adulteresses:] There it is written, "You will love your neighbor as yourself" (Lev. 19:18), meaning, Choose for him a mode of execution as painless as possible. [That accounts for the leniency.]

[J]   But here: "And all women may take warning and not commit lewdness as you have done" (Ezek. 23:48) [which accounts for the stringency] [cf. M. 1:6D–E].

The Talmud's treatment of the Mishnah is fairly systematic, and the exegesis is close and consistently relevant. Units **I**, **II**, **IV** take up the Mishnah's laws, and, predictably, we close with attention to the secondary matter of comparing opinions assigned to authorities here with those in the same names elsewhere.

1:6

[A]   *[If] she was clothed in white clothing, he puts black clothes on her.*

[B]   *[If] she had gold jewelry, chains, nose rings, and finger rings on, they take them away from her to put her to shame.*

[C]   *Then he brings an Egyptian rope [alt.: a rope made out of twigs] and ties it above her breasts.*

[D]   *And whoever wants to stare at her comes and stares, except for her slave boys and slave girls, since in any case she has no shame before them.*

[E]   *And all women are allowed to stare at her, since it is said, "That all women may take warning not to commit lewdness (Ezek. 23:48).*

[I.A]   The Mishnah pericope [at M. 1:6A] speaks of a case in which [black clothes] are not becoming to her.

[B]   But if they were becoming to her, it is not in such a case [that this law pertains, but she is left in white].

[II.A] *He brings an Egyptian rope [M. 1:6C].*

[B]   And why an Egyptian rope?

[C]   Said R. Isaac, "Because she did the sort of thing that Egyptians do."

[III.A] R. Jeremiah raised the question, "Is the Egyptian rope essential to the rite? Is the Egyptian basket [referred to at M. Sot. 2:1] essential to the rite?" [This inquiry is not answered.]

[B]   Who provides them?

[C]   The answer is in accord with that which Rabbi said, for Rabbi said, "Providing funds for the water channel, the wall of the city and its tower, and all the needs of the city, is from the money left over in the Temple treasury, and here the same rule applies.''

The Talmud's systematic exegesis of the Mishnah is clear.

1:7

[A]   *By that same measure by which a man metes out [to others], they mete out to him:*

[B]   *She primped herself for sin, the Omnipresent made her repulsive.*

[C]   *She exposed herself for sin, the Omnipresent exposed her.*

[D]   *With the thigh she began to sin, and afterward with the belly, therefore the thigh suffers the curse first, and afterward the belly.*

[E]   *(But the rest of the body does not escape [punishment].)*

[I.A]   **R. Meir did say [following the Tosefta's version]: "On what basis do you rule that by the same measure by which a man metes out, they mete out to him [M. 1:7A]?**

[B]   **"Since it is said, 'By measure in sending her away thou dost contend with her' (Is. 27:8)—I know only that he measured out with a seah. How do I know that [if] he measured out with a qab, a half-qab, a third-qab, a half-third-qab, a quarter-qab, a half-quarter-qab, an eighth-qab, twentieth-qab [the same rule applies]?**

[C]   **"Since it says, 'For all the armor of the armed man in the tumult' (Is. 9:5), lo, you have here many measures.**

[D]   **"I know only that this applies to something which comes by measure.**

[E]   **"How do I know that a few perutot add up to a large sum?**

[F]   **"Since it is said, 'Laying one thing to another to find out the account' " [Qoh. 7:27] [T. 3:1].**

[G]   [The rule of measure for measure applies in yet another way.] In worldly affairs, [if] someone commits a transgression, on account of which people are liable to death at the hands of heaven, [it may be exacted little by little, until it adds up, as at E–F]. [Thus:]

[H]   His ox dies, his chicken is lost, his flask breaks, he breaks his finger, and the account is complete.

[I]   Another matter: One happens and joins the next, the account is complete.

[J]   And how much is completing the account? Even one transgression [will not be overlooked].

[II.A]   It was taught: **R. Meir says [following the Tosefta's version]: "Just as there are diverse tastes in regard to food and drink, so there are diverse tastes in regard to women['s behavior].**

[B]   **"You can find a man on whose cup a fly flits by. He will put it aside but won't taste what's in that cup. This one is a bad lot for women, for he is [always] contemplating divorcing his wife.**

[C]   **"You can find a man in whose cup a fly takes up residence, and he tosses [the fly] out but does not drink what is left in it. Such a one is like Pappos b. Judah, who used to lock his door to keep his wife inside when he went out.**

[D]   **"And you can find a man into whose cup a fly falls. He tosses it away but drinks what is in the cup.**

[E]   **"This is the trait of ordinary man, who sees his wife talking with her neighbors or with her relatives and leaves her be [M. Sot. 4:4C].**

[F]   **"And you have a man into whose meal a fly falls, and he picks it up and sucks it [for the soup it absorbed] and tosses it away, and then eats what is on his plate.**

[G]   **"This is the trait of a bad man, who sees his wife going around with her hair in a mess, with her shoulders uncovered, shameless before her servant boys, shameless before her servant girls, going out and doing her spinning in the marketplace, bathing, talking with anybody at all."**

[H]   It is a religious duty to divorce such a woman, as it is said, "When a man takes a wife and marries her, if then she finds no favor in his eyes because he has found some indecency in her, and he writes her a bill of divorce and puts it in her hand and sends her out of his house, and she departs out of his house" (Deut. 24:1).

[I] "And if she goes and becomes another man's wife" (Deut. 24:2)—and Scripture calls him "a different man"—because he is not his match.

[J] The first man puts her away because of transgression, and this other one comes along and stumbles through her.

[K] The second husband, if he has merit in Heaven, puts her away. And if not, in the end, she buries him,

[L] since it is said, "Or if the latter husband dies, who took her to be his wife" (Deut. 24:3)—

[M] this man is deserving of death, for he received such a woman into his house [T. Sot. 5:9].

[N] Samuel said, "They keep distant from a loose woman [and do not marry her], but they need not keep distance from her daughter."

[O] Now this view of his accords with that which R. Yohanan said, "A married woman who committed adultery—

[P] "the offspring are assigned the status of the husband,

[Q] "for the greater part of the act of sexual relations derives from the husband."

[III.A] One Scripture says, ". . . make your body swell and your thigh fall away" (Num. 5:22).

[B] And another Scripture says, ". . . her body shall swell, and her thigh shall fall away" (Num. 5:27).

[C] And yet another verse of Scripture says, "When the Lord makes your thigh fall away and your body swell" (Num. 5:21).

[D] Does one verse of Scripture determine the meaning of two other Scriptural verses? [What does the water really affect?]

[E] Said R. Mana, "In one instance, the verse refers to what actually happens [to the belly], and in another, to the stipulation [specified by the priest]."

[F] Said R. Abin, "And even if you say the several verses refer to what actually happens, they also refer to the stipulation."

[**IV**.A] "To make the belly swell and to cause the thigh to fall away" refers to the lover.

[B] "And her belly swelled and her thigh fell away" refers to the wife.

[C] Now that is quite reasonable.

[D] With the thigh the sin first began, and afterward the whole belly got involved.

[E] Therefore the thigh is smitten first, and then the whole belly—and finally the whole body is not exempt.

[F] R. Abba son of R. Papi made the following interpretation:

[G] "Now if in the case of the application of the measure of punishment, which is minimal, a single limb is smitten, and the rest of the limbs feel it,

[H] "in the case of the measure of goodness, which is abundant, all the more so!"

The Talmud is made up principally of the Tosefta, which is presented and then interpreted at units **I** and **II**, with an exegesis of the relevant verses of Scripture at units **III** and **IV**.

1:8

[A] *Samson followed his eyes [where they led him], therefore the Philistines put out his eyes, since it is said, "And the Philistines laid hold on him and put out his eyes" (Judg. 16:21).*

[B] *Absalom was proud of his hair, therefore he was hung by his hair (2 Sam. 14:25–26).*

[C] *And since he had sexual relations with ten concubines of his father, therefore they thrust ten spear heads into his body, since it is said, "And ten young men that carried Joab's armor surrounded and smote Absalom and killed him" (2 Sam. 18:15).*

[D] *And since he stole three hearts—his father's, the court's, and the Israelites', since it is said, "And Absalom stole the heart of the men of Israel" (2 Sam. 15:6)—therefore three darts were thrust into him, since it is said, "And he took three darts in his hand, and thrust them through the heart of Absalom" (2 Sam. 18:14).*

[I.A]   It was taught: Rabbi says, "Since the beginning of his ruin took place in Gaza, therefore he was punished in Gaza."

[B]   And it is not written: "Samson went down to Timnah, [and at Timnah he saw one of the daughters of the Philistines]" (Judg. 14:1)?

[C]   Said R. Samuel bar Nahman, "The one [woman] in Timnah he took in marriage."

[D]   One verse of Scripture states, "Samson went down to Timnah, [and at Timnah he saw one of the daughters of the Philistines]" (Judg. 14:1).

[E]   And yet another verse of Scripture states, "And when Tamar was told, 'Your father-in-law is going up to Timnah [to shear his sheep],' she put off her widow's garments, and put on a veil, wrapping herself up, and sat at the entrance to Enaim, which is on the road to Timnah" (Gen. 38:13–14).

[F]   Rab said, "As to the usage, 'going up' or 'going down' to Timnah, the meaning is that there were two Timnahs, one involving Judah, the other involving Samson."

[G]   R. Simeon said, "There was only a single Timnah. And the reason that going up and going down are both used in that regard is that the one involving Judah was an ascent, for Heaven's sake. Therefore it is written in that regard, 'going up.'

[H]   "The one involving Samson, since it was not for the sake of Heaven, is referred to as 'going down.' "

[I]   Said R. Aibu bar Nigri, "It is like a spring, to which they go down when going from Paltetah and to which they come up from Tiberias."

[II.A]   It is written, "[Then Samson went down with his father and mother to Timnah,] and he came to the vineyards of Timnah" (Judg. 14:5).

[B]   Said R. Samuel bar R. Isaac, "This teaches that his father and his mother showed him the vineyards of Timnah, sewn in mixed seeds, and they said to him, 'Child! Just as [17b] their vineyards are sewn with mixed seeds, so their daughters are sewn with mixed seeds.' "

[C]   "His father and mother did not know that it was from the Lord; for he was seeking an occasion against the Philistines" (Judg. 14:4).

[D]   Said R. Eleazar, "In seven places it is written, 'You should not intermarry with them.' "

[E]   Said R. Abin, "This is to prohibit intermarriage with the seven peoples [of the land].

[F]   "And here why does it say [that Samson was punished for marrying a Philistine woman, when there is no prohibition in the Torah against marrying Philistines]?"

[G]   Said R. Isaac, " 'Toward the scorners he is scornful, [but to the humble he shows favor]' (Prov. 3:34). [Since Samson got involved with scornful people, he was punished.]"

[III.A]   It is written, "And the spirit of the Lord began to stir him in Mahaneh-dan, between Zorah and Eshtaol" (Judg. 13:25).

[B]   There are two Amoraim who interpret this passage.

[C]   One of them said, "When the Holy Spirit rested upon him, his footsteps were as if from Zorah and Eshtaol."

[D]   The other one said, "When the Holy Spirit rested on him, his hair grew stiff like a bell, and the sound went as between Zorah and Eshtaol."

[IV.A]   "[And the woman bore a son, and called his name Samson; and the boy grew] and the Lord blessed him" (Judg. 13:24).

[B]   R. Huna in the name of R. Yosé: "For [despite his great strength,] his sexual capacities were like those of any other man [Qorban ha'edah: and so he could enjoy sexual relations with a normal woman]."

[V.A]   It is written, "[Then Samson called out to the Lord and said, 'O Lord God, remember me, I pray thee, and strengthen me, I pray thee, only this once, O God,] that I may be avenged upon the Philistines for one of my two eyes' " (Judg. 16:28).

[B]   Said R. Aha, "He said before him, 'Lord of the world! Give me the reward of one of my eyes in this world, and let the reward for the other eye be readied for me in the world to come.' "

[**VI**.A]   One verse of Scripture states, "He judged Israel forty years." [This verse is not in the present version.]

[B]   And yet another verse of Scripture says, "He had judged Israel twenty years" (Judg. 16:31).

[C]   Said R. Aha, "It teaches that the Philistines feared him for twenty years after his death just as they feared him for twenty years when he was alive."

[**VII**.A]   *Absalom was proud of his hair, [Therefore he was hung by his hair] [M. 1:8B].*

[B]   R. Haninah said, "It was like a large carob tree."

[C]   Might you think [that Absalom with his head of hair was slender, looking] like a *kindon* tree?

[D]   R. Bibi in the name of R. Yohanan, "They were arranged in single stalks."

[E]   Said R. Haninah, "When I came up here [to the land of Israel], I took the garment of my son and the garment of my son-in-law and wrapped it around the trunk of a carob of the land of Israel, but they did not suffice to reach around it.

[F]   "And I cut down the branch of a carob, and my hands filled up with its sap."

[G]   Said R. Jonathan, "Better were the leavings of the orchards, which we ate in our youth, than the peaches which we eat in our old age.

[H]   "For in the passage of time the world changes."

[I]   Said R. Hiyya bar Ba, "In olden times a *seah* of Arbelit grain would yield a *seah* of fine flour, a *seah* of flour would yield a *seah* of inferior wheat, a *seah* of fine flour would yield a *seah* of bran.

[J]   "And nowadays, the yield is not even one for one."

[**VIII**.A]   It is written, "Now in all Israel there was no one so much to be praised for his beauty as Absalom" (2 Sam. 14:25).

[B]   Is it possible that this was in all ways?

[C]   [Indeed so.] Scripture says, "From the sole of his foot to the crown of his head, there was no blemish in him" (2 Sam. 14:25).

[D]   It is written, "And he had a son whose name was Saul, a hand-some young man. There was not a man among the people of Israel more handsome than he" (1 Sam. 9:2).

[E]   Is it possible that this was in all ways?

[F]   Scripture states, "From his shoulders upward he was taller than any of the people" (1 Sam. 9:2).

[G]   But with regard to Abner, what does it state?

[H]   "[And the king said to his servants,] "Do you not know that a king and a great man has fallen this day in Israel?" (2 Sam. 3:38).

[I]   Why was Abner killed?

[J]   R. Joshua b. Levi, R. Simeon b. Laqish, and rabbis:

[K]   R. Joshua b. Levi said, "It was because he treated the blood of youths as if it were a light thing: '[And Abner said to Joab,] 'Let the young men arise and play before us' " (2 Sam. 2:14).

[L]   R. Simeon b. Laqish said, "It was because he placed his name before the name of David."

[M]   This is in line with that which is written in Scripture: "And Abner sent messengers to David where he was, saying, 'To whom does the land belong?' " (2 Sam. 3:12).

[N]   And it thus is written, ". . . from Abner to David . . ."

[O]   And rabbis say, "It was because he did not allow Saul to be appeased by David."

[P]   This is in line with that which is written, "See, my father, see the skirt of your robe in my hand" (1 Sam. 24:11).

[Q]   He said to him, "What do you make of the self-glorification of this one! It got caught on a thorn and the skirt was torn off."

[R]   When they came to Maagel, he said to him, "[And David called to the army, and to Abner the son of Ner, saying,] 'Will you not answer, Abner?' " (1 Sam. 26:14).

[S]   "In regard to the skirt, you said it was ripped off by a thorn. Have your spear and shield [conjectural: SPHT = waffle] been ripped off?"

[T] And there are those who say, "It was because there was sufficient doubt so that it was in his power to forgive Nob, the city
of the priests, and he did not forgive them."

[IX.A] *And since he stole three hearts—his father's, the court's, and
the Israelites'—*

[B] His father's, as it is written, "And at the end of forty years
[Absalom said to the king, 'Pray let me go and pay my vow,
which I have vowed to the lord, in Hebron]' " (2 Sam. 15:7).

[C] The whole reign of David was only forty years, and here it says
this?

[D] But when the Israelites sought a king: "For your servant
vowed a vow [while I dwelt at Geshur in Aram, saying, 'If the
Lord will indeed bring me back to Jerusalem, then I will offer
worship to the Lord]' " (2 Sam. 15:8).

[E] [David] said to [Absalom], "What do you want here?"

[F] He said, "Write out an order that two men whom I will take
may come with me."

[G] He said to him, "Tell me whom you wish to take, and I shall
write the order."

[H] He said to him, "Write it out blank, and I'll choose whomever
I want."

[I] He wrote the order with blank spaces.

[J] He went and chose his men, two by two, until he reached two
hundred men.

[K] This is in line with that which is written: "With Absalom went
two hundred men from Jerusalem who were invited guests, and
they went in their simplicity, and knew nothing. And while
Absalom was offering the sacrifices he sent for Ahithophel" (2
Sam. 15:11).

[L] "Invited" by David.

[M] "Going in their simplicity" because of Absalom.

[N] "And they knew nothing" of the conspiracy of Ahithophel.

[O] R. Huna in the name of R. Aha: "And all of them were heads
of sanhedrins."

[P]   When they saw things going opposite to the will of the king, they said, "Lord of all ages, let us fall into the hand of David, and let David not fall into our hand.

[Q]   "For if we fall into David's hand, lo, he will have mercy on us.

[R]   "But if, God forbid, David should fall into our hand, we shall not have mercy on him."

[S]   That is in line with what David said: "He will deliver my soul in safety from the battle that I wage, for many are arrayed against me" (Ps. 55:19).

[T]   *And the heart of the court:* "Absalom said moreover, 'O that I were a judge in the land!' " (2 Sam. 15:4).

[U]   "Thus Absalom did [to all of Israel who came to the king for judgment]" (2 Sam. 15:6).

[V]   *And the heart of all Israelites:* "So Absalom stole the hearts of the men of Israel"(2 Sam. 15:6).

The Talmud provides to the Mishnah a massive repertoire of thematically relevant materials.

1:9

[A]   *And so is it on the good side:*

[B]   *Miriam waited for Moses, since it is said, "And his sister stood afar off" (Ex. 2:4),*

[C]   *therefore, Israel waited on her seven days in the wilderness, as it is said, "And the people did not travel on until Miriam was brought in again" (Num. 12:15).*

[I.A]   Said R. Yohanan, "The following verse was stated through the Holy Spirit."

[B]   "And his sister stood at a distance, [to know what would be done to him]" (Ex. 2:4).

[C]   "I saw the Lord standing beside the altar" (Amos 9:1).

[D]   "*His sister:* 'Say to wisdom, You are my sister' " (Prov. 7:4).

[E]   *"From a distance:* 'The Lord appeared to him from afar' "
(Jer. 31:3).

[F]   *"To know:* 'The earth shall be full of the knowledge of the
Lord [as the waters cover the sea]' " (Is. 11:9).

[G]   *"What would be done to him:* 'Surely the Lord does nothing,
without revealing his secret to his servants the prophets' "
(Amos 3:7).

The Talmud presents a filigree of verses, a group illustrating
each word of the cited verse of the Mishnah, as indicated.

1:10

[A]   *Joseph had the merit of burying his father, and none of his
brothers was greater than he, since it is said, "And Joseph went
up to bury his father . . . and there went up with him both
chariots and horsemen" (Gen. 50:7, 9).*

[B]   *We have none so great as Joseph, for only Moses took care of
his [bones].*

[C]   *Moses had the merit of burying the bones of Joseph, and none
in Israel was greater than he, as it is said, "And Moses took the
bones of Joseph with him" (Ex. 13:19).*

[D]   *We have none so great as Moses, for only the Holy One,
blessed be he, took care of his [bones], as it is said, "And he
buried him in the valley" (Deut. 34:6).*

[E]   *And not of Moses alone have they stated [this rule], but of all
righteous people, since it is said, "And your righteousness shall
go before you. The glory of the Lord shall gather you [in
death]" (Is. 58:8).*

[I.A]   Said R. Isaac, "The glory of the Life of the Ages was with
them [when they went to bury Jacob.]"

[B]   It is written, "When they came to the threshing floor of Atad
[thorn]" (Gen. 50:11).

[C]   Now do they thresh thorns?

[D]   Said R. Samuel bar Nahman, "We have examined the whole of
Scriptures and have not found a place called Atad.

[E]   "But what is the meaning of Atad [as thorns]?

[F]   "These are the Canaanites, who were worthy of being put to death through threshing in thorns [when the Israelites conquered the land]."

[G]   By what merit were they saved?

[H]   It was by the merit of [the following action]: "The inhabitants of the land, the Canaanites, saw the mourning on the threshing floor of Atad, and they said, 'this is a grievous mourning to the Egyptians' " (Gen. 50:11).

[I]   And what form of mourning did they carry out for him?

[J]   R. Eleazar said, "They let their garments loose."

[K]   R. Simeon b. Laqish said, "They untied the shoulder knots on their garments."

[L]   Rabbis say, "They bowed down."

[M]   Said R. Yudan bar Shalom, "They pointed with the finger and said, 'This is a grievous mourning to the Egyptians' " (Gen. 50:11).

[N]   Now if these Canaanites, who performed a rite of burial neither with their own hands nor even with their feet [by walking to the grave], see how the Holy One, blessed be he, has given them a reward—

[O]   the Israelites, who carry out the rites of burial with their own hands and feet, with their adults and with their minors—how much the more so [will they be rewarded for their actions]!

[17c/   Said R. Abbahu, "All those seventy days which passed between
II.A]   the letters [sent by Haman, on the one side, and Mordecai, on the other, the thirteenth of Nisan and the twenty-third of Sivan] corresponded to the seventy days in which the Egyptians were occupied in burying our father, Jacob."

[III.A]   It is written, "And David lamented with this lamentation over Saul and Jonathan his son, and he said . . . that the use of the bow should be taught to the people of Judah" (2 Sam. 1:17–18).

[B]   This is surely odd [that the Judaeans would have to learn how to use a bow].

[C]   He could not have meant to teach the Judaeans [since he came from a different area].

[D]   What could this mean?

[E]   But David said, "Since the righteous take their leave, and those who hate Israel come and oppress them, [the Judaeans had best learn to protect themselves]."

[IV.A]   "Behold, is it not written in the book of the Upright" (2 Sam. 1:18)—

[B]   Two Amoras [treat this matter].

[C]   One said, "This is the book of Genesis."

[D]   The other said, "This is the book of Numbers."

[E]   For him who said it was the book of Genesis, there are no problems.

[F]   But as to him who said this refers to the book of Numbers, what war is there [in that book]?

[V.A]   "The people of Israel journeyed from Beeroth Bene Jaakan to Moserah. There Aaron died" (Deut. 10:6).

[B]   Now did Aaron die in Moserah? And was it not at Mount Hor that he died?

[C]   That is in line with the following verse of Scripture: "And Aaron, the priest, went up Mount Hor at the command of the Lord, and died there" (Num. 33:38).

[D]   But once Aaron died, the clouds of glory departed from Israel, and the Canaanites sought to make trouble for Israel.

[E]   This is in line with the following verse of Scripture: "When the Canaanite, the king of Arad, who dwelt in the Negeb, heard that Israel was coming by the way of Atharim, he fought against Israel" (Num. 21:1).

[F]   What is the meaning of "By the way of Atharim"?

[G]   He heard that Aaron, their great wayfarer, had died, for he would show the way [tar] for them.

[H]   "Come and let us fight them."

[I]   The Israelites wanted to go back to Egypt and journeyed to the rear for eight journeys, but the tribe of Levi ran after them and slew eight families.

[J]   They slew four of them.

[K]   That is in line with that which is written:

[L]   "Of the Aramites, the Izharites, the Hebronites, and the Uzzielites" (1 Chron. 26:23).

[M]   When did they go back? In the time of David.

[N]   That is in line with that which is written, "In his days the righteous one flourishes" (Ps. 72:7).

[O]   They said, "Who caused all this bloodshed for us?"

[P]   They said, "It was because we did not perform the proper burial rights for that righteous man."

[Q]   So they went and arranged a eulogy for him and performed the proper obsequies for that righteous man.

[R]   And the Scripture treated the matter in their regard as if he had died there and been buried there,

[S]   for they performed the proper obsequies for that righteous man.

[VI.A]   ["And Moses took the bones of Joseph] with him" (Ex. 13:19)—

[B]   R. Qerispai in the name of R. Yohanan: " 'With him'—with your own soul you have done [this deed]."

[C]   Said R. Hama bar Haninah, "It may be compared to a king who was marrying off his son. A hyparch came to demand the right to be carried in a palinquin, and he did not allow him.

[D]   "Said the king, 'Let him be. Sometime soon he will marry off his daughter, and I shall deal honorably with him out of that with which he has honored me.' "

[E]   This is in line with that which is written:

[F]   "I will go down with you to Egypt, and I will also bring you up again" (Gen. 46:4).

[G]   What is the meaning of that which is stated, "I also will bring you up again"?

[H]   He said, "You I shall bring up, and all the rest of the tribes shall I bring up as well."

[I]   This teaches that every tribe brought up the bones of its founder with it.

[VII.A]   It was taught in the name of R. Judah, "If the matter were not written in Scripture, it would not be possible to say it at all."

[B]   [Following the Tosefta's version:] **Moses acquired merit [through burying] the bones of Joseph, so only the Omnipresent, blessed be he, took care of him, since it is said, "And he buried him in the valley" (Deut. 34:6) [M. Sot. 1:9E–F].**

[C]   **This teaches that when Moses died, Moses was laid upon the wings of the Presence for four mils, from the portion of Reuben to the portion of Gad.**

[D]   **For he died in the field of a portion of Reuben but he was buried in a field in the portion of Gad.**

[E]   **Now how do we know that he died in the midst of a field of the portion of Reuben? Since it is said, "Ascend this mountain of the Abarim, Mount Nebo" (Deut. 32:49). And Nebo belongs only in the portion of Reuben, as it is said, "And the sons of Reuben built Heshbon, Elealeh, Kiriathaim, Nebo, and Baal-meon" (Num. 32:37–38).**

[F]   **Now how do we know that he was buried in a field in the portion of Gad? Since it is said, "And of Gad he said, 'Blessed be he who enlarges Gad! Gad couches like a lion, he tears the arm, and the crown of the head. He chose the best of the land for himself, for there a commander's portion was reserved' " (Deut. 33:20–21) [T. Sot. 4:8].**

[VIII.A]   The Holy One, blessed be he, said, "He came to the heads of the people" (Deut. 33:21).

[B]   The ministering angels said, "The just decrees of the Lord" (Deut. 33:21).

[C]   And the Israelites said, "With Israel he executed the commands" (Deut. 33:21).

[D]   These and those would say, "He enters into peace; they rest in their beds who walk in their uprightness" (Is. 57:2).

The Talmud provides to the Mishnah a massive repertoire of thematically relevant materials.

[F]   Now that statement poses no problems in regard to the *zab*, *zabah*, and *mesora* [for minors, after all, may be afflicted in these ways].

[G]   But as to a woman after childbirth, does a minor woman give birth?

[H]   Have not R. Redipah and R. Jonah in the name of R. Huna [stated], [read with Qorban ha'edah:] "If a woman became pregnant and gave birth before she reached puberty, she and her infant will live. If she became pregnant before, and gave birth after, she reached puberty, she will survive, but the baby will die"?

[I]   How then [does Yohanan know that one may separate an offering for a minor who has given birth]?

[J]   Since he has married her off, she already has left his domain.

[K]   But [the reason we seek for the husband's right to separate the offering not in the wife's knowledge and consent is] that a man may separate an offering for his wife who is a deaf-mute.

[L]   But here in the case of a minor wife accused of adultery, you cannot maintain that it is the case [that the husband may set aside the offering; since a deaf-mute cannot go through the ordeal].

[M]   For R. Zeira and R. Yosa in the name of R. Yohanan: "A minor who committed adultery—she has no will to be prohibited to her husband.

[N]   "And as to a deaf-mute wife, you cannot [maintain that the husband has the right to set aside the offering].

[O]   "For it is written, 'And the woman shall say, Amen, Amen' (Num. 5:22), [and this one cannot make those sounds]."

[P]   Said R. Abin, "Since it is written, '. . . and you shall rejoice, you and your household' (Deut. 14:26)—because he is prevented from rejoicing with her [if the rite is not carried out], he has every right to separate the required offering in her behalf without her knowledge and consent. [He has every right to do so, because he must be able to participate in the rejoicing specified in connection with the festivals in Jerusalem, and he will be unable to do so if the rite is not carried out.]"

[Q]   [At this point we have proved that, because the husband must
       be able to participate in the Temple cult, he has the right to
       make it possible for his wife to do so, even without her knowl-
       edge and consent. That would indicate he may do so also for
       the woman after childbirth who lacks the required offering for
       her to be able to go into the Temple. But if the operative rea-
       son is to allow entry into the Temple, then the whole of Yo-
       hanan's position is not validated, only that part of it which
       concerns the offering needed to permit the woman to enter the
       Temple. This is the force of what follows.] R. Aha in the name
       of R. Ila: "Without her knowledge and consent he separates
       not the burnt offering of fowl but the sin offering of fowl [Lev.
       12:8], for it is only the latter which renders the woman after
       childbirth fit to eat meat deriving from Temple sacrifices."

[R]   [Along these same lines] it was taught, "He separates in her be-
       half only something which permits her to [eat sacrificial
       meat]."

[S]   Said R. Yosé, "You have only this [consideration, namely, the
       sin offering of fowl, and hence you may not allow the husband
       to separate without the wife's knowledge and consent the offer-
       ing of the accused wife]. [Only the stated purpose—the hus-
       band's need to be able to go to the Temple—justifies his doing
       so, and, as is clear, that limits the occasions on which he has
       the right to separate offerings for his wife to those which affect
       him as well.]"

[T]   It was taught, "Just as this prevents the wife from eating meat
       of sacrificial beasts, so that [namely, the rite of the accused
       wife] prevents her from doing so, [and, consequently, the hus-
       band may separate the offering of the accused wife without her
       knowledge and consent, just as he may do so for the wife who
       has just given birth].

[U]   "And since he is prevented from rejoicing [by eating the festal
       sacrifices with her], so he is prevented from eating meat deriv-
       ing from sacrifices [as just now explained]."

[V]   It was taught: "Even the offerings required at the end of Naz-
       irite vows which may yet be required of her prevent her from
       eating sacrificial meat [and hence the husband may separate
       those offerings without her knowledge and consent],

[W]   "for since she is disfigured [prior to the completion of those
       rites, since she cannot drink wine], he is prevented from rejoic-

ing with her, so it follows that just as he is prevented from rejoicing with her, it is as if he is prevented from eating the
sacrificial rites."

[X]   It was taught: R. Judah says, "A man may bring in behalf of
his wife every offering which she owes.

[Y]   "Even if she ate prohibited fat, or even if she has inadvertently
violated the law of the Sabbath [he provides her offering]."

[Z]   So did R. Judah say, "Once he has divorced her, he is no
longer liable, for so does he write to her, 'And obligations
which may come to me on your account from now on [I shall
no longer bear].' "

[IV.A]   [In reference to M. 2:1B, *All meat offerings at the outset and at
the end are in a utensil of service,*] has it not been taught:

[B]   The manner in which meal offerings are brought is as follows:
They bring the offering from home in a silver or gold utensil,
[and not as specified].

[C]   But [the offering under discussion] is suitable to be brought in
a utensil of service [and that is the Mishnah's meaning].

[V.A]   [As to M. 2:1D–E, the omission of oil and frankincense:] R.
Simeon B. Yohai taught, "On what account have they ruled,
'All sin offerings and guilt offerings in the Torah do not re-
quire drink offerings [along with them]'?

[B]   "So that the offering of a sinner should not be adorned [in a
lovely way]. [And the same consideration applies here.]"

[C]   They objected: "Lo, the sin offering and the guilt offering
brought by a *mesora* [do require drink offerings, so M. Men.
9:6C].

[D]   "And if you say that the *mesora* is not deemed a sinner, has not
R. Isaac stated, 'This is the law of the leper' (Lev. 14:1)—this
is the law of the gossip [*mesora—mosi shem ra*]?' "

[E]   He said to him, "Since he has been afflicted [by his illness, he
has atoned for his sin of gossiping].

[F]   "And it is written, 'Lest . . . your brother be degraded in your
sight' (Deut. 25:3).

[G]   "After being punished] is he like one who is not a sinner?"

[VI.A]   R. Yohanan in the name of R. Ishmael, "It is written, '[If you offer a cereal] offering [of first fruits to the Lord, you shall offer for the cereal offering of your first fruits crushed new grain from fresh ears, parched with fire]' (Lev. 2:14).

[B]   "And it is written, '[. . . and bring] the offering [required of her, a tenth of an *ephah* of barley meal]" (Num. 5:15).

[C]   "Just as meal offering stated in the latter context consists of barley, so that in the former likewise it is made up of barley."

[D]   Said R. Eleazar, "Here, new grain is stated [at Lev. 2:14], and in connection with the plagues of Egypt, new grain is stated (Ex. 9:30).

[E]   "Just as 'new grain' mentioned in connection with the plagues in Egypt refers to barley ['the barley was in ear'], so 'new grain' mentioned in connection with the present case is barley."

[F]   R. Aqiba says, "In regard to a meal offering of the community, bringing first fruits is mentioned in connection with Passover, and bringing first fruits is mentioned in connection with Pentecost [the former: the *omer;* the latter: the two loaves of bread].

[G]   "If then we find that of that species of grain which the individual brings in fulfillment of his obligation, the community brings in fulfillment of its obligation on Pentecost—

[H]   "[then] of what species does the individual bring to fulfill his obligation? It is barley.

[I]   "So the community should bring in fulfillment of its obligation only barley.

[J]   "Another matter: Should you say that the *omer* was offered of wheat, then the two loaves would not be first fruits (Lev. 23:17). [The two loaves are supposed to be the first meal offering of wheat of the year. If the *omer* is made of wheat, then they would not be the first meal offering of wheat.]"

[VII.A]   [With reference to M. 2:1, sifted flour,] there we have learned, *Pounded wheat, groats, and grits are susceptible to uncleanness in all circumstances* [being dampened before milling] (M. Makh. 6:2H).

[B]   R. Jonah [explained], "Pounded wheat is split into two, groats into three, and grits into four parts [when they are milled]."

[C]   R. Yosé b. R. Bun asked, "Is it so, then, that from that point onward [if ground into more parts], they are deemed flour? Then it is not necessary to winnow flour from them."

Units **I** and **II** provide a close reading of the Mishnah's language, in the former case, measured against that of Scripture, in the latter, compared to available law. Unit **III** then vastly expands the range of discourse, occupying the bulk of this passage of the Talmud. The issue is clearly spelled out at the beginning. The unpacking of the argument on whether or not the husband may bring offerings for the wife without her knowledge and consent could not be more thorough. The operative criterion is whether or not his own participation in the cult is affected. Since the condition of the wife governs the husband's participation, as the Talmud indicates, he is able to bring those offerings without her knowledge and consent. Unit **III** is generated by unit **II**'s exegesis of the Mishnah's language. Units **IV** and **V** proceed to the exegesis of the Mishnah once more. Unit **VI** takes up the matter of using barley (M. 2:1G), and unit **VII**, the matter of sifting. So, in all, what the Talmud gives us is a disciplined and sustained analysis of the Mishnah's facts and language.

2:2

[A]   *He [the husband] would bring a clay bowl and put it in a half-log of water from the laver.*

[B]   *R. Judah says, "A quarter-log."*

[C]   *As [Judah] calls for less writing, so he calls for less water [M. 2:3H].*

[D]   *And [the priest] goes into the hekhal and turns to his right.*

[E]   *Now there was a place, an amah by an amah, with a marble flagstone, and a ring was attached to it.*

[F]   *And when he raised it [the stone], he took the dirt from under it and put it [into the bowl of water],*

[G]   *sufficient to be visible on the water,*

[H]   *since it says, "And of the dust that is on the floor of the taber-*
nacle the priest shall take and put it into the water" (Num.
5:17).

[I.A]   It was taught [in a Tannaite tradition] "[The husband would
bring a] new [clay bowl . . .]"

[B]   The Mishnah formulation [before us accords with the view] of
R. Eleazar.

[C]   For we have learned there: *He would bring a new flask of clay*
[M. Neg. 14:1B].

[D]   Who teaches that it is to be a new flask?

[E]   It is R. Eleazar, for he interprets the verse as follows:

[F]   "In an earthen vessel over running water . . ." (Lev. 14:5)—
Just as the water is of a sort with which no [prior] work has
been done, so the earthen vessel must be of a sort with which
no [prior] work has been done.

[G]   Now that interpretation validates the position that, [in connection with the purification rite of a *mesora,* a new clay utensil is
to be used], for he expounds [the language pertinent to that
rite], ". . . in an earthen vessel over running water. . . ."

[H]   But what have you to say here [with regard to the accused
wife, in which case there is no parallel language at all]?

[I]   Said R. Yohanan, "[The Tanna who maintains that a new
utensil is to be used here] concurs with the position of R. Ishmael [in the following]."

[J]   It has been taught: *Water from the laver* (M. 2:2A)—

[K]   R. Ishmael says, "It is to be spring water."

[L]   And sages declare the rite valid with water of any character.

[M]   Lo, R. Eleazar accords with R. Ishmael's position on the
water, and R. Ishmael accords with R. Eleazar's position on
the use of the new utensil.

[N]   It is found taught as follows: *A new clay bowl.*

[O]   R. Ishmael says, "There are Tannaim who teach as follows: 'A
clay bowl, and not a sherd.'

[P]   "And there are Tannaim who teach as follows: 'Even a sherd'
[suitable for holding water is acceptable for the rite]."

[Q]   Now they wanted to propose the following theory of the authorities behind this saying:

[R]   The one who said "A clay utensil, not a sherd" is R. Eleazar.

[S]   Those who said "Even a sherd" are the rabbis.

[T]   The whole of the cited tradition belongs to the rabbis. The one who said "The clay utensil, not a sherd" speaks of a case in which the larger part of the bowl is missing and the smaller part is available; [in such a case, the sherd is not suitable].

[U]   And the one who said "With a sherd" speaks of a case in which the bowl is lacking only its smaller part, but the larger part is in hand.

[V]   There are Tannaim who teach: "With a clay utensil, not with a sooty one."

[W]   There are Tannaim who teach, "Even with a sooty one."

[X]   They [once more] proposed to conclude that the one who said, "A clay utensil, not a sooty one" is R. Eleazar.

[Y]   Those who said "Even with a sooty one" are the rabbis.

[Z]   The whole of it accords with the position of the rabbis.

[AA]   He who says "With a clay utensil, not a sooty one" cites the view of the rabbis, and he who says "Even with a sooty one" also cites the view of the rabbis.

[II.A] There we have learned: *A hyssop with which one has sprinkled [a person unclean with purification water] is fit for use [also] in purifying a leper [M. Par. 11:8A].*

[B]   R. Imi in the name of R. Eleazar: "This [pericope of the Mishnah] excludes the position of R. Eleazar."

[C]   For it has been taught: **A hyssop which is fit for the [18a] purification rite is fit for the leper. If one sprinkled with it for the purification rite, it is fit for use for a leper. R. Eleazar says, "Cedar wood, hyssop, and a red thread mentioned in the Torah are to be articles with which work has not been done [which have never been used before]"** [T. Neg. 8:2].

[D]   Said R. Yose, "Now it is not an argument a fortiori [that if one used the hyssop to sprinkle purification water, the hyssop may not be used for sprinkling someone else requiring pruification water]?

[E]   "Now if in the case of a *mesora*, in which articles required for use in his connection are not rendered invalid by use for some other purpose, if one has sprinkled with a hyssop for purification water the hyssop is invalid for use with a *mesora*,

[F]   "in the case of purification water, in which articles required for use in this connection are rendered invalid by use for some other purpose, is it not logical that hyssop used for purification water one time may not be used for purification water another time?"

[G]   If one has used a hyssop for a given *mesora*'s purification rite, what is the law as to then using the hyssop to validate another *mesora*? [This question is addressed to the position of Eleazar. Do we maintain that it is as if he has sprinkled purification water, and the hyssop is invalid for another *mesora*, or do we maintain that use for the purification rite is separate and not taken into consideration in the case of a second use for a *mesora*?]

[H]   [There is a dispute in this regard.] One who says "It is valid" maintains that it is the view of R. Judah, with which R. Eleazar concurs [in the story that follows at J].

[I]   One who says "It is invalid" holds that it is not the view of R. Judah, with which R. Eleazar concurs.

[J]   It was taught: **Said R. Judah, "It was my Sabbath to be at R. Tarfon's house. He said to me, 'Judah, my son, give me my sandal,' and I gave it to him. He put his hand out of the window, and took a staff from there. He said to me, 'Judah, son, with this staff here I have declared clean three lepers.' And I learned from that case seven laws [concerning the staff]: it is of cypress wood; its head is planed; it is a cubit in length; its breadth is a fourth of the thickness of the leg of a bed, divided one into two, then two into four parts; they sprinkle, repeat, and do it a third time [with the same piece of wood]; they declare clean [a mesora] both while the Temple is standing and not while the Temple is standing; and they effect a rite of purification in the provinces" [T. Neg. 8:2D].**

[III.A]   ["And in his hand the priest shall have the water of bitterness that brings the curse" (Num. 5:18).] "Water . . ."

[B]   Is it possible that the water should have the hue of normal water?

[C]   Scripture has said, ". . . that brings the curse . . ." [not normal water].

[D]   Is it possible that it should be the color of ink?

[E]   Scripture has said, "Water."

[F]   How so?

[G]   The water should have the appearance of water and the appearance of bitterness [brought about by the dirt from the ground].

[H]   Sages have given as its measure *a half-log of water from the laver [M. 2:2B].*

[I]   And lo, it has been taught: *R. Judah says, "A quarter-log" [M. 2:2A].*

[J]   What R. Judah says here is consistent with a position held elsewhere, for we have learned,

[K]   *As Judah calls for less writing, so he calls for less water [M. 2:2C].*

[IV.A]   There we have learned: *Helene, his mother, set a golden candlestick over the door of the sanctuary. She also made a golden tablet on which was written the pericope of the accused wife [M. Yom. 3:10D–E],*

[B]   **so that when the sun rises, sparks of golden light sparkle forth from it, so people know that the sun is rising [T. Yom. 2:3C].**

[C]   How was the passage written thereon?

[D]   R. Simeon b. Laqish said in the name of R. Yannai, "It was written only in *alef-bet* [that is, the beginnings of the words of the pericope, but not fully spelled out]."

[E]   And lo it has been taught: In the writing used here, he wrote there [that is, he wrote the scroll and followed the way the scroll's text was given on the golden tablet], not with thick nor with thin but with middling letters. [That is, the priest would write the scroll by copying what was on the golden tablet. This then implies that he copied everything out, not merely the beginning letters of each word.]

[F]   Interpret the passage to mean that he copied an *alef* from the tablet onto the scroll, and so to with a *bet*, and so on.

[G]   R. Hoshaiah taught [contrary to the foregoing view], "The entire pericope of the accused wife was completely written out on the scroll.

[H]   "For from that scroll did he read and interpret all of the details of the pericope."

[**V**.A]   And why these matters of water, dirt, and writing [prior to the ordeal itself, as inducements to confess her sin]?

[B]   "Water" indicating the place from which she came.

[C]   "Dirt" indicating the place to which she goes.

[D]   "Writing" indicating before whom she is destined to give a full account.

[E]   There we have learned:

[F]   *Aqabiah b. Mehallalel says, "Reflect upon three things, and you will not fall into the clutches of transgression: [know from whence you come, whither you are going, and before whom you are going to have to give a full account of yourself. From whence do you come? From a putrid drop. Whither are you going? To a place of dust, worms, and maggots. And before whom are you going to have to give a full account of yourself? Before the King of Kings of Kings, the Holy One, blessed be he]"* [M. Abot 3:1].

[G]   R. Abba son of R. Papi, and R. Joshua of Sikhnin in the name of R. Levi: "All three of them did R. Aqabiah derive from a single verse of Scripture: 'Remember your Creator' (Qoh. 12:1:BWR'K).

[H]   " 'Remember your well (B'RK), your pit (BRK), your Creator (BWR'K).'

[I]   " 'Your well'—the place from which you came.

[J]   " 'Your pit'—the place to which you go.

[K]   " 'Your Creator'—before whom you are going to give a full account of yourself."

[**VI**.A]   Three matters must be done for the particular woman at hand [and may not be made ready in advance for anyone who may come along]:

[B]   [The writ of divorce]: "He will write for her" (Deut. 24:1).

[C]   [The rites of the accused wife]: "He will do for her all of this law" (Num. 5:30).

[D]   [The writ of emancipation of a slave woman] "not yet given her freedom" (Lev. 19:20).

[E]   [Tosefta's version:] **Three things must be visible on the surface of the water: the dust of the red cow, the dust of the accused wife, and the blood of the bird [used to purify mesora (Lev. 14:6).**

[F]   **The dust of the red cow—sufficient to be visible on the surface of the water.**

[G]   **The dust of the accused wife—sufficient to be visible on the surface of the water [M. 2:2G].**

[H]   **The blood of the bird of a mesora—sufficient to be visible on the surface of the water.**

[I]   **The spit of a deceased, childless brother's wife—sufficient to be visible to the sight of the elders [T. Sot. 1:8].**

[J]   [Yerushalmi's version omits *the blood of the bird,* etc., and so] R. Ishmael taught: "Also the blood of the bird used to purify the *mesora.*"

[K]   Said R. Zeira, "They took the measure of the matter and laid down the following rule:

[L]   "The blood of a small bird is not fully diluted in a quarter-*log* of water, and the blood of a large bird does not blot out the water in a quarter-*log* of water."

[M]   This is in line with that which is stated, "In blood" (Lev. 14:1).

[N]   "In the blood [of the bird that was killed over the running water]" (Lev. 14:6)—Is it possible that it should be only blood [with no appearance of water in the mixture]?

[O]   Scripture says, "Running water."

[P]   If it calls for "running water," is it possible that it should be wholly water?

[Q]   Scripture says, "Blood."

[R]   How so?

[S]   It must be running water in which the blood of the bird is to be recognized.

[T]   Sages gave us the measure [for such a mixture] a quarter-*log*.

[VII.A]   R. Pedat in the name of R. Yohanan: "Water used for the rite of the accused wife is invalidated if left standing overnight."

[B]   R. Aha in the name of R. Abina, "Any sort of material, part of which is not destined for the altar itself, is in no way rendered invalid by being left overnight."

[VIII.A]   "[And the priest shall take] some of the dust [that is on the floor of the tabernacle and put it into the water]" (Num. 5:17).

[B]   Might one think that the dirt may be taken from an available pile of dirt in a basket [and not from the floor of the Temple (for the reading, cf. Qorban ha‛edah]?

[C]   Scripture specifies, "From the dust that is on the floor of the tabernacle."

[D]   If the requirement is that the dust be from the floor of the tabernacle, it is possible to suppose that the dirt is valid only if the priest will dig it up with a spade?

[E]   Scripture says, "Which will be . . ."

[F]   How so?

[G]   If there is no dirt there, he brings some and puts it there.

[H]   Said R. Abin, "Accordingly it has been said:

[I]   " 'Is it possible that it will be valid only if one will come and dig up some dirt with a spade?

[J]   " 'Scripture says, "Which will be there . . ."—deriving from any source [in the courtyard].' "

[K]   "The tabernacle"—to encompass also [dirt from] the tabernacle, also that from the high places of Nob, Gibeon, and Shilo, and the eternal house [to be rebuilt when the Messiah comes].

The exercise of unit **I**, to find the authority behind the Mishnah, is important in establishing a correct text for the Mishnah, since, as we see, whether or not the bowl must be unused prior to its service for the rite of the accused wife is at issue. Sifting the several sayings assigned to Tannaitic authority then leads to some secondary questions. Unit **II** is continuous with the main inquiry of unit **I**, namely, Eleazar's position. Unit **III** proceeds to the Scriptural foundations for the law. Unit **IV** provides a repertoire of materials relevant to copying out the curse on a scroll ("book"): how the text is supplied to the priest, the materials in use, and the like. Unit **V** turns to a homily on the Mishnah's requirements. Unit **VI** is relevant at G, which cites the Mishnah; but it adds nothing to the interpretation of the Mishnah. I give the Tosefta's version, which gives four items for the promised three, and should lose either I, as we now have it, or in light of J, G. It is not an important problem. The kind of exegetical exercise for Lev. 14:6 is followed for Num. 5:17, regarding the dust on the floor of the tabernacle, at unit V,III. Then Abin states a further exegesis of the same verse in the same form. The relevance to the Mishnah is clear.

2:3

[A]   *He came to write the scroll.*

[B]   *From what place did he write?*

[C]   *From, "If no man has lain with thee . . . but if thou hast gone aside with another instead of thy husband . . ." (Num. 5:19f.).*

[D]   *But he does not write, "And the priest shall cause the woman to swear" (Num. 5:21).*

[E]   *And he writes, "The Lord make thee a curse and an oath among thy people . . . and this water that causeth the curse shall go into thy bowels and make thy belly to swell and thy thigh to fall away."*

[F]   *But he does not write, "And the woman shall say, Amen, Amen!"*

[G]   *R. Yosé says, "He made no break."*

[H]   *R. Judah says, "He writes, in fact, only, 'The Lord make thee a curse and an oath . . . and this water that causeth the curse shall go into thy bowels. . . .'*

[I]   *"And he did not write, 'And the woman shall say, Amen, Amen!' "*

[I.A]   R. Qerispai said, "There is a dispute between R. Yohanan and R. Simeon b. Laqish.

[B]   "One said, 'The priest imposes the oath and then he writes [the curse down in the scroll, as at Num. 5:19, 5:23].'

[C]   "The other one said, 'He writes [the curse down in the scroll], and afterward he imposes the oath.' "

[D]   They proposed to make the following statement:

[E]   He who said, "He imposes the oath and afterward writes the scroll" follows the order in which the Scripture states matters: "[Then the priest shall make her] take an oath" (Num. 5:19), "[Then the priest] shall write [these curses in a book . . .]" (Num. 5:23).

[F]   He who said "He writes the curses and then he imposes the oath" holds that position so as to set the oath immediately prior to the actual administration of the bitter water.

[G]   There are those who teach, "Both the various conditions specified of the rite and the oath itself are essential to the performance of the rite."

[H]   There are those who teach, "The taking of the oath is essential to the rite; the other specifications and conditions are not essential to the rite."

[I]   They proposed to theorize as follows:

[J]   The one who said "both the various conditions specified for the rite and the oath itself are essential to the performance of the rite" maintains that where the words "ordinance" and "Torah" are mentioned, all details in the cited pericope are essential to the correct performance of the rite described therein.

[K]   And he who says "The taking of the oath is essential to the rite; the other specifications and conditions are not essential to the rite" does not hold that view.

[L]   No, that is not so. He does hold that view, but he maintains that they are not listed in the necessary order [that is, Scripture tells what must be done, but it does not specify the order in which the rites must be carried out].

[M]   Now the dispute just now spelled out is in line with the one spelled out earlier.

[N]   That is to say, he who says "Both the various conditions speci-fied of the rite and the oath itself are essential to the perfor-mance of the rite" accords with the other who said "He imposes the oath and afterward writes the scroll," just as Scrip-ture specifies.

[O]   He who says "The taking of the oath is essential to the rite; the other specifications and conditions are not essential to the rite" holds the view of the one who says "He writes the scroll and afterward imposes the oath."

The Talmud's exercise is formally perfect and exposes all of the logical possibilities of the cited disputes, first, one by one, then in sequence. The whole is clear as given.

2:4

[A]   *He writes neither on a tablet, nor on papyrus, nor on unpre-pared hide, but only on [parchment] scroll,*

[B]   *since it is written, "In a book" (Num. 5:23).*

[C]   *And he writes neither with gum, nor with coppera, nor with anything which makes a lasting impression [on the writing ma-terial], but only with ink,*

[D]   *since it is written, "And he will blot it out"—*

[E]   *writing which can be blotted out.*

[I.A] Levi bar Sisi raised the question before Rabbi: "As to the scroll written for the accused wife, what is the law on its im-parting uncleanness to the hands?"

[B]   He said to him, "That is a valid question."

[C]   Said R. Yosé, "It is not a valid question.

[D]   "Is it not so that they decreed that scrolls should impart un-cleanness to the hands only because of their holiness?

[E]   "But this scroll is written to be blotted out, [so it is not holy to begin with and does not require the protection of the cited law]."

[F]   No, it remains a pressing question.

[G]   For it is only because the Scripture has specified that the scroll is to be blotted out that it is blotted out. [But otherwise it would be holy, like any other scroll, and hence the question is a valid one.]

[II.A]   And how many [excess] letters may be written in [the scroll], such that it is no longer a valid [scroll], with the result that the blotting out is not required [by Scripture], so that one [who goes ahead and blots it out] will be liable on that account [for needlessly erasing the name of God]?

[B]   R. Hanin taught:

[C]   "The House of Shammai say, 'One.'

[D]   "And the House of Hillel say, 'Two.' "

[E]   Said R. Hila, "The reason for the position of the House of Hillel is that the two letters should be sufficient to write Yah [God]."

[III.A]   R. Yudan raised the question, "If one wrote the scroll from memory [and did not copy it from a copy before him, and then blotted it out], what is the law?

[B]   "If he blotted it out in dirt [what is the law]?

[C]   "If he wrote it part by part and blotted it out as he went along, [what is the law]?" [These questions are not answered.]

[IV.A]   It was taught:

[B]   R. Eleazar b. Shammua says, "They do not write it on the hide of an unclean beast."

[C]   Said R. Simeon, "Since you have said that the scroll is written to be blotted out, why should he not write it [on such a hide]?"

[D]   It was taught: R. Eleazar b. Simeon says, "I concur with the position of R. Eleazar b. Shammua, rather than with the position of father.

[E]   "For the woman may say that she will not drink the water, and the holy name written on the scroll will be [permanently] hidden away on the hide of an unclean beast."

[F]   [Simeon said,] "Here it is written, 'book' (Num. 5:23).

[G]   "And there [in connection with the writ of divorce], 'book' is
      written (Deut. 24:1).

[H]   "Here [in regard to a writ of divorce] you say that it may be
      written on any thing which is not attached to the ground, and
      here you say this [requiring a hide of only one type of beast]?"

[I]   He said to him, "No. There is a significant difference.

[J]   "Here it is written, 'On a book, and he will write' [thus differ-
      entiating the two passages]."

[V.A] Is it possible that he writes with ink, red ink, ink prepared
       with gum, or vitriol?

[B]   Scripture says, "And he will blot out . . ."

[C]   Since it says, "And he will blot out . . . ," is it possible that it
      may be written with any sort of liquid (milk, blood, etc., [M.
      Makh. 6:4]) or with fruit juice?

[D]   Scripture says, "And he will write."

[E]   How so?

[F]   It must be writing which can be blotted out.

[G]   And what is such writing as that?

[H]   It is writing in ink which is not prepared with gum.

[I]   And has it not been written, "If it is blotted out of the scroll,
      it is valid"?

[J]   Interpret that statement in line with the following tradition, as
      it has been taught:

[K]   Said R. Meir, "So long as we studied with R. Ishmael, we
      never put vitriol in ink."

Unit I asks whether the scroll prepared for the present occasion
enjoys the same status as other scrolls containing passages of
the Torah. The discussion leaves nothing out, except the answer. Units II and III set forth other questions, also not fully
answered. Units IV and V deal with M. 2:4C–E. As a whole,
we have an anthology of relevant materials, but, unlike the
foregoing, the exegetical logic of the several units is not fully
and finally exposed.

2:5

[A]   *To what does she say, "Amen, Amen"?*

[B]   *" 'Amen' to the curse" (Num. 5:21, " 'Amen' to the oath"*
       (Num. 5:19).

[C]   *" 'Amen' that it was not with this particular man," " 'Amen'*
       that it was with no other man."

[D]   *" 'Amen' that I was not made unclean, and if I was made un-*
       clean, may [the bitter water] enter into me."

[E]   *" 'Amen' that I have not gone aside while betrothed, married,*
       awaiting levirate marriage, or wholly taken in levirate
       marriage."

[F]   *R. Meir says, " 'Amen' that I was not made unclean, 'Amen'*
       that I shall not be made unclean."

[18b/   R. Eleazar in the name of R. Yosé b. Zimrah, "[In saying the
I.A]   word 'Amen' in an oath, one makes three affirmations, as fol-
         lows:] 'Amen' to receiving the oath, 'Amen' to the oath [itself,
         as at Num. 5:19], 'Amen' to confirm what has been said in the
         oath."

[B]   [The fact that saying] Amen [after the statement of the oath
       constitutes] acceptance [of what has been said] derives from the
       rite of the accused wife [who simply states "Amen" after the
       officiating priest spells out the oath and its conditions].

[C]   [The fact that saying] Amen [confirms the standing of] the oath
       [itself] [derives from the following verse:] ". . . that I may per-
       form the oath which I swore to your fathers, to give them a
       land flowing with milk and honey, as at this day. Then I an-
       swered, 'Amen [so be it], Lord' " (Jer. 11:5).

[D]   [The fact that saying] Amen [after the statement of the oath]
       confirms all the matters [stated in the oath] derives from the
       following: "And Benaiah the son of Jehoiada answered the
       king, 'Amen! May the Lord, the God of my lord the king say
       so. As the Lord has been with my lord the king, even so may
       he be with Solomon . . .' " (1 Kings 1:36–37).

[E]   [Referring to Num. 5:21 (Qorban ha'edah vs. Pené Moshe),]
       said R. Tanhuma, "If it is from the verse just now cited, then
       saying Amen to an oath [as indicated in that verse] proves

nothing, [for the woman says Amen to the curse, not to the oath (Qorban ha'edah)].

[F]   "But rather the following verse is what proves the case: 'That you may enter into the covenant of the Lord your God and into its curse' (Deut. 29:12).

[G]   "And there is no 'curse' except an oath, as you say in Scripture, 'Let the priest make the woman take the oath of the curse' " (Num. 5:21).

[II.A]   Now how do we know that [sages] have learned to transfer the oath [from one matter to yet others relevant to the same party]? It is from the accused woman. [That is, how do we know that the same oath may cover more than the provisions for which it originally was invoked: It is from the case of the accused wife.]

[B]   "And the woman shall say, 'Amen, Amen' " (Num. 5:22).

[C]   " 'Amen' that it was not with this particular man," " 'Amen' that it was with no other man" [M. 2:5C].

[D]   Up to this point we learn that one may insert into the oath matters concerning which it is appropriate to impose the oath upon the woman [such as, an oath that she has not committed adultery with anyone at all].

[E]   How do we know that one may insert into an oath matters concerning which it is not appropriate to impose the oath, [in that the matters are not congruent to the original cause of the oath, e.g., that there has been no theft of slaves, property, deeds, and the like]?

[F]   Said R. Yosé b. R. Bun, "Let us derive the answer from the following: 'Amen' that I have not gone aside while betrothed, married, awaiting levirate marriage, or wholly taken in levirate marriage [M. 2:5E]."

[G]   Now are the matters of the levirate connection [awaiting marriage, or standing in a fully consummated marriage] appropriately included within the oath? [Clearly they are not, since the law is that the woman in a levirate connection is not required to undergo the ordeal of the accused wife.]

[H]   And even so, you say that they assign the oath to cover these relationships as well.

[I]   Accordingly, one includes in an oath matters which, to begin with, are not appropriate to its original cause.

[**III**.A]   There are Tannaim who repeat the tradition as follows: Just as the accused wife is subjected to a curse along with the oath, so all others who are subjected to an oath are subjected to both a curse and an oath.

[B]   And there are Tannaim who repeat the tradition as follows: This particular one is subjected to a curse along with the oath, but no others who are subjected to an oath are subject to both a curse and an oath.

[C]   [Since the law of taking an oath derives from the analogy of the case of the accused wife,] they wanted to propose the following: As to the position of the one who said "Just as the accused wife is subjected to a curse along with the oath, so all others who are subjected to an oath are subject to both a curse and an oath." [That position] poses no problems, [because, as noted, the governing analogy is fully worked out in such a rule].

[D]   But as to the position of the one who says "This particular one is subjected to a curse along with the oath, but no others who are subjected to an oath are subject to both a curse and an oath," [there is a problem].

[E]   For you derive [from the law governing the accused wife] the fact that one may apply the oath to matters not originally covered by its cause. And yet, it would appear, you are not willing to derive [from the law governing the accused wife] the fact that both a curse and an oath apply. [So you are not consistent.]

[F]   There are Tannaim who repeat the tradition as follows: Just as the accused is subject to saying "Amen . . . Amen," so all others who are subjected to an oath say "Amen . . . Amen."

[G]   And there are Tannaim who repeat the tradition as follows: This particular one is subject to saying "Amen . . . Amen," but all others who are subject to an oath do not say "Amen . . . Amen."

[H]   They wanted then to propose the following: As to the position of the one who said "Just as the accused wife is required to say 'Amen . . . Amen,' " so all others who are subjected to an oath say 'Amen . . . Amen,' " there is no problem [for the same reason as is stated at C].

[I]   But as to the position of the one who says "This particular one
        is required to say 'Amen . . . Amen,' but no others who are
        subjected to an oath are required to say 'Amen . . . Amen,' "
        [there is a problem].

[J]   For you derive [from the law governing the accused wife] the
        fact that one may apply the oath to matters not originally cov-
        ered by its cause. And yet, it would appear, you are not willing
        to derive [from the law governing the accused wife the fact that
        all those who take an oath must say] "Amen . . . Amen."

[IV.A] Said R. Ba bar Mamel, "Who taught that the deceased, child-
        less brother's wife awaiting levirate marriage [is subject to the
        oath, as at M. 2:5E]? It is R. Aqiba.

[B]   "For R. Aqiba maintains that a woman in a levirate marriage
        [who has illicit sexual relations] produces a *mamzer* [a totally il-
        legitimate offspring]. [It follows that if she has committed adul-
        tery, she is prohibited to remain with her levirate husband.]"

[C]   R. Ili said to him, "What difference does the matter of produc-
        ing a *mamzer* make in regard to the expression of jealousy [and
        consequent ordeal]?

[D]   "The Torah has stated, '. . . and he is jealous of his wife . . .'
        (Num. 5:14).

[E]   "[This includes] even the case of a woman who is only partly
        his wife [that is, who is not firmly within the marital bond].
        [Hence rabbis vis-à-vis Aqiba, who hold that a woman in a le-
        virate marriage who had illicit sexual relations and produces a
        child does not impart to that child the status of *mamzer*, be-
        cause her marital relation is not so firm as that of a woman in a
        normal marriage, still concur with the rule of M. 2:5E.]"

[F]   [Rejecting this objection of Ili,] said R. Shimi, "And has not
        R. Yannai stated, 'Thirty-and-some-odd sages voted: How do
        we know that the relationship of consecration of a wife to one
        husband does not apply [at all] in the case of a levirate
        marriage?

[G]   " 'Scripture states, 'The wife of the deceased shall not be mar-
        ried outside the family to a stranger; her husband's brother
        shall go in to her, and take her as his wife' (Deut. 25:5).

[H]   " '[The meaning is that] she will not stand in a complete rela-
        tionship with another [that is, be deemed completely wed to

another; there is no consideration of consecration to any man at all]. [Accordingly, (Shimi maintains,) rabbis vis-à-vis Aqiba will not concur in the clause of M. 2:5E].' "

[I]   Said to him R. Yohanan, "Now [why should such a vote have been required at all]? Is it not a statement explicitly made in the Mishnah [so what need was there for an exegetical debate]?

[J]   *"He who betrothes a woman and said, 'Lo, you are betrothed to me after your levir will perform the rite of removing the shoe'—she is not betrothed [M. Qid. 3:5H].* [Since at this point she is not subject to consecration for marriage to anyone, even afterward the statement made now is null.]"

[K]   R. Yannai broke out in praises [of Yohanan, on account of this statement of his, citing the following verses of Scripture]: "Those who lavish gold from the purse" (Is. 46:6); "My son, keep sound wisdom and discretion; let them not escape from your sight" (Prov. 3:21); "Be wise, my son, and make my heart glad" (Prov. 27:11); "Give instruction to a wise man, and he will be still wiser" (Prov. 9:9); "The wise man also may hear and increase in learning" (Prov. 1:5).

[L]   Said to him R. Simeon b. Laqish, "Even after all these verses of praise, I can interpret the Mishnah's rule in line with the position of R. Aqiba, who has ruled that a woman in a levirate marriage who commits adultery produces a *mamzer*" [cf. Pené Moshe].

[M]   [Delete: And let them object: "What difference does the matter of producing a *mamzer* make in a case in which there is a valid act of consecration?" etc.]

[V.A]   A woman awaiting levirate marriage who [in the interim] committed adultery—

[B]   R. Eleazar said, "She is [thereafter] permitted to have sexual relations with the levirate husband [and so to enter marriage with him]."

[C]   R. Joshua b. Levi said, "She is forbidden from having sexual relations with the levirate husband [and may not then marry him]."

[D]   Rabbis state [the following question which] R. Mana said, "Has not R. Jacob bar Aha said in the name of R. Eleazar, 'A woman awaiting levirate marriage who died—the levir is permitted to marry her mother'? [That would indicate that, when she is alive, he may not marry her mother, even prior to his entering levirate marriage with her. It follows that there is a marital bond between the woman and the levir sufficient to prohibit his marrying her mother. It must further follow that if, while awaiting the levirate marriage, she committed adultery, she should be prohibited from marrying the levir, just as she would if she were engaged to him and committed adultery. That statement poses a problem to the position of Eleazar, B.]"

[E]   [There is yet a further problem to Eleazar:] Since we have learned, *This is the general principle: Concerning any situation in which she may have sexual relations in such wise as not to be prohibited to her husband, the husband may make no condition whatsoever with her [regarding the effect of the ordeal]* [M. 2:6C].

[F]   Now who can be the Tanna who stands behind that statement? It can be neither rabbis nor R. Aqiba. [For M. 2:5E has a stipulation effective for the woman awaiting levirate marriage. Aqiba and rabbis must agree with that statement, as we have seen above, unit **IV**. It then follows that, so far as Eleazar is concerned, the authority behind M. 2:6C is not to be located. It must further follow that the dispute between Eleazar and Joshua b. Levi requires reinterpretation, and it is to that task that we now proceed.]

[G]   But thus must we interpret the matter [to make sense of the question raised at E–F]:

[H]   He [Eleazar] who said that she is permitted to marry accords with rabbis and not with R. Aqiba.

[I]   And he [Joshua b. Levi] who said that she is forbidden to marry accords with R. Aqiba and not with rabbis.

[**VI**.A]   Said R. Yannai, "A woman awaiting levirate marriage who committed adultery is permitted to marry [the levir later on]."

[B]   And it has been taught likewise: ". . . and it is hidden from the eyes of her husband" (Num. 5:13)—and not from the eyes of her levir.

[C]   R. Jacob bar Zabedi in the name of R. Abbahu: "There was a case, and it involved a woman awaiting levirate marriage to a priest, and sages nonetheless permitted her to have sexual relations with the levir."

[D]   Said R. Yosé b. R. Bun, "Even a flogging does not apply to her case."

[**VII**.A]   [With reference to M. 2:5F, Meir's statement, " *'Amen' that I was not made unclean, 'Amen' that I shall not be made unclean,* "]it is not that R. Meir maintains, "The water tests her from this point," but rather, "the water is deposited in her, so that, if she should become unclean, they will test her retroactively."

[**VIII**.A]   "This is the law in cases of jealousy" (Num. 5:29)—the law governing all ages.

[B]   A woman does not drink the bitter water and then repeat the ordeal.

[C]   Said R. Judah, "Nehemiah of Sihin gave testimony for R. Aqiba: 'A woman does drink the bitter water and repeat the process.'

[D]   "Said R. Aqiba, 'I shall then explain the matter. As regards adultery with one particular man she does not drink the bitter water and repeat the ordeal.

[E]   " 'But as regards an accusation covering two men, she does drink the bitter water and repeat the ordeal.' "

[F]   But sages say, "Whether it is by reason of one man or of two men [that she is accused of having adultery], she does drink the bitter water and repeat the ordeal [should the occasion arise].

[G]   "Korkemit proves the matter, for she drank the bitter water, repeated the rite, and did so yet a third time, on the instructions of Shemaiah and Abtalion, and it was by reason of suspicion involving only one man."

[**IX**.A]   *There we have learned: [Aqabya b. Mahallel said], "They do not administer the bitter water to a proselyte or a freed slave-woman." And sages say, "They do administer the bitter water [to a proselyte or a freed slave woman]" [M. Ed. 5:6].*

[B]   Now how shall we explain this dispute?

[C]   If it concerns an Israelite who married a proselyte woman, it has been written, "The children of Israel" (Num. 5:12)—and not proselytes.

[D]   If it is the case of a proselyte who married an Israelite girl, it is written, "Then the man shall bring his wife to the priest" (Num. 5:15).

[E]   But we must interpret the matter to apply to the marriage of a proselyte man and a proselyte woman.

[F]   What is the Scriptural basis for the position of Aqabya?

[G]   "The children of Israel"—not proselytes.

[H]   What is the Scriptural basis for the position of sages?

[I]   "And you will say to them" (Num. 5:12) is meant to encompass all which is stated in the pericope.

[J]   And what is stated in the pericope?

[K]   "If a man lies with her carnally" (Num. 5:13).

[L]   Her act of sexual relations is what prohibits her. Then her husband becomes jealous of her and administers the water. [This applies also to the proselytes' marriage.]

[X.A] "And it is hidden from the eyes of her husband" (Num. 5:13)—this excludes a blind man, who cannot see.

[B]   If he is a blind man and she is a blind woman—

[C]   the Mishnah teaching of R. Judah declares him exempt from all of the religious requirements which are stated in the Torah.

Unit **I** takes up the meaning of M. 2:5A, "Amen, Amen." Unit **II** proceeds to prove that the oath, once it is administered, may cover matters not originally included within it. The oath of the accused wife serves as the generative metaphor for all other oaths, as at **II**.F. This then yields the discussion of unit **III**, which is fully and handsomely spelled out. The issue is drawn, again, in terms of the limitations of the governing metaphor. Unit **IV** proceeds to M. 2:5E, the status of the woman awaiting levirate marriage. If the oath is valid in such a case, it means that a woman awaiting levirate marriage is deemed in some way to be set aside for, or subject to the marital bond of, the levir. Consequently, if the woman has sexual relations, it is not as a completely free agent, and, it follows, the levir may be taken into account in the oath. This view is Aqiba's. An effort is made to show that both rabbis and Aqiba, within the same frame of argument, will concur. **IV.**L, M. pose some textual problems, which I cannot solve. Certainly L requires a fuller statement than we have before us. Unit **V** goes over exactly the same ground, this time with its own set of authorities. The remaining units, **VI–X**, are brief and undeveloped. What we have is essentially an anthology of further, relevant materials. But the successful, protracted discussions of the earlier units are not equaled here.

2:6 [Leiden MS and *editio princeps:* 2:6–7]

[A]   *All concur that he [the husband] may make no stipulation with her about anything which happened before she was betrothed or after she may be divorced.*

[B]   *[If after she was put away,] she went aside with some other man and became unclean, and afterward he [the first husband] took her back, he makes no stipulation with her [concerning such an event].*

[C]   *This is the general principle: Concerning any situation in which she may have sexual relations in such wise as not to be prohibited [to her husband], he [the husband] may make no stipulation whatsoever with her.*

[I.A]   Said R. Yannai, "It is self-evident that a man may retract his expression of jealousy [prior to the woman's actually going in secret with the named man].

[B]   "If he divorced the wife, is it as if he has retracted the expression of jealousy?"

[C]   What would be a practical case?

[D]   If he expressed jealousy to his wife, then divorced her, then he took her back, and finally, she went aside with the named man.

[E]   If you say that if he divorced his wife, it is as if he has retracted the expression of jealousy, then he has to express jealousy a second time.

[F]   If you say that if he divorced her, it is not as if he has retracted the original expression of jealousy, then he does not have to express jealousy to her as second time.

[G]   But if he expressed jealousy to her, and then she went aside with the named man, and he knew about it, and then he divorced her, and then he took her back, and she went aside a second time, then drank the water, and the water did not affect her, [what is the law]?

[H]   Is she deemed to be clean?

[I]   Or, since the water did not affect the woman because she was forbidden when she was taken back by her husband [for the husband took her back after she had gone aside with the named man, is she deemed to be unclean? [The question is not answered.]

The Talmud's sustained inquiry is clear as given. What is important is at G–I. The Mishnah is ignored.

3 Yerushalmi Sotah
Chapter Three

3:1

[A] *He would take her meal offering from the basket made of twigs and put it into a utensil of service and lay it into her hands.*

[B] *And a priest puts his hand under hers and waves [the meal offering].*

[C] *He waved it (Num. 5:25) and brought it near the altar.*

[D] *He took a handful [of the meal offering] and burned it up [on the altar].*

[E] *And the residue is for the priests to eat.*

[I.A] It is written, "Then the priest shall take the cereal offering of jealousy out of the woman's hand, and shall wave the cereal offering before the Lord . . ." (Num. 5:25).

[B] Now does he do it himself? [The Mishnah specifies that he puts his hand under hers and waves the offering which she holds. Further, the standard procedure is for the sacrifier (he who benefits from the offering) to wave the meal offering, not the priest.]

[C] And does he not wave it [while it is yet] in her hand?

[D] But: On the basis of the cited verse, we derive the fact that he takes the meal offering from an unconsecrated utensil and puts it into a utensil consecrated for the Temple service.

[II.A] *And a priest puts his hand under hers and waves [the meal offering] [M. 3:1B].*

[B] But such a procedure is unseemly [that he should put his hand on hers].

82

[C]   He brings a cloth.

[D]   But it will not interpose properly.

[E]   Then he brings an aged priest [who will not be aroused by contact with the woman].

[F]   You may even say that they bring a child, who has not yet reached the time of sexual desire.

[III.A]   R. Hiyya taught, "In the case of an accused wife who is lacking hands, two priests wave the meal offering in her behalf [one standing in for her]."

[IV.A]   Said R. Yosé, "Under all circumstances [of the waving of the meal offering], it is only one point of information which the rabbis require.

[B]   "What does he touch against the altar, the meal offering or the utensil?" [The answer is that he touches the body of the utensil against the altar.]

[V.A]   As to the acts of waving meal offerings, how do we know that they come before the acts of touching the utensil containing the meal offering against the altar?

[B]   R. Jeremiah in the name of R. Pedat: "They derived that law from the rules governing the rite of the accused wife. ['The priest shall take the cereal offering . . . and wave it before the Lord and [then] bring it to the altar' (Num. 5:25).]"

[C]   Said R. Yosé, "The laws governing the accused wife are singled out because they innovate [for their own case alone], and a matter which is singled out for its innovation does not supply laws [governing routine rites]."

[D]   R. Bun bar Hiyya derived the fact from the following: " 'This is the law of the cereal offering. The sons of Aaron shall offer it before the Lord' (Lev. 6:14). Now if reference is made to offering it [that is, bringing it into contact with the altar], then where is provision made for waving it? That already has taken place."

[E]   Said R. Yosé, "Interpret the passage to refer to those meal offerings which to begin with do not require waving, in which case there is no implication whatever to be drawn from the cited passage."

[F]   Then whence do they derive evidence of the fact [that waving is prior to bringing near]?

[G]   It is from this verse: "And you shall bring the cereal offering that is made of these things to the Lord; and when it is presented to the priest, he shall bring it to the altar" (Lev. 2:8).

[H]   "You shall bring" encompassing the meal offering of the first sheaf, indicating that it requires bringing near.

[I]   "And bring it near" encompassing the meal offering of the accused wife, that it too requires bringing near.

[J]   And it is written thereafter: "And he shall raise up" (Lev. 2:9).

[K]   Now where, in the cited passage, is reference made to waving the meal offering? [Since no such reference indeed is to be found, that must mean] that it already had been done.

[VI.A]   There we have learned: *These are meal offerings from which the handful is taken, and the residue of which belongs to the priests: [the meal offering of fine flour, the meal offering prepared in a baking pan and in a frying pan, the loaves, the wafers, the meal offering of gentiles, the meal offering of women, the meal offering of the first sheaf, the meal offering of a sinner, and the meal offering of jealousy]* [M. Men. 6:1A–B].

[B]   R. Ba bar Mamel and R. Samuel b. R. Isaac were in session. R. Ba bar Mamel raised the following question before R. Samuel b. Isaac: "In the case of the meal offering of the first sheaf, how do we know that what is left over is eaten [by the priests]?"

[C]   He said to him, "And did not R. Yohanan say in the name of R. Ishmael, 'It is written, [If you offer] a cereal offering [of first fruits to the Lord, you shall offer for the cereal offering of your first fruits crushed new grain from fresh ears, parched by fire]' (Lev. 2:14).

[D]   " 'And it is written [. . . and bring] the offering [required of her, a tenth of an *ephah* of a barley meal]' (Num. 5:15).

[E]   " 'Just as the meal offering stated in the latter context consists of barley, so that in the former [that is, in the case of the meal offering of the first sheaf] likewise is made up of barley.' [Cf. Y. Sot. 2:1 VI.]

[F]   "And it follows: Just as in the case of the meal offering
brought by the accused wife, what is left over is eaten by the
priests, so in the case of the meal offering of the first sheaf,
what is left over is eaten by the priests." [Delete: Said R.
Aqiba.]

[G]   When they had completed this discourse, R. Ba bar Mamel
arose with R. Jeremiah. He said to him, "Now look at this
novice in the law of yours! How indeed do we know that in the
case of the meal offering of the accused wife itself, what is left
over is eaten by the priests?!"

[H]   R. Zeira came to R. Isaac of Attush and taught as follows:
" 'And every cereal offering, mixed with oil and dry, shall be
for all the sons of Aaron, one as well as another' (Lev. 7:10).

[I]   "Now how shall we interpret the cited passage? If it refers to a
meal offering soaked in oil and made from wheat, that has already been treated [at Lev. 2:3: 'And what is left of the cereal
offering shall be for Aaron and his sons'].

[J]   "So if it does not deal with a meal offering soaked in oil made
from wheat, then assign the rule to one soaked in oil made
from barley.

[K]   "And the other said, 'How shall we deal with this passage? If it
is in reference to a dry meal offering made of wheat, that too
has already been dealt with.

[L]   " 'But if it does not deal with a dry meal offering made with
wheat, then apply the rule to a dry meal offering made with
barley [such as that brought by the accused wife].' "

[M]   For R. Yosé has stated, "We deal with an oil-soaked meal offering made from wheat and a dry meal offering made from
wheat [18d], and the passage was stated because it was
required.

[N]   " '. . . shall be for all the sons of Aaron, one as well as another' (Lev. 7:10): A male priest takes a share, even though he
is blemished.

[O]   "But a minor does not take a share, even though he is
blemished."

[P]   Said R. Yosé b. R. Bun, "Because the Torah has treated a passage as encompassing other matters for one particular purpose,
you now wish to treat the matter as encompassing every sort of
matter.

[Q]   "But what is essential is the repeated reference to 'memorial.'
[That is, we may prove that the residue of the meal offering of
the first sheaf is eaten by the priests by the repeated use of the
word 'memorial,' both at Lev. 7:10, for any meal offering, and,
for the one under discussion (Lev. 2:16): 'And the priest shall
burn as its memorial portion. . . .']

[R]   "Just as in the case of the use of the word 'memorial' later on
[at Lev. 2:2, 2:9, etc.], the meaning is that what is left over
may be eaten, so in the case of the use of the word 'memorial,'
here [in the case of the accused wife (Num. 5:26), in the case
of the first sheaf (Lev. 2:16)], what is left over may be eaten."

[S]   Whence did they derive evidence of that fact?

[T]   [It is from the verse] "And you shall bring the cereal offering
that is made of these things to the Lord; and when it is presented to the priest, he shall bring it to the altar" (Lev. 2:8).

[U]   "You shall bring" encompassing the meal offering of the first
sheaf, that it requires bringing near.

[V]   "And bring it near" encompassing the meal offering of the accused wife, that it too requires bringing near.

[W]   And it is written thereafter: "And what is left of the cereal offering shall be for Aaron and his sons; it is a most holy part of
the offerings by fire to the Lord" (Lev. 2:10).

Units I–V take up M. 3:1A–B. Only unit V is amply spelled
out. The final proof, V.F–K, simply derives its proof text from
a more appropriate passage; the exegesis, G–I, is independent
of the present context. The repetition at VI.Rff. makes little
sense. It appears that the little pericope is inserted whole, without revision for the needs of context. Only VI.V is pertinent in
the repetition of the material. In relationship to the Mishnah,
units I–V are essential. Unit VI deals with the theme of M.
3:1E, but not with its detailed law.

3:2

[A]   *He would give her the water to drink.*

[B]   *And [only] afterward he would offer up her meal offering.*

[C]   *R. Simeon says, "He would offer up her meal offering.*

[D]   *"And afterward he would give her the water to drink,*

[E]   *"since it is said, 'And afterward he gives the woman the water to drink' (Num. 5:26).*

[F]   *"But if he gave her the water to drink and afterward he offered up her meal offering, it is valid."*

[I.A]   What is the Scriptural basis for the position of rabbis [at M. 3:2A–B]?

[B]   "[And he shall make the woman drink . . . and the water . . .] shall enter into her . . ." (Num. 5:24). ["And the priest shall take the cereal offering of jealousy . . . and wave . . ." (Num. 5:25).]

[C]   What is the Scriptural basis for the position of R. Simeon?

[D]   "And afterward he gives the woman the water to drink" (Num. 5:26).

[E]   How does R. Simeon interpret the Scriptural basis for the position of rabbis, namely, "And the water will enter into her"?

[F]   [It means] all of the water and not only part of it.

[G]   And how do rabbis interpret the Scriptural basis for the position of R. Simeon, "And afterward he gives the woman the water to drink"?

[H]   [This means] that they do so against her wishes, not by her grace.

[I]   R. Simeon concurs with sages [i.e., rabbis] that *if he gave her the water to drink and afterward he offered up her meal offering, it is valid [M. 3:2F].*

[J]   And sages concur with R. Simeon that if he offered up her meal offering and afterward he gave her the water to drink, it is valid.

[K]   What then is the difference between them?

[L]   [It is defining what is] the religious duty involved, [that is, whether the crucial element is the meal offering or the water].

[M]   Rabbis maintain that it is a meal offering, meaning that the meal offering serves to subject the woman to the test.

[N]   R. Simeon holds, [by contrast], that it is the water which subjects [Leiden MS and *editio princeps:* does not subject] the woman to the test.

[O]   What is the Scriptural basis for the position of rabbis?

[P]   "It is a cereal offering of jealousy, a cereal offering of remembrance, bringing iniquity to remembrance" (Num. 5:15).

[Q]   What is the Scriptural basis for the position of R. Simeon?

[R]   "And the water that brings the curse shall enter into her and cause bitter pain" (Num. 5:24).

[S]   How do the rabbis interpret the Scripture on which R. Simeon rests his case, ". . . and it will enter into her"?

[T]   This teaches that [the water] diffuses throughout all her limbs.

[U]   And how does R. Simeon interpret the Scriptural basis for the position of rabbis, "It is a cereal offering of jealousy, a cereal offering of remembrance, bringing iniquity to remembrance"?

[V]   [This verse] teaches that all the sins which the woman has against her come to remembrance at that very hour.

[W]   Rabbis say, "[The priest] writes, blots out the scroll, administers the water, then offers the meal offering."

[X]   R. Simeon says, "He writes the scroll, offers the meal offering, blots out the scroll, then administers the water."

[Y]   All parties then concur that the blotting out is done alongside the administration of the waters.

[Z]   But rabbis say, "He writes, blots out, administers the water, and makes the offering."

[AA]   And R. Simeon says, "He writes, offers the offering, blots out, then administers the water."

[BB]   It has been taught: **But under all circumstances she has the power to repent for her behavior, until her meal offering has been offered.**

[CC]   **Once her meal offering has been offered, if she said, "I am not going to drink," they force her and make her drink it against her will [T. Sot. 2:3G–H].**

[DD]   This accords with the view of R. Simeon.

[EE]   But in the view of rabbis, [how can we make sense of this, for] the woman already has drunk [the water prior to the offering of the meal offering]? [Accordingly, Simeon's position is taken for granted here.]

[FF]   We have learned: *She has hardly sufficed to drink it before her face turns yellow, etc. [M. 3:4A].*

[GG]   There are those who teach, *She does not move from there before* [and the above clause will follow].

[HH]   He who said, *She hardly sufficed . . .* is R. Simeon, [since her meal offering already will have been offered up].

[II]   Those who said *She did not move from there* are the rabbis, [since the water does not do its work until her meal offering has been offered up].

The formal and logical perfection of the Talmud before us leaves no room for further comment. That the issue of the Mishnah exhaustively worked out is self-evident.

3:3

[A]   *[If] before the scroll is blotted out, she said, "I am not going to drink the water," her scroll is put away, and her meal offering is scattered on the ashes.*

[B]   *But her scroll is not valid for the water ordeal of another accused wife.*

[C]   *[If] her scroll was blotted out and then she said, "I am unclean," the water is poured out, and her meal offering is scattered on the ashes.*

[D]   *[If] her scroll was blotted out and then she said, "I am not going to drink it," they force her to make her drink it against her will.*

[I.A]   It was taught: **Her scroll [M. 3:3A] was put away under the hinge [of the gate] of the Temple [T. Sot. 2:2K].**

[B]   Why?

[C]   So as to wear it out.

[D]   There was a small passage there, into which the water would be poured.

[E]   It was taught: No trace of sanctity applies [to that water].

[F]   What is the law as to using that water for kneading mud?

[G]   What difference would it make? The water is poured out in any event.

[H]   But it was taught [to the contrary]: A trace of sanctity applies [to that water].

[II.A]   *If her scroll was blotted out, and then she said, "I am unclean," the water is poured out, and her meal offering is scattered on the ashes [M. 3:3C].*

[B]   That is to say that the meal offering of the accused wife is deemed holy [even] before the scroll is written out. [For it is as if the scroll had not been written at all.]

[C]   Said R. Yosé, "More than this did R. Hiyya teach: 'While the woman is yet en route [to the Temple, if one set aside meal for the meal offering], the meal offering set aside for her is deemed holy.' "

[D]   Said R. Yosé b. R. Bun, "The Mishnah [itself] has made that same point: *[These are the ones whose meal offerings are to be burned]: . . . the one whose husband has sexual relations with her on the way to Jerusalem [M. 3:6H].* [The meal offering has to be burned because it was deemed consecrated, and then became useless.]"

[III.A]   *If her scroll was blotted out and then she said, "I am not going to drink it," they force her and make her drink it against her will [M. 3:3D].*

[B]   Why?

[C]   Because she caused the Holy Name of God to be blotted out.

[D]   How much [of the Name] is to be blotted out [in order to invoke the cited rule]?

[E]   R. Hanina taught: "The House of Shammai say, 'One letter.'

[F]   "And the House of Hillel say, 'Two.' "

[G]   Said R. Ili, "The basis for the ruling of the House of Hillel is that enough should be blotted out to be sufficient to write the word 'Lord' (YH)."

[IV.A]   **[R. Judah says, "With iron tongs they force her mouth open, and they force her and make her drink it against her will."]**

[B]   **Said R. Aqiba, "And why do we have to test her any further? Is it not to test her? And lo, she is now tested and proved to be degraded [by her refusal to drink]!" [T. Sot. 2:3E–F].**

[C]   But R. Aqiba had the theory, "She who says, 'I am not going to drink' is equivalent to the one who says 'I am unclean for you.' "

[D]   Then R. Aqiba does not maintain that *they force her to drink* [by strangling her to force her mouth open] *until her face turns yellow and force her to drink against her will* [M. 3:3D]?

[E]   He maintains that that is the case if she has already begun to drink the water [and, at that point, she no longer is able to decline to do so].

The Talmud systematically analyzes the Mishnah's materials, at units **I**, **II**, and **III**. Then unit **IV** cites and analyzes the relevant passage of the Tosefta.

3:4

[A]   *She hardly has sufficed to drink it before her face turns yellow, her eyes bulge out, and her veins swell.*

[B]   *And they say, "Take her away! Take her away!"*

[C]   *so that the Temple court will not be made unclean [by her corpse].*

[D]   *[But if nothing happened,] if she had merit, she would attribute [her good fortune] to it.*

[E]   *There is the possibility that merit suspends the curse for one year, and there is the possibility that merit suspends the curse* for two years, and there is the possibility that merit suspends the curse for three years.

[F]   On this basis Ben Azzai says, "A man is required to teach Torah to his daughter.

[G]   "For if she should drink the water, she should know that [if nothing happens to her], merit is what suspends [the curse from taking effect]."

[H]   R. Eliezer says, "Whoever teaches Torah to his daughter, it is as if he teaches her sexual satisfaction."

[I]   R. Joshua says, "A woman wants a qab [of food] with sexual satisfaction more than nine qabs with abstinence."

[J]   He would say, "A foolish saint, a smart knave, an abstemious woman,

[K]   "and the blows of abstainers (perushim)—

[L]   "lo, these wear out the world."

[I.A]   [We note that even before she has drunk all the water, but only part of it, the water begins to take effect.] Now did we not propose to maintain [above] that all the water, but not part of the water, [is what carries out the test of the woman]?

[B]   It [does not mean that she had not drunk it all, but it] is a usage along the lines of what someone must say, "Mr. So-and-so had not sufficed to drink before his body trembled."

[II.A]   There is the possibility that merit suspends the curse for one year, there is the possibility that merit suspends the curse for two years, and there is the possibility that merit suspends the curse for three years [M. 3:4E].

[B]   There is the possibility that merit suspends the curse for one year: This derives from Nebuchadnezzar, "At the end of twelve months . . ." (Dan. 4:29).

[C]   There the possibility that merit suspends the curse for two years: This derives from Amnon, "After two full years . . ." (2 Sam. 13:23).

[D]   And there is the possibility that merit suspends the curse for three years: This derives from Ahab, "For three years Syria and Israel continued without war" (1 Kings 22:1).

[E] Said R. Yosé, "It is said, 'Throughout those twelve months he kept busy doing religious duties, and throughout all those two years he kept busy studying Torah.' "

[F] Now where do we find evidence for that statement in Scripture?

[G] "For three years Syria and Israel continued without war."

[III.A] ["A cereal offering of remembrance, bringing iniquity to remembrance" (Num. 5:15):] "A cereal offering of remembrance" constitutes a general statement.

[B] "Bringing iniquity to remembrance" then serves as a limiting statement.

[C] When we have a generalization followed by such a qualification, then we include in the generalization only what is specified in the qualifying statement.

[D] If that is how you phrase matters, then will it not come out that the attribute of strict justice is buried?

[E] Now if it is the measure of strict punishment, which is lesser, lo, which the [meal offering] serves to call to mind, the measure of goodness, which is abundant, how much the more so [will the meal offering call it to mind].

[F] Then: "A cereal offering of remembrance" applies if the woman has merit.

[G] "Bringing iniquity to remembrance" applies if she has no merit.

[IV.A] It was taught: R. Tarfon says, "All references to remembrance stated in the Torah are meant for good, except for this one, which is meant to speak of punishment."

[B] Said to him R. Aqiba, "Had the Scripture said, 'Bringing iniquity to remembrance' (Num. 5:15) and nothing more, then matters I should have ruled just as you do.

[C] "But lo, it states, 'A meal offering of remembrance'—only in reference to goodness."

[V.A] It was taught: **R. Judah b. Petera said in the name of Eleazar b. Matya, "What is the meaning of the Scripture 'Now if the woman has not been made unclean'?**

[B]   "Now do we not know that if the woman was not made unclean, then she is clean? Why does Scripture say so?

[C]   "But in the end, the Omnipresent compensates her for her humiliation.

[D]   "For if she was barren, she will become pregnant.

[E]   **"If she used to give birth with pain, now she will give birth in comfort. If she used to produce females, now she will produce males. If she used to produce ugly children, now she will produce pretty babies. If she used to produce dark ones, now she will produce fair ones. If she used to produce short ones, now she will produce tall ones. If she used to produce one by one, now she will produce two by two" [T. Sot. 2:3R–S].**

[F]   Said to him R. Simeon b. Laqish, "If so, then every woman will go and behave badly so as to be visited [in this way]."

[G]   Now does R. Simeon not concur in the statement "But if the woman has not defiled herself and is clean, then she shall be free and shall conceive children" (Num. 5:28)?

[H]   She will conceive valid seed, not invalid seed.

[VI.A]   Ben Azzai [M. 3:4F] does not concur with R. Eleazar b. Azariah. For it has been taught: MᶜSH B: **R. Yohanan b. Beroqah and R. Eleazar Hisma came from Yabneh to Lud and they greeted R. Joshua in Peqiin.**

[B]   **Said to them R. Joshua: "What was new in the schoolhouse today?"**

[C]   **They said to him, "We are all your disciples and we drink your water."**

[D]   **He said to them, "Even so, it is hardly possible that there should be nothing new in the schoolhouse every day. Whose week was it?"**

[E]   **They said to him, "[It was the week of] R. Eleazar b. Azariah."**

[F]   **He said to them, "And whence was the narration?"**

[G]   **"Assemble the people, men, women, and children, and the sojourner within your towns, that they may hear and learn to fear the Lord your God" (Deut. 31:12).**

[19a/H]   **He said to them "And what did he explain in this connection?"**

[I]   **They said to him, "Rabbi, thus did he explain in its connection: 'Now if the men came along to study, the women came along to listen, why did the children come along? To provide a reward to the people who brought them' " [T. Sot. 7:9].**

[J]   **He said to him, "The generation in which R. Eleazar flourishes is not orphaned" [T. Sot. 7:12D].**

[VII.A]   A Roman matron asked R. Eleazar [better: Eliezer], "How is it that, though only one sin was committed in connection with the golden calf, those who died, died by three kinds of execution?"

[B]   He said to her, "Woman has no wisdom except at the distaff, for it is written, 'And all the women that were wise-hearted did spin with their hands' " (Ex. 35:25).

[C]   Said to him Hyrcanus, his son, "So as not to answer her with a single teaching from the Torah [cf. M. 3:4H], you have lost out on three hundred *kors* of tithe per year!"

[D]   He said to him, "Let the teachings of the Torah be burned, but let them not be handed over to women."

[E]   When she went out, his disciples said to him, "Rabbi, this one you have pushed away.

[F]   "To us what will you say?"

[G]   R. Berekhiah, R. Abba bar Kahana in the name of R. Eliezer: "Any one who was subject to the testimony of witnesses, who had been properly admonished also, died in a court trial.

[H]   "Whoever was subject to the testimony of witnesses but was not given an admonition was subjected to the ordeal of water that brings the curse, like the unfaithful wife.

[I]   "Whoever had neither witnesses nor an admonition died in the consequent plague."

[J]   Both Rab and Levi bar Sisi say, "If a person slaughtered an animal to the golden calf, offered up incense, and poured out a drink offering, he died following a regular court trial.

[L]   "If he clapped hands, danced, or played before the calf, he was subjected to the ordeal of the water that brings a curse, like the accused wife.

[M]   "If he merely rejoiced in his heart [at the making of the calf], he died in a plague."

[VIII.A]   What is meant by *a foolish saint* [M. 3:4J]?

[B]   If one saw a child drowning in a river and said, "When I shall remove my phylactery, I shall save him,"—

[C]   while this one is taking off his phylacteries, the other one gave up the ghost.

[D]   If he found a fig which was the first of the season, and said, "Whomever I shall meet first, I shall give it to him [so as not to benefit from first fruits]," if he then saw a betrothed maiden and ran after her [for that purpose]—

[E]   this is in line with that which we have taught:

[F]   *He who runs after his fellow to kill him, after a male, after a betrothed maiden . . . [M. San. 8:7].*

[IX.A]   *A smart knave* [M. 3:4J]: R. Zeriqan in the name of R. Huna, "This is one who applies lenient rulings to himself and strict rulings to other people."

[B]   That is in accord with the following which has been taught:

[C]   **[Under all circumstances does the decided law follow the opinion of the House of Hillel.]**

[D]   **He who wishes to impose upon himself a more stringent rule,**

[E]   **to follow the rule in accord with both the House of Shammai and the House of Hillel,**

[F]   **concerning such a person is said the following verse: "[The wise man has his eyes in his head,] but the fool walks in darkness" [Qoh. 2:14].**

[G]   **He who latches onto the lenient rulings of the House of Shammai and to the lenient rulings of the House of Hillel is an evil man.**

[H]   But if it is to be in accord with the opinions of the House of Shammai, then let it be in accord with both their lenient rulings and their strict rulings.

[I]   And if it is to be in accord with the opinions of the House of Hillel, then let it be in accord with both their lenient rulings and their strict rulings [T. Yeb. 1:13].

[J]   That ruling which you have stated just now [about following the rulings of either house] applies before the echo went forth.

[K]   But once the echo had gone forth and made its declaration, the law under all circumstances accords with the view of the House of Hillel.

[L]   And whoever transgresses the position of the House of Hillel is liable to the death penalty.

[M]   It was taught: The echo went forth and declared, "These views and those views are the teachings of the living God. But the law accords with the House of Hillel under all circumstances."

[N]   Now where did the echo come forth?

[O]   R. Bibi in the name of R. Yohanan: "In Yavneh the echo came forth."

[**X**.A]   *An abstemious woman* [M. 3:4J]: This is one who sits and quotes biblical phrases in a suggestive way:

[B]   "And she said, 'You must come in to me, for I have hired you with my son's mandrakes and he lay with her that night' " (Gen. 30:16).

[C]   Said R. Abbahu: "It was as if it already was in mind."

[D]   "In any case he knew that it was in her mind only so as to produce a founder of a tribe."

[**XI**.A]   *Blows of abstainers* [M. 3:4J]: This is the sort of person who gives advice to heirs of an estate on how to keep the widow from getting her rightful maintenance.

[B]   It is in line with the following:

[C]   The widow of R. Shobetai was wasting his estate [by supporting herself in high style from his estate].

[D] The heirs came and complained to R. Eleazar. He said to them, "Now what can we do for you? You are fools. Pay off her marriage settlement."

[E] He said to them, "I shall tell you what to do. Pretend that your are going to sell [the land], and she will then lay claim on her portion, and thereby she will lose all claim on maintenance from the estate."

[F] They did exactly that. In the evening she came and complained to R. Eleazar.

[G] She said to him, "This is a case in which the blows of the abstainers have injured me.

[H] "May [terrible things] happen to me if I ever intended such a thing to happen."

[I] A disciple of Rabbi had two hundred *zuz* less a *denar* [in which case he was permitted to accept poor man's tithe, having too little money to be deemed well-off].

[J] Rabbi was accustomed to give over to him his poor man's tithe every third year [when it was due] as the tithe owing to those who were in need.

[K] One time the other disciples treated the student in a mean way by making up [the *denar*, so that he had the two hundred *zuz* and was no longer eligible to receive the poor man's tithe].

[L] [Rabbi] came and wanted to hand over to him the poor man's tithe as he had been accustomed to do.

[M] He said to him, "Rabbi, I have the requisite sum of money, [and so I am not eligible]."

[N] He said, "In the case of this one, *the blows of the abstainers* have smitten him."

[O] He instructed his disciples, and he took him up to a tavern and made him one *qarat* poorer.

[P] And then Rabbi handed over to him the poor man's tithe as he had been accustomed to do.

[XII.A] They added to the list [of M. 3:4J], *a self-afflicting girl,* who afflicts herself so as to lose her hymen.

[B] *A widow who is a gadabout,* who is always out gossiping and who gives herself a bad name.

[C] *A precocious child:*

[D] R. Helqiah in the name of R. Simon, "This is one who is great in Torah before he reaches maturity and so humiliates his elders."

[E] Said R. Yosé, "This is one who is nine years old, but who is sexually mature as a twelve-year-old.

[F] "If such a one should have sexual relations with any one of the women who are listed in the Torah as prohibited to him, they are put to death on his account, and he goes free."

The Talmud systematically works through and supplements the Mishnah's materials. Units **I–IV** deal with the ordeal of its effects. Units **V–XII** go on to the Mishnah's appended materials. Unit **VII** stands within the framework of the Mishnah's announced themes, to illustrate Eliezer's misogyny. The rest glosses the Mishnah's language.

3:5

[A] *R. Simeon says, "Merit does not suspend the effects of the bitter water.*

[B] *"And if you say, 'Merit does suspend the effects of the bitter water,' you will weaken the effect of the water for all the women who have to drink it.*

[C] *"And you give a bad name to all the women who drink it who turn out to be pure.*

[D] *"For people will say, 'They are unclean, but merit suspended the effects of the water for them.' "*

[E] *Rabbi says, "Merit does suspend the effects of the bitter water.*

[F] *"But she will not bear children or continue to be pretty. And she will waste away, and in the end she will have the same [un-pleasant] death."*

[I.A] Said R. Hamnuna, "A woman who [after drinking the water] is ailing all over her body [but does not suffer locally as predicted for the faithless wife (Num. 5:27)] is permitted to have sexual relations with her husband."

[B]   This is in line with the following, which was taught:

[C]   R. Simeon b. Eleazar says, "Even a clean woman who drank the water—in the end she will die of an unpleasant sickness,

[D]   "because she has brought herself into this situation of over-whelming doubt."

[II.A]   "But if the woman has not defiled herself and is clean, then she shall be free . . ." (Num. 5:28)—

[B]   This one is clean, and not one against whom witnesses have come to indicate that she is unclean.

[C]   "If the woman has not defiled herself and is clean"—this one is clean, not one who depended [for surviving the rite of the water that brings the curse] upon merit.

[D]   This is in line with the opinion of the one who says "Merit suspends the punishment, even if it is not recognized that that is the fact."

[E]   But in line with the opinion of the one who says "Merit suspends the punishment, and that fact will be recognized," [this thought is not completed].

[F]   Said R. Isaac, "Thus we interpret the matter [of B]: If a woman drank the water and the water did not put her to the test it is so that you may not say that they are false witnesses.

[G]   "Therefore the water did not put her to the test.

[H]   "This comes to tell you that the water does not put to the test a woman who is prohibited from having sexual relations with her husband, [as is one who is subject to testimony to her adultery]."

[I]   Said R. Judah, "And is this in line with the view of the one who said 'Merit suspends the punishment [= M. 3:5E], and it is not even known that that is the fact' [vs. F]?

[J]   "And why is it not known?

[K]   "Because merit suspends the punishment from coming upon her."

[III.A]   "The man shall be free from iniquity" (Num. 5:31).

[B]   He does not scruple that merit has suspended the punishment for her.

[C]   Is it possible to suppose that she too should not take that into account?

[D]   Scripture says, "And the woman shall bear her iniquity" (Num. 5:31).

[E]   And this is in accord with the one who says that merit suspends punishment and that fact may not be known. [Consequently, if she knows the truth, that she has committed adultery, the failure of the ordeal to prove it does not mean that she may resume sexual relations. Merit may simply have suspended the punishment for the time being.]

The Talmud goes over the issue of whether merit suspends the punishment, on the one side, and whether, if that has happened, people will know it, on the other. The Mishnah's materials are closely examined, and its positions explored.

3:6

[A]   *[If] her meal offering was made unclean before it was sanctified in a utensil,*

[B]   *lo, it is in the status of all other such meal offerings and is to be redeemed.*

[C]   *And [if this takes place] after it is sanctified in a utensil,*

[D]   *lo, it is in the status of all other such meal offerings and is to be burned.*

[E]   *And these are the ones whose meal offerings are to be burned:*

[F]   *the one who says "I am unclean to you," and the one against whom witnesses come to testify that she is unclean;*

[G]   *the one who says, "I am not going to drink the water," and the one whose husband does not want to make her drink it;*

[H]   *and the one whose husband has sexual relations with her on the way to Jerusalem [M. 1:3].*

[I]   *And all those who are married to priests—their meal offerings are burned.*

[I.A]   It was taught:

[B]   *[If] her meal offering was made unclean before it was sanctified in a utensil, lo, it is in the status of all other such meal offerings.*

[C]   *It is redeemed [M. 3:6A–B]* **and eaten.**

[D]   *[If her meal offering was made unclean] after it was sanctified in a utensil,*

[E]   **its appearance is allowed to rot and it goes out to the place of burning [M. 3:6C–D] [T. Sot. 2:4].**

[II.A]   *She who says "I am unclean" [M. 3:6F]—*

[B]   Is her meal offering not in the status of an animal set aside as a sin offering, the owner of which has died? [Why is it burned?]

[C]   For as to an animal set aside for a sin offering, the owner of which has died, money set aside for the purchase of such an animal is to go off to the Dead Sea. [So the meal should be thrown into the sea.]

[D]   [No,] it is to be compared to a suspensive guilt offering [in line with H, below].

[E]   If it is to be compared to a suspensive guilt offering, then even after it was sanctified in a utensil [it should remain in its status, and it should be offered up].

[F]   Said R. Matteniah, "It is to be compared to a guilt offering which has already been slaughtered."

[G]   For we have learned there:

[H]   *[He who brings a suspensive guilt offering and is informed that he did not commit a sin]—if after it was slaughtered he was informed, the blood is to be poured out, and the meat goes forth to the place of burning [M. Ker. 6:1A, G–I].* [Now we have a viable analogy.]

[III.A]   It was taught: **[If the meal offering was sanctified, but there was not time to offer up the handful before her husband died,**

[B]   **or [if] she died [so she will not drink],**

[C]   **the residue is prohibited [to the priest] [= M. 3:6E–H].**

[D]   **[If] the handful was offered,**

[E]   **and afterward she died, or the husband died,**

[F]   the residue is permitted.

[G]   For to begin with it was brought in a case of doubt.

[H]   Her doubt has been atoned for and gone its way [T. Sot. 2:5].

[I]   [If] witnesses came against her to testify that she was unclean,

[J]   one way or the other the meal offering is prohibited.

[K]   [If] they turned out to be conspiring witnesses, one way or the other the meal offering is treated as unconsecrated. In the case of any woman married to a priest, whether she is a priest girl, or a Levite girl, or an Israelite girl, her meal offering is not eaten [M. 3:6I], for he has a share in it. But the offering is not wholly consumed in the fire, because she has a share in it [T. Sot. 2:6].

[L]   What is the meaning of "One way or the other"?

[M]   Whether the handful of the meal offering had been removed or had not been removed,

[N]   whether it had been offered up or it had not been offered up.

[O]   R. Ila said, "It means, 'Whether the handful had been taken or had not been taken, in a case in which it had not been offered up.'

[P]   "But once the meal offering has been offered up, the residue is permitted to the priests. [It was suitably offered, and the priests have every right to their part.]"

[IV.A]   There we learned: *R. Simeon says, "[From] the meal offering of a priest who was a sinner [Lev. 6:16], the handful is taken [even though the whole of it in any case is offered on the altar]; then the handful is offered up by itself, and the residue thereof is offered up by itself" [M. Men. 6:1C].* [Rabbis say no handful is taken; the whole is burned on the altar.]

[B]   And both of them interpret the same verse of Scripture: "And the remainder shall be for the priest, as in the cereal offering" (Lev. 5:13).

[C]   Rabbis say, "Lo, it is like a meal offering brought by a priest as a free-will offering.

[D]   "Just as a meal offering brought as a free-will offering is wholly burned up on the altar,

[E]   "so this too is wholly burned up on the altar."

[F]   [And] R. Simeon says, "Lo, the tenth of an *ephah* of fine flour brought by a priest is like a tenth of an *ephah* of fine flour brought by an Israelite.

[G]   "Just as the tenth of an *ephah* of fine flour brought by an Israelite has removed from it a handful [for offering up on the altar], so a handful is taken out of this and offered up on the altar.

[H]   "If [then you wish to say], 'Just as the residue of [an Israelite's] meal offering is eaten, so this is eaten,'

[I]   "Scripture states, 'Every meal offering of the priest shall be wholly burned up' " (Lev. 6:23).

[J]   As to these remnants of the offering, on what account are they brought up to the altar [in Simeon's view]? [In the opinion of rabbis, there is no residue, since there is no handful.]

[K]   Is it on account of the handful of meal, or on the account of their being residue?

[L]   If you say it is on account of the handful, then one may not put them on the altar at night; he may not put them on the altar if the sacrifier has died; and the priest's attitude has no effect upon them [to render them refuse]. [If the priest forms the intention to eat the remnant outside of its normal time, or to burn it outside of its normal place, then that intention renders the offering refuse. That qualification applies, specifically, to an offering which is subject to the priest's utilization once a given act has taken place to permit the offering to be subject to the priest's utilization. In the case of the meal offering, once the handful is taken, the residue is available for the priest's use. Hence when we distinguish the handful from the residue, we also invoke the consideration of refuse. These facts form the foundation of what follows.]

[M]   But if you say that it is on account of their being mere residue,

[N]   then he does put them on the altar by night, and he does put them on the altar if the sacrifier has died.

[O]   What is the law as to taking account of the priest's attitude? [For the priest has no share in the residue anyhow.]

[P]   Let us derive the answer to that question from the following:

[Q]   **R. Eleazar b. R. Simeon says, "The handful is offered by itself, and the residue is scattered on the ashes" [T. Sot. 2:6I].**

[R]   R. Yohanan raised the question, "How do we interpret this matter?

[S]   "If it is the ashes above [the altar itself], then R. Simeon has already said the rule [at M. Men. 6:1].

[T]   "But if it is not a matter of speaking of the ashes above, then apply it to the matter of the ashes which are below [the place of burning]."

[U]   [That is, they are treated as ordinary residue. If they were treated as the handful, Eleazar would have nothing to add to what his father has said. So it follows:] This is in line with that which has been said:

[V]   They put them on by night, they put them on the ashes after the death of the sacrifier, and the attitude of the priest affects them.

[W]   [Differing from this view,] said R. Yosé b. R. Bun, "One does not take account of the priest's attitude to them, for they are not made suitable either for human consumption or for the consumption of the altar. [Cf. Leiden MS: There is no point at which an act affecting the handful permits the residue for priestly use.]"

[X]   R. Ba bar Mamel raised the question, "Does this statement of R. Eleazar b. R. Simeon follow the theory of his father, or does it follow the theory of sages?

[Y]   "If it follows the theory of his father, then [the handful and residue] are to be offered above [on the altar—which is not Eleazar's view]!

[Z]   "If it follows the theory of sages, then one should not take a handful [of the meal offering at all, for reasons already specified]. [That is, as at A–I, above, which analogy governs?]

[AA]   It follows the theory of his father.

[BB]   R. Simeon says, "Lo, the tenth of an *ephah* of fine flour brought by a priest is like the tenth of an *ephah* of fine flour brought by an Israelite.

[CC]   "Just as the tenth of an *ephah* of fine flour brought by an Israelite has a handful removed from it [for offering up on the altar], so a handful is taken out to this [meal offering and offered up on the altar].

[DD]   "If then you wish to say, 'Just as the residue of [an Israelite's] meal offering is eaten, so this one [of a priest] is eaten,'

[EE]   "Scripture states, 'Every meal offering of the priest shall be wholly burned up; it shall not be eaten' (Lev. 6:23).

[FF]   "[Then why does Eleazar not have the meal offering burned on the altar, as his father wishes? It is because the analogy is limited to the rule,] 'And let it be wholly burned up and not eaten.'

[GG]   "But the analogy does not extend to the rule 'It will be wholly offered up [without the removal of a handful].' "

[HH]   Said R. Yosé, "Rabbi [at M. 3:6I] accepted the opinion of R. Eleazar b. R. Simeon and he taught in accord with his view."

[II]   R. Ba bar Kohen raised the following question before R. Yohanan: "And what difference does it make to me whether the rule accords with R. Eleazar b. R. Simeon?

[JJ]   "It may even accord with R. Simeon his father [since M. 3:6I does not say where the burning takes place]."

[KK]   He said to him, "Offering [the meal offering] is on top of the altar, but burning [M. 3:6I] is not on top of the altar."

[LL]   Objected R. Haninah before R. Mana, "And lo, R. Hiyya taught this matter and stood at variance with the stated position.

[MM]   "[Thus did Hiyya teach:] To offer it up completely cannot be done, because of the share owned by the wife.

[NN]   "To eat it also cannot be done, because of the share of the husband [who was a priest].

[OO]   "He said to him, 'A handful is taken out of it, for the sake of the woman. Then the handful is offered up by itself, and the

residue by itself [since the priest may not eat the residue of his
now meal offering]' " [cf. Y. 2:1 I D–F].

[PP] [Mana] said to [Haninah], "Rabbi [at M. 3:6I] accepted the
view of R. Eleazar b. R. Simeon, and R. Hiyya the Elder [in
the cited passage] accepted the view of R. Simeon, his father
[who wants the handful and the residue to be offered, each by
itself, on the altar itself]."

Units **I–III** cite and gloss the Mishnah. At issue at unit **II** is a
viable analogy for the procedure specified in the Mishnah. This
prepares the way for the much more sophisticated inquiry into
governing analogies, worked out, after the intervention of unit
III's citation and explanation of the Tosefta, at unit **IV**. What
we have at **IV** is a sustained and truly brilliant exercise, fully
realizing the logical promise of the materials. We begin with
the basic fact that there is a dispute on the governing analogy
for the priest's offering. Simeon maintains that the priest's
meal offering is like anyone else's, except in the detail that the
priest does not get to eat the residue. Rabbis say that the governing analogy is the offering of a priest. What is invoked is
the free-will meal offering of a priest, from which no handful is
taken; the whole is simply burned on the altar. So the analogy
tells you whether or not the handful must be removed at all.
The argumentation at **IV**.C–E for rabbis, and **IV**.F–J, for Simeon, is fully exposed. Then a secondary question, with its implications carefully specified, is presented, K–N. Paragraph O
is deceptive. It appears to wish merely to clarify a detail of the
foregoing, namely, the issue of the priest's attitude. As explained, the problem is whether or not the consideration of refuse is to be introduced at all. Simeon's son, Eleazar, is cited in
this context, along with Yohanan's clarification of Eleazar's
statement. At once the problem becomes a fresh one. If Eleazar's position is introduced to clarify one issue, then his position must be fully compared with that of his father on a related
and intersecting issue. That accounts for R–T, and, we see, V
ties the whole thing together. Then the deepest logical implications of father's and son's positions are exposed by Ba bar Mamel, X–Z. Once more, the issue is completely spelled out. A
problem for Eleazar's position is introduced and answered at
FF–GG. HH–PP tie up the loose ends of the argument. As I
said, it would be difficult to find a better example than this one

of a fully worked out, subtle, rich, and significant discourse in the logic of legal exegesis.

3:7

[A]   *An Israelite girl who is married to a priest boy—her meal offering is burned.*

[B]   *And a priest girl who is married to an Israelite boy—her offering is eaten [by the priests].*

[C]   *What is the difference between a priest boy and a priest girl?*

[D]   *The meal offering of a priest girl is eaten, the meal offering of a priest boy is not eaten.*

[E]   *The priest girl may be deconsecrated [declassed], but a priest boy may not be deconsecrated [declassed].*

[F]   *A priest girl contracts corpse uncleanness, and a priest boy does not contract corpse uncleanness.*

[G]   *A priest boy eats Most Holy Things, but a priest girl does not eat Most Holy Things.*

[I.A]   *What is the difference between a priest boy and a priest girl? The meal offering of a priest girl [married to an Israelite boy] is eaten, the meal offering of a priest boy is not eaten [M. 3:7C–D].*

[B]   This is in line with that which is written, "Every cereal offering of a priest shall be wholly burned; it shall not be eaten" (Lev. 6:23)—not a priest girl.

[C]   R. Abbahu raised the following question before R. Simeon b. Laqish: "And lo, it is written, 'But if a priest buys a slave as his property for money [the slave may eat of it]' (Lev. 22:11).

[D]   "Shall we once more say, 'A priest boy, and not a priest girl' [meaning that the slaves of a priest girl may not eat food in the status of heave offering]? [So long as she is not declassed, they may do so.]"

[E]   Why then [is the meal offering of a priest girl eaten by the priests, while one of the priest boy is not]?

[F]   "The priest from among Aaron's sons, who is anointed to suc-
ceed him, [shall offer it to the Lord as decreed forever; the
whole of it shall be burned]" (Lev. 6:22).

[G]   [This encompasses] the one whose son takes his place, thus excluding the priest girl, whose son does not take her place [that
is, the son of a priest girl married to an Israelite is an Israelite].

[II.A] *The priest girl may be deconsecrated [declassed], but a priest
boy may not be deconsecrated [M. 3:7E].*

[B]   This is in line with that which is written: "[He shall take to
wife a virgin of his own people,] that he may not profane his
children among his people; [for I am the Lord who sanctify
him]" (Lev. 21:15).

[C]   I know only that the child is subject to deconsecration.

[D]   How do I know that the priest girl herself [who violates the
laws of her caste] may be deconsecrated?

[E]   It is a logical inference to be made.

[F]   Now if the [child], who committed no transgression, lo, he is
deemed deconsecrated, she herself, who did perform a
transgression [e.g., by marrying an unsuitable person]—is it
not logical that she should be deconsecrated?

[G]   The priest boy himself may prove to the contrary. For he may
have performed a transgression [that is, married someone not
fit for his caste], but he will not be deconsecrated.

[H]   No, if you have said that that is the case for the male, who is
not deconsecrated under any circumstances,

[I]   will you say the same of the female, who may be deconsecrated
under all circumstances?

[J]   Since she may be deconsecrated under all circumstances [e.g.,
when she marries an ordinary Israelite, she looses her status as
a priest girl], she also may be deconsecrated [in the special cir-
cumstance before us].

[K]   What do you wish to say?

[L]   He should not profane (YHL) [his children among his people]
[might have been written]. Instead it says, "He will not suffer
deconsecration (YHLL)."

[M]   Also he who had been fit and was deconsecrated [remains a priest].

[**III**.A]   *A priest girl contracts corpse uncleanness, but a priest boy does not contract corpse uncleanness [M. 3:7F].*

[B]   R. Dosa of Malehayya and R. Aha in the name of R. Eleazar: "A priest girl is permitted to go abroad."

[C]   What is the Scriptural basis for that statement?

[D]   "[And the Lord said to Moses,] 'Speak to the priests, [the sons of Aaron, and say to them that none of them shall defile himself for the dead among his people' " (Lev. 21:1)—not to the priest girls.

[E]   Now if so, what shall we have to say? Since she is subject to the decree, she should not go abroad?

[F]   Then let her be subject to the decree and not go abroad!

[G]   If you say so, you turn out to ignore the pericope covering sources of uncleanness [which addresses male, not female priests, as at D].

[**IV**.A]   *A priest boy eats Most Holy Things, but a priest girl does not eat Most Holy Things [M. 3:7G].*

[B]   This is in line with that which is written, "Every male among the priests may eat of it; [it shall be eaten in a holy place; it is most holy]" (Lev. 7:6).

The Talmud systematically provides an exegetical foundation for the Mishnah's several rules. Yerushalmi's text at **II**.K–M is faulty.

3:8

[A]   *What is the difference between a man and a woman?*

[B]   *A man goes around with unbound hair and torn garments, but a woman does not go around with unbound hair and torn garments (Lev. 13:44–45).*

[C]   *A man imposes a Nazirite vow on his son, and a woman does not impose a Nazirite vow upon her son [M. Naz. 4:6].*

[D]   *A man brings the hair offering for the Nazirite vow of his father, and a woman does not bring a hair offering for the Nazirite vow of her father [M. Naz. 4:7].*

[E]   *The man sells his daughter, and the woman does not sell her daughter (Ex. 21:6).*

[F]   *The man arranges for a betrothal of his daughter, and the woman does not arrange for the betrothal of her daughter [M. Qid. 2:1].*

[G]   *A man [who incurs the death penalty] is stoned naked, but a woman is not stoned naked.*

[H]   *A man is hung [after being put to death], and a woman is not hung [M. San. 6:3–4].*

[I]   *A man is sold [to make restitution] for having stolen something, but a woman is not sold to [make restitution] for having stolen something (Ex. 22:2).*

[**I**.A]   "Man" (Lev. 13:44). I know only that the law [that the leper goes around with unbound hair] applies to a man.

[B]   How do I know that the law covers a woman?

[C]   Scripture says, "Leprous"—applying to anyone, man, woman, child.

[D]   If so, why does it say, "A man"?

[E]   To apply to them [C] the law which follows. [Thus] *A man goes around with unbound hair and torn garments, but a woman does not go around with unbound hair and torn garments [M. 3:8B].*

[**II**.A]   *A man imposes a Nazirite vow on his son. . . . A man brings the hair offering for the Nazirite vow of his father . . . [M. 3:8C, D].*

[B]   R. Yohanan in the name of R. Meir: "There are twenty-four rulings in which the House of Shammai take the lenient position, and the House of Hillel take a stringent position, and this is one of them.

[C]   "The House of Shammai say, 'A man does not impose a Nazirite vow on his son.'

[D]   "And the House of Hillel say, 'A man does impose a Nazirite vow on his son.' "

[**III**.A]   *The man sells his daughter [M. 3:8E].*

[B]   This is in line with that which is written, "When a man sells his daughter as a slave, [she shall not go out as the male slaves do]" (Ex. 21:7).

[**IV**.A]   *The man arranges for a betrothal of his daughter [M. 3:8F].*

[B]   This is in line with that which is written, "[And the father of the young woman shall say to the elders,] 'I gave my daughter to this man to wife, and he spurns her' " (Deut. 22:16).

[**V**.A]   *A man is stoned naked, but a woman is not stoned naked [M. 3:8G].*

[B]   This is in line with that which is written, "[You shall bring them both out to the gate of the city,] and you shall stone them to death [with stones]" (Deut. 22:24).

[C]   "Stone him"—not his garment.

[D]   R. Haggai raised the following question before R. Yosé: "And is it not written, '[You shall bring them both out to the gate of the city,] and you shall stone them to death with stones' (Deut. 22:24).

[E]   "If that is so, then '[Stone] them'—not their garments [in which case, both male and female should be stoned in the nude]."

[F]   What then is the proof of the matter?

[G]   A man, because if naked he does not suffer much humiliation, is stoned naked. A woman, who suffers much humiliation [if she is seen naked] is not stoned naked.

[**VI**.A]   *A man is hung and a woman is not hung [M. 3:8H].*

[B]   This is in line with that which is written, "[And if a man has committed a crime punishable by death and he is put to death,] and you hang him [on a tree, his body shall not remain all night upon the tree]" (Deut. 21:22–23).

[C]   That is to say, "Hang him"—not her.

[**VII**.A]   *A man is sold to make restitution for having stolen something [M. 3:8I].*

[B]   [He is sold] "for that which he has stolen"—not for paying the double indemnity which he owes.

[C]   "For that which he has stolen"—not for having perjured himself in [such a regard and for owing compensation to the
victim].

[D]   "For that which he has stolen"—he is not sold and then sold
another time.

[E]   "If he has nothing"—on the basis of that phrase, we draw the
conclusion, "On account of one theft, but not on account of
two acts of theft, he is sold."

[F]   R. Jeremiah raised the question, "If he stole from a partner-
ship, how do you treat such a case?

[G]   "Is this deemed tantamount to a single act of theft, or to two
distinct acts of theft?" [This question is not answered.]

[H]   If he was stealing and taking out objects all night,

[I]   then we rule as follows:

[J]   if the owner was aware of the matter, they constitute two
[many distinct] acts of theft.

[K]   And if not, it constitutes a single [protracted] act of theft.

The Talmud again provides a systematic exegesis of the Mishnah, mostly in the form of proof texts.

4 Yerushalmi Sotah
Chapter Four

4:1 [Leiden MS and *editio princeps:* 4:1–2

[19c/A] *A betrothed girl and a childless brother's widow awaiting Levirate marriage, neither undergo the ordeal of drinking the water nor receive a marriage contract,*

[B] *since it is written "When a wife, being subject to her husband, goes astray" (Num. 5:29)—*

[C] *excluding the betrothed girl and the childless brother's widow awaiting levirate marriage.*

[D] *A widow married to a high priest, a divorcée, and a woman who has undergone the rite of halisah married to an ordinary priest, a mamzer girl and a Netinah girl married to an Israelite, an Israelite girl married to a mamzer or to a Netin,*

[E] *neither undergo the ordeal of drinking the water nor receive a marriage contract.*

[I.A] [And why should the husbands-to-be not] administer the water [to the women named at M. 4:1A]? [Since, after all, they do express jealousy to these potential wives, as is indicated by the fact that they do not receive the marriage settlement that is coming to them, they should be allowed to go through the ordeal.]

[B] It is a decree of Scripture itself: "Then the man shall bring his wife to the priest" (Num. 5:15) [so the reference to wife is exclusive].

[C] Then let him [also] not express jealousy [to the women listed at M. 4:1A]!

114

[D]   Scripture says, "And he is jealous of his wife" (Num. 5:14)—
       even [of a woman who is only] partly his wife [at that point].

[II.A] Does the Mishnah's rule accord [also] with the view of the
       House of Shammai, for the Shammaites [at M. 4:2H–I] hold
       that a woman may receive the marriage contract while not
       undergoing the ordeal of drinking the water? [Here the two are
       treated as mutually exclusive; if one does not do the one, she
       does not get the other.]

[B]   [Yes, that is the case. There is a special consideration operative
       at M. 4:2H–I, for] said R. Yosé, "There the reason the House
       of Shammai [give her the marriage settlement] is that she may
       say, 'Bring me my husband, and I shall drink the water.'
       [Since it is possible for her to prove herself to be clean, she is
       not punished for having been alone with a man other than her
       husband.]

[C]   "But here, she knew full well that a betrothed girl does not
       drink the water. Why in the world did she [go off with some
       man so as to] subject herself to this great doubt and invalidate
       her right to collect her marriage settlement? [Since this woman
       cannot prove herself clean, she should not have risked being
       alone with a man. It is her own fault that she loses the mar-
       riage settlement, based on the risk she herself took.]"

[III.A] [As to I.D, above,] R. Judah raised the question, "As to that
       which you have said there, 'And he is jealous of his wife
       (Num. 5:14)—even of a woman who is only partly his wife as
       of that point,'

[B]   "do we say the same [in reference to the curse, 'If no man has
       lain with you, and if you have not turned aside to uncleanness]
       while you were under your husband's authority . . . ' (Num.
       5:19)—even if he was your husband only in part? [This then
       would contradict M. 4:1A–C.]" [The question is not
       answered.]

[IV.A] What would be an example [of the rule of M. 4:1A, that a be-
       trothed girl or childless brother's widow awaiting levirate mar-
       riage neither undergo the ordeal of drinking the water nor
       receive a marriage contract]? [In fact M. 4:1A applies only if
       the entire ordeal is completed with the woman in the stated
       status.]

[B]   [If, however,] the husband expressed jealousy to her when she
       was still betrothed, consummated the marriage, and she went
       aside with the named man, then he makes her drink the water
       by reason of the original expression of jealousy. [So this exem-
       plifies the other side of the rule, the point at which the status
       specified at M. 4:1A does not exempt the woman from
       undergoing the ordeal.]

[C]   [Again:] if he expressed jealousy to her while she was yet await-
       ing marriage with the levir, then he consummated the mar-
       riage, then he requires her to drink the water by reason of the
       original expression of jealousy.

[D]   If he expressed jealousy to her while she was yet betrothed,
       and he married her, and then she went aside, and only there-
       after did he have sexual relations, then she goes forth along
       with collecting her marriage settlement. [This is in line with
       M. 4:2E: because of his having sexual relations with her, she
       loses the opportunity to undergo the ordeal, hence collects.]

[E]   But if not, she goes forth without collecting her marriage
       settlement.

[F]   If her husband expressed jealousy to her, then died, and she
       fell before the levir [for levirate marriage], and he married her,
       and she went aside with the man originally named by the now-
       deceased husband, the levir requires her to drink the water by
       reason of the expression of jealousy of the original husband [the
       levir's brother].

[G]   If her husband did not express jealousy to her, and he died,
       and she fell before the levir, and he, for his part, expressed
       jealousy to her about the named man, and he had not consum-
       mated the marriage to her before he too died, and then she fell
       before his brother [yet a further levir], he does not have the
       right to impose on her the ordeal of the water,

[H]   for she has fallen to him [as a wife] only because of the rela-
       tionship to the first brother, [her original husband, who never
       issued an expression of jealousy to begin with].

[I]   But if the levir [the second brother] had expressed jealousy to
       her and married her and then died, and she then fell before the
       second levir, and he married her, and she went aside with the
       named man, he has every right to impose the rite of drinking

the water upon her by reason of the expression of jealousy of the second brother.

[**V**.A]   There we have learned: *A barren woman and a woman past menopause and a woman who cannot give birth do not undergo the ordeal of drinking the water and do not receive the marriage contract [M. 4:3C].*

[B]   For it is written, "But if the woman has not defiled herself and is clean, then she shall be free and shall conceive children" (Num. 5:28). This applies to one who is suitable to conceive.

[C]   It then excludes this one, who is not suitable to conceive.

[D]   They objected: "Lo there is *the widow married to a high priest [M. 4:1D].*

[E]   "Lo, she is suitable to conceive [yet does not undergo the ordeal of drinking the water nor does she receive a marriage contract]. [So C cannot be the operative consideration.]"

[F]   Her case is subject to a different consideration, for it is written, "He shall not defile himself as a husband among his people and so profane himself" (Lev. 21:4). [The usual consideration is capacity to produce children.]

[G]   There we have learned, *A mamzer invalidates and validates for eating. How so? [An Israelite girl married to a priest, or a priest girl married to an Israelite, who gives birth to a son with him, and the son goes and trifles with a slave girl, and she produces a son from him—lo, this boy is a slave. If the mother of the slave's father was an Israelite girl married to a priest, if the father and son die, she does not eat heave offering, by reason of the grandson. If she was a priest's daughter married to an Israelite, despite the grandson, she does eat heave offering (M. Yeb. 7:5M–S).]* [It follows that a priest's child who is invalid still is deemed a child for the stated purposes, as just explained.] And here you say this [namely, F, that we totally ignore the priest's invalid offspring for the present purpose]!

[H]   Said R. Tanhuma, "There it says, '[If a priest's daughter is married to an outsider, she shall not eat of the offering of the Holy Things. But if a priest's daughter is a widow or divorcée] and has no child [and returns to her father's house as in her youth, she may eat of her father's food]' (Lev. 22:12–13).

[I]   "[That is, she has no offspring] deriving from any source what-
        ever [even invalid offspring].

[J]   "But in the present instance, [we speak] only of valid off-
        spring, not invalid offspring [thus excluding from the provi-
        sions of Num. 5:28, cited above, the widow married to a high
        priest and the others listed at M. 4:1D]."

[VI.A] [As to the reason behind M. 4:1D–E,] said R. Yosé b. R. Bun,
        "Do the waters not come [and leave her unmarked] except in
        order to permit her once more to have sexual relations with her
        husband? [That is why the women in invalid marriages do not
        drink the water, for in any case they should not be married to
        their present husbands.]

[B]   "But in the case of this one, once she has gone aside with the
        named man, he says to her, 'Get out.' [She is permanently for-
        bidden to the husband and he may not remain in the marriage
        in any event.]"

Once more we have a full account of the Mishnah's problems
and their solutions. Units **I** and **III** take up the most fundamental question, namely, the distinction on which the Mishnah
is based. Unit **II** asks about the authority for the Mishnah's position. Unit **IV** then exemplifies the basic consideration of the
Mishnah, namely, that we deal with a complete process. If the
process of warning, going aside, and drinking the water, should
be interrupted, e.g., by a change in the woman's status, then it
is null. The cases of unit **IV** are both important and self-ex-
planatory. Unit **V** goes to the next material of the Mishnah and
asks how we distinguish the operative consideration here (the
absence of valid children or children not deemed legal entities)
from the operative consideration in a related case, in which invalid offspring were treated as legal entities. The distinction is
carefully worked out on the basis of Scripture's language, V.H–
J. Unit **VI** offers yet another reason for the Mishnah's rule.

4:2 [Leiden MS and *editio princeps:* 4:3]

[A]   *And these do not undergo the ordeal of drinking the water or
        receive a marriage contract:*

[B]   *She who says "I am unclean," or against whom witnesses came to testify that she is unclean;*

[C]   *and she who says "I will not drink."*

[D]   *[If, however,] her husband said "I will not make her drink,*

[E]   *or [if] her husband had sexual relations with her on the way [to Jerusalem],*

[F]   *she receives her marriage contract but does not undergo the ordeal of drinking the bitter water.*

[G]   *[If] their husbands died before they drank the bitter water—*

[H]   *The House of Shammai say, "They receive the marriage contract and do not undergo the ordeal of drinking the bitter water."*

[I]   *And the House of Hillel say, "They do not undergo the ordeal of drinking the bitter water and do not receive the marriage contract."*

[I.A]   Said R. Josiah, "Zeira told me in the name of the men of Jerusalem, 'There are three cases in which, if [the aggrieved parties] wish to forgive [the malefactor], they are allowed to do so: the accused wife, the incorrigible son, and the rebellious elder. . . .' "

The Talmud here alludes to a saying which is not fully cited (cf. B. Sot. 25a).

4:3 [Leiden MS and *editio princeps:* 4:4]

[A]   *"A woman who was pregnant by another husband [who died or divorced the woman] and a woman who was giving suck to a child by another husband do not undergo the ordeal of drinking the bitter water and do not receive the marriage contract,"* the words of R. Meir.

[B]   *And sages say, "He has the power to set her apart and then to take her back after a while."*

[C]   *A barren woman and a woman past menopause and a woman who cannot give birth do not undergo the ordeal of drinking the bitter water and do not receive the marriage contract.*

[D]   *R. Eliezer says, "He has the power to marry another woman
      for purposes of procreation."*

[E]   *And all other women either undergo the ordeal of drinking the
      bitter water or do not collect the marriage contract.*

[I.A] A man should not marry a woman made pregnant by his fellow
      or one who is giving suck to the infant of his fellow.

[B]   And if he did marry a woman in such a condition, Scripture
      says of him, "Do not remove an ancient landmark or enter the
      fields of the fatherless" (Prov. 23:10).

[C]   "He who marries a woman made pregnant by his fellow or a
      woman nursing the infant of his fellow must divorce her and
      [as a penalty] may never remarry her," the words of R. Meir.

[D]   *And sages say, "He may put her away but then take her back
      after a proper period of time" [M. Sot. 4:3B].*

[E]   Now in all such matters [in which scribes have imposed a strict
      ruling and a person has violated the scribes' rule], does R.
      Meir impose so heavy a penalty [as just now indicated]?

[F]   Let us derive the answer to that question from the following:

[G]   *A minor who performed the rite of halisah should perform the
      rite of halisah again when she grows up. But if she did not per-
      form the rite of halisah [later on], her [original] performance of
      halisah is confirmed as valid [M. Yeb. 12:4E–F].*

[H]   [We shall now find out that the cited statement belongs to
      Meir, and we shall then see how it answers the original ques-
      tion.] R. Mana cited this statement without cited authority.

[I]   R. Isaac son of R. Hiyya the Elder in the name of R. Yohanan:
      "It belongs to R. Meir, [for R. Meir] said, 'They do not effect
      the rite of *halisah* or permit a levirate marriage in the case of a
      minor girl, lest she turn out to be barren [so the entire rite will
      not have been required]. [Accordingly, Meir in this case does
      not impose a strict penalty. To begin with, one should not per-
      form the rite; but if it has been performed, it is valid, and no
      penalty is exacted.]'" [That answers the original question.]

[II.A] It was taught: "**A nursing mother whose husband died, lo,
      she should not be betrothed nor wed until twenty-four
      months have passed,**" the words of R. Meir.

[B]   **And R. Judah says, "Eighteen months."**

[C]   **R. Jonathan b. Joseph says, "The House of Shammai say,
      'Twenty-four months,' and the House of Hillel say, 'Eighteen
      months.' "**

[D]   **Said Rabban Simeon b. Gamaliel, "In accord with the opin-
      ion of the one who says 'twenty-four months,' she is in fact
      permitted to be wed in twenty-one months. In accord with
      the opinion of the one who says 'eighteen months,' she may
      be wed in fifteen months. For the milk begins to deteriorate
      only three months after conception [in the case of a preg-
      nancy from the new marriage"] [T. Nid. 2:2].**

[E]   R. Jacob bar Aha said, "Aqabiah asked R. Simeon b. Laqish
      about the law, and he instructed him that the interval is
      twenty-four months."

[F]   R. Jeremiah: "Aqabiah asked R. Hanina, and he informed him
      that it is twenty-four months."

[G]   What [is going on here]?

[H]   There were two cases.

[I]   In one [he ruled] in the name of R. Haninah [19d] and in one,
      in the name of R. Simeon b. Laqish.

[J]   R. Mana ruled, "Eighteen months," and he fasted on the en-
      tire day [on which he gave that ruling].

[K]   R. Mar Uqba gave instruction in Arbela that it was twenty-four
      months, and that applies even if the infant [of the former mar-
      riage] dies.

[III.A] [With reference to M. 4:3D,] sages concur with R. Eleazar that
         if the man already has a wife and children [in the case of M.
         4:3C], the barren woman drinks [the bitter water] and may col-
         lect her marriage settlement. [Eleazar differs only where the
         man has no other wife or children.]

[B]   If he had a wife and children and they died, between the time
      that he expressed jealousy and the time that the wife went in
      private with the named man,

[C]   she has already been proved appropriate to undergo the ordeal
      [even though he has no other wife and children now].

[D]   If he had no wife and children and then between the time of
      his expressing jealousy and the time of her going in private
      with the named man, he got both,

[E]   she has already been proved inappropriate to undergo the ordeal. [We follow the situation which prevails at the time of the expression of jealousy in applying M. 4:3D.]

Units **I** and **II** deal with the Mishnah's theme but not with the Mishnah's law, since they ignore the issue of the ordeal. Only at unit **III** do we reach the Mishnah's materials, and then, as is clear, the Talmud has little to add, except a minor clarification, stated at **III**.E, of Eleazer's position.

4:4 [Leiden MS and *editio princeps:* 4:5]

[A]   *The wife of a priest drinks the bitter water and [if proved innocent] is permitted [to go back] to her husband.*

[B]   *The wife of a eunuch undergoes the ordeal of drinking the bitter water.*

[C]   *On account of [men in] all sorts of prohibited relationships to the women,] wives are subjected to warning,*

[D]   *except for a minor,*

[E]   *and for one who is not human.*

[**I**.A]   [Why should M. 4:4A tells us that the woman returns to her husband? That surely is self-evident. She has drunk the water and survived the ordeal.] If not, what should we have said? [Surely,] since she drank the water, and the water did not put her to the test, she is clean.

[B]   [No.] I might say that merit suspended the punishment [and hence, perhaps the woman should be prohibited from going back to her husband on the possibility that, indeed, she was guilty, but the ordeal did not prove it]. [Consequently M. 4:4A must be made explicit.]

[C]   That explanation is valid from the viewpoint of the one who said "Merit suspends the punishment, and that fact [of the woman's uncleanness] may not be known."

[D]   But in accord with the view of the one who said "Merit suspends the punishment, and that fact will be known," [what is there to say about M. 4:4A]?

[E]   Said R. Isaac, "Thus do we interpret the matter: It applies to a case in which she drank the water, and it did not put her to the test. [In this case the woman was raped, so the water is null.] Since the water does not put to the test the woman who was raped, but only the one who was seduced, since this one was raped, [it may not have worked].

[F]   [Now, furthermore, since the rule in the priesthood is that] a woman who was raped is in the same status as the woman who had sexual relations willingly, in the case of an ordinary Israelite, on that account it is necessary to state that [the wife of a priest in particular] is permitted to go back to her husband. [We do not assign to rape the failure of the water to put the woman to the test. She returns to her husband. This is not a self-evident point, and that is why the Mishnah must make it explicit.]

[G]   Now how do we know that sexual relations which take place contrary to the woman's will invalidate a married woman to remain married to a priest?

[H]   Now if in the case of creeping things, which are a minor sort of uncleanness, the law has treated contamination effected them by accident to contamination effected by them deliberately,

[I]   an accused wife, who is subject to a far more stringent law, all the more so!

[II.A]   R. Jacob bar Idi taught before R. Jonathan: " 'But if you have gone astray, though you are under your husband's authority, and if you have defiled yourself, and some man other than your husband has been with you . . .' (Num. 5:20)—

[B]   "This then excludes a case of rape.

[C]   "How do you derive [that fact from the reference to 'under your husband's authority']?"

[D]   He said to him, "Just as 'under your husband's authority' means 'of her own free will,' so in the present case, [the prohibited act of sexual relations must be] of her own free will [excluding a case of rape, in which the rite does not apply]."

[E]   "[If a man lies with her carnally, and it is hidden from the eyes of her husband, and she is undetected though she has defiled herself, and there is no witness against her,] since she was not taken in the act" (Num. 5:13).

[F]   Lo, if she were caught in the act, she would be permitted! And is there a woman who was found out in Israel, who would be forbidden [under these circumstances]? And who is that? It is the one who began to have sexual relations willingly, but ended up being raped.

[G]   And is there one who is not detected in Israel and yet she would be permitted?

[H]   And who is that? It is one who to begin with was subjected to rape, but in the end completed the sexual act willingly.

[I]   It would, for example, accord with the case of a woman who came to R. Yohanan. She said to him, "I was raped."

[J]   He said to her, "But in the end wasn't it nice for you?"

[K]   She said to him, "Now if someone should dip his finger into honey and put it into his mouth on the Day of Atonement, is it not bad for him at the beginning, but in the end isn't it nice for him?"

[L]   And he accepted her view.

[III.A]   "But if you have gone astray though you are under your husband's authority, and if you have defiled yourself and some man other than your husband has lain with you" (Num. 5:20)—

[B]   This is added to encompass (Leiden MS and *editio princeps:* to exclude) the wife of a eunuch [M. 4:4B].

[C]   "And some other man . . . has lain with you"—

[D]   This is said to encompass a eunuch [who seduces a married woman]—

[E]   *except for a minor and for one who is not human [M. 4:4D–E].*

The Talmud restricts its discussion to the Mishnah's language and law. Unit I points out that the Mishnah's rule is self-evident and hardly requires specification. A careful discussion demonstrates that that is not the case under the specified circumstances. Unit II, familiar from Y. 1:2 I, goes on to the case of a woman who is raped. She is not subjected to the ordeal and is guiltless. Unit II.A–D pose no problems, nor do G–L.

The rhetoric of E–F is puzzling, though the analogy of G leaves no doubt as to F's meaning. Unit **III** poses no problems.

4:5 [Leiden MS and *editio princeps:* 4:6]

[A]   *And these are the women whom a court subjects to warning [in behalf of the husband]:*

[B]   *A woman whose husband became a deaf-mute or an imbecile, or was imprisoned—*

[C]   *not to impose upon her the ordeal of drinking the water did they state the rule, but to invalidate her for receiving her marriage contract.*

[D]   *R. Yosé says, "Also it serves to impose upon her the ordeal of drinking the water.*

[E]   *"When her husband goes free from prison, he may then impose the ordeal of drinking the bitter water."*

[**I**.A]   And the Lord said to Moses, "Say to the people of Israel, [If any man's wife goes astray and acts unfaithfully against him . . . and if the spirit of jealousy comes upon him, and] he is jealous of his wife . . . and he will make the woman drink the water . . .' " (Num. 11–14, 24).

[B]   It is a decree of the Scripture [that a court also may warn the wife, since Scripture speaks of the whole people of Israel, not only to the husband].

[C]   "Then the man shall bring his wife to the priest" (Num. 5:15).

[D]   And should a court [also] not express jealousy to the woman [vs. A–B]?

[E]   The Torah has said "he is jealous of his wife" even if she is only partially his wife, [and even a court may do so].

[**II**.A]   In the case of sexual relations with those who are invalid for marriage to a woman—how do we know that she is invalidated [for marriage to the priesthood on that account]?

[B]   How do we interpret the matter?

[C]   If she is in the status of a married woman, she is subject to a strict rule [that is, subject to extirpation].

[D]   If it is a widow married to a high priest, it already is stated, "And the man will bring his wife to the priest" (Num. 5:15), [excluding her, since she is not legitimately wed to him].

[E]   The common trait applying to them is this:

[F]   One whose offspring is invalid—his act of sexual relations with her invalidates [her for marriage into the priesthood].

[G]   And one whose seed is not invalid—his act of sexual relations also does not invalidate [her for marriage into the priesthood].

[H]   And these are they:

[I]   **A nine-year-and-one-day-old boy of Ammonite, Moabite, Egyptian, Edomite, or Samaritan origin, [or] a Netin or mamzer [of that age or older], who had sexual relations with the daughter of a priest, Levite, or Israelite, has rendered her invalid for marrying into the priesthood.**

[J]   **R. Yosé says, "Any one whose seed is valid—she is valid [for marrying into the priesthood]. And any whose seed is invalid—she is invalid, [thus delisting the Egyptian]."**

[K]   **Rabban Simeon b. Gamaliel says, "Any whose daughter you are permitted to marry—you are permitted to marry his widow; and any whose daughter you are not permitted to marry—you are not permitted to marry his widow. [Thus Ammonites and Moabites are delisted]" [T. Yeb. 8:1].**

Unit I.A–B explain the Scriptural basis for the Mishnah's rule. Unit I.C–D ask why the court may not express jealousy. A–B have proved that the court may do just that. E, which purports to be an answer, in no way responds to C–D (unless we add the language inserted by me, in line with Qorban ha'edah and Pené Moshe). I am at a loss to explain why unit II has been added. Even if it continues I.E—as it surely should—it is difficult to justify introducing the issues of II.A here. The cited passage of Tosefta spells out those who are under discussion. The clear intent is to take account of how sexual relations may invalidate a woman for marriage into the priesthood. But that issue is not before us. In all, I cannot properly interpret the place or argument of I.E or II.

5 Yerushalmi Sotah
Chapter Five

5:1

[20a/A]   *"Just as the water puts her to the test, so the water puts him [the lover] to the test,*

[B]   *"since it is said, 'And it shall come . . . , And it shall come' (Num. 5:22, 24).*

[C]   *"Just as she is prohibited to the husband, so she is prohibited to the lover,*

[D]   *"since it is said, 'And she will be unclean . . . , And she will be unclean' " (Num. 5:27, 29), the words of R. Aqiba.*

[E]   *Said R. Joshua, "Thus did Zekharyah b. Haqqassab expound [the Scripture]."*

[F]   *Rabbi says, "The two times at which 'If she is made unclean,' 'She is made unclean' are stated in the pericope refer, one to the husband and one to the lover."*

[I.A]   We have learned the formulation of the Mishnah as "It shall come . . . it shall come."

[B]   There are Tannaim who teach the Mishnah in the language, "And it shall come . . . and it shall come."

[C]   He who said that the Mishnah pericope reads "It shall come . . . it shall come" is R. Aqiba [who deems the repetition of the same word to signify two distinct meanings, purposes, or applications].

[D]   The one who said that the Mishnah pericope reads "And it shall come . . . and it shall come" is R. Ishmael [who emphasizes the use of the conjunction "and" as encompassing, and who does not think that the mere repetition of a given word bears special meaning, because, in his view, the Torah uses the language ordinarily used by people].

[E]   [Along these same lines,] we have learned in the formulation of the Mishnah, "She will be unclean . . . she will be unclean."

[F]   There are Tannaim who teach the Mishnah in the language, "*And* she will be unclean . . . *and* she will be unclean."

[G]   The one who said that the Mishnah pericope reads "She will be unclean . . . she will be unclean" is R. Aqiba.

[H]   The one who said that the Mishnah pericope reads "*And* she will be unclean . . . *and* she will be unclean" is R. Ishmael.

[I]   It was taught: "[It is written,] 'BW [come] and BH [into her].' "

[J]   And so is it written.

[K]   [The explanation of the fact] accords with that which R. Ami said in the name of R. Yohanan: "For the purposes of exegesis they remove [the W] from the beginning [of the word in which it appears, and they set it at] the end [of the word, thus as if it were written, BW and BH, 'into him' and 'into her,' so in line with M. 5:1A]."

[L]   R. Haninah in the name of R. Jeremiah: "And that is the case even of a letter found in the very middle of a word.

[M]   " 'And you shall put oil upon it [the meal offering]' (Lev. 2:15). This means, 'You will pour oil on the meal offering.'

[N]   "It serves to encompass all meal offerings [meaning that all of them have to have oil poured on them].

[O]   "May I then say that it includes the meal offering baked in the oven? [Surely not!]

[P]   "The text therefore states, 'Oil thereon,' excluding some kinds of meal offering. [The word 'LYH is now read 'LH, meaning, on *it*, not on some other kind, and the Y then is removed from the middle of the word, as Jeremiah has said. For a better version of the exegesis, see B. Men. 75a.]"

[Q]   "[Water that] brings the curse" (HM'RRYM)—R. Tanhuma said, "Why does it say 'HM'RRYM?' [Because letters contain the numerical value of 496, for the 248 limbs of the woman, and the 248 limbs of the man [thus the water brings the curse throughout the bodies of both the woman and her lover].

[R]   That is in line with what we have learned: *Just as the water puts her to the proof, so the water puts him to the proof.*

[**II**.A]   Just as she is forbidden to the husband, so she is forbidden to the lover.

[B]   Just as she is forbidden to the brother of her husband [should he die childless], so she is forbidden to the brother of her lover [under the same circumstances]. [Consequently, her lover's brother cannot marry her.]

[C]   Just as the water puts her to the test for each act of sexual relations which she has with her husband after she has had sexual relations with her lover, so they put him to the test.

[D]   [M. 5:1A implies that if the water does not put her to the proof, then it does not put him to the proof, even though he has violated the law by having sexual relations with a married woman. Why should this be so?] As to her, since it is her lot to be prohibited both to him and to another party [both to the husband and the lover], she is put to the test.

[E]   But as to him, [only] when she drinks is he tested.

[F]   If the water put him to the test but did not put her to the test [so that he suffered the ill-effects and she did not], I say that merit suspended the working of the water.

[G]   This poses no problems to the one who holds that the merit suspends the punishment, and that fact may not be known at all.

[H]   But in the view of him who says that when merit suspends the punishment, the fact is clearly known, lo, in this case, that fact is not [clearly] indicated, [since, after all, one of the two parties has suffered the ill-effects of drinking the water].

[I]   But is such a case I maintain that [the lover] drank water which had been left uncovered [and it was poisoned by a snake, and] he was poisoned thereby.

[J]   Do they require that the water put him to the test only in the specified manner [in the right order of symptoms, as specified above]?

[K]   But I say, [The man was affected by the water because] he went in private with other women [besides this one, and he is punished for what he has done in other cases].

[L]   But to begin with did we not theorize: When she drinks, he is put to the test?

[M]   Interpret the case to be one in which he did the act deliberately, but she did it inadvertently.

[N]   Consequently, the water put him to the test and did not put her to the test. [This completes the solution.]

[O]   If the water put her to the test but did not put him to the test, I maintain that merit suspended the punishment coming to him.

[P]   That view poses no problems to the one who says that merit suspends the punishment, and that fact may not be known at all.

[Q]   But in the view of the one who says that merit suspends the punishment, but if so, that fact is certainly known, lo, in this case it was not indicated!

[R]   But I maintain that she drank water which had been left uncovered [and had been poisoned], and so she was poisoned.

[S]   Do they not require that the water put her to the test only in the specified manner?

[T]   But I say, [The woman was affected by the water because] she went in private with other men [besides this one, and she is punished for what she has done in other cases].

[U]   If that is the case, then if the husband divorced her, the suspected lover, unaffected by the water, should be permitted to marry her. [That is contrary, in fact, to the law.]

[V]   Interpret the case to be one in which he did the act inadvertently [unaware that she was a married woman], and she did it deliberately. [Consequently] the water put her to the test and did not put him to the test.

[W]   Now if he did it deliberately and she did it inadvertently, it is obvious that she is permitted to have sexual relations with her husband.

[X]   If the husband divorced her, what is the law as to [the lover's] now being permitted to marry her?

[Y]   Surely it is not possible to say that, to begin with, he deliberately had sexual relations with her and now is permitted to marry her! And will you say this?

[Z]   If he did it inadvertently and she did it deliberately, it is obvious that she is prohibited to have sexual relations with her husband.

[AA] If the husband divorced her, what is the law as to [the lover's] being permitted to marry her?

[BB] Surely it is not possible to say that she goes forth from the husband's domain! And will you say this?

[CC] And how do we know that the matter depends wholly on her [in the case in which the lover acted innocently, and the married woman intentionally]?

[DD] Simeon bar Ba in the name of R. Yohanan: "It is written 'You shall not have sexual relations with your neighbor's wife and defile yourself through her' (Lev. 18:20)—'through her' is the matter decided.

[EE] "If she did the deed deliberately, she is forbidden. If she did it inadvertently, she is permitted."

The Talmud admirably focuses upon the central issue of the Mishnah, the liability of both the lover and the faithless wife to the effects of the water that brings the curse. The theme is worked out first through exegesis of Scripture, then through the application of practical reason to the facts of the matter. The exegetical materials of unit **I** pose a problem of text only at **I.L–P**, in which I follow the sense of the cited passage of **B**. The interesting side to unit **II** is in the inquiry into the correlation of what happens to the accused wife and what happens to her lover. This produces a set of paired exercises going over familiar issues, especially the matter of whether or not the effects of merit's suspending punishment are or are not to be discerned. If they are, then, at each point, we have to take account of the water's failing to do its work.

5:2 [Leiden MS and *editio princeps:* 5:2–4]

[A] *On that day did R. Aqiba expound [as follows]: " 'And every earthen vessel whereinto any of them falls, whatsoever is in it conveys uncleanness' (Lev. 11:33). It does not say, 'It will be unclean' but 'will convey uncleanness'—that is, to impart uncleanness to other things.*

[B] *"Thus has Scripture taught concerning a loaf of bread unclean in the second remove, that it imparts uncleanness in the third remove [to a loaf of bread with which it comes into contact]."*

[C] *Said R. Joshua, "Who will remove the dirt from your eyes, Rabban Yohanan b. Zakkai, for you used to say, 'Another generation is going to come to declare clean a loaf of bread in the third remove [from the original source of uncleanness].'*

[D] *"For there is no Scripture in the Torah which indicates that it is unclean.*

[E] *"But now has not Aqiba, your disciple, brought Scriptural proof from the Torah that it is indeed unclean,*

[F] *"since it is said, 'And whatsoever is in it shall impart uncleanness' " (Lev. 11:33).*

[I.A] [With regard to Aqiba's view that a loaf of bread unclean in the second remove from the original source of uncleanness has the capacity to impart uncleanness to food with which it comes into contact, hence, at the third remove from the original source of uncleanness,] R. Yosé b. R. Bun said, "Rab and Samuel [disputed about this matter].

[B] "One of them said, 'Whether the food is in the status of heave offering [and hence, more sensitive to becoming unclean, and also more capable of imparting uncleanness], or in the status of unconsecrated food, [R. Aqiba's opinion applies].'

[C] "The other of them said, 'If the food is in the status of heave offering, [R. Aqiba's opinion applies], but food [unclean in the second remove] which is not consecrated [does] not [have the power to impart uncleanness to food with which it comes into contact]. [Hence there is no third remove in the matter of unconsecrated food's contracting uncleanness. Unconsecrated food in the third remove from the original source of uncleanness itself is completely clean and does not receive uncleanness from

food in the second remove from the original source of
uncleanness.]'

[D]   "Now we do not know which one of them held one opinion,
and which one held the other.

[E]   "But on the basis of that which R. Yosé in the name of R.
Jonah, and some say that Rab said it in the name of R. Hiyya
the Elder, namely, 'What is unclean in the third remove from
the original source is unclean because of the effects of the dead
creeping thing,' [which was that original source, and that is
stated without differentiation as to the character of the food—
unconsecrated, consecrated—which receives the uncleanness], it
follows that it is he who has said that R. Aqiba's position applies both to heave offering and to unconsecrated food alike."

[F]   [Now that we have established the grounds for dispute, we
turn to other laws of the Mishnah to test the more controversial
of the two positions, namely, Rab's.] The Mishnah pericope
[which follows] stands at variance with the position of Rab:

[G]   *Produce of tithe which was rendered susceptible to uncleanness
by liquid and which a Tebul Yom [one who has immersed and
who now awaits sunset to complete the process of purification
from uncleanness] touched, or [which] dirty hands [touched,
which are unclean in the second remove]—they separate from
that produce in the status of tithe heave offering of tithe in a
state of cleanness, [and said heave offering is clean], because it
is in the third remove, and the third remove from the original
source of uncleanness is clean so far as unconsecrated food is
concerned [M. T.Y. 4:1]* [So there is no status of uncleanness
imputed to food which is not consecrated and which suffers
contact with food unclean in the second remove. Surely Aqiba
has been misinterpreted by Rab, or Aqiba must differ from the
cited pericope.]

[H]   Interpret the passage as a lenient ruling in regard to uncleanness affecting the hands, since the perpetual uncleanness of the
hands [in the second remove] is merely by reason of a decree of
the scribes.

[I]   But lo, we have learned [that the same rule applies to] Tebul
Yom [so it cannot be a leniency accorded only to the hands]!

[J]   Interpret the rule to apply to a Tebul Yom who has immersed
himself by reason of the doubtful uncleanness imparted by

being in a grave site [which may or may not contain corpse matter sufficient to impart uncleanness. Since we do not know for sure that the person was originally made unclean by a corpse, we also have no reason to impose the full stringencies of the law, hence the stated leniency as to food in the third remove from the original source of uncleanness. But, in general, there is indeed a third remove of uncleanness affecting ordinary, not consecrated, food.]

[K]   Said R. Zeira, "[There is a still better solution]. Even if you say that the Tebul Yom under discussion is unclean by reason of an uncleanness specified by the Torah, the case of the Tebul Yom still is different. He is described in Scripture as both clean and unclean. He is clean so far as unconsecrated food is concerned even while it it yet day, and he is clean for heave offering only after the sun has set."

[L]   R. Haggai objected before R. Yosé, "[There is an alternative explanation for the usage of the words 'unclean' and 'clean' with regard to the Tebul Yom]. One may say that [the entire passage speaks only of food in the status of heave offering]. The Tebul Yom [during the day before the sun set] is clean so far as touching the consecrated food is concerned, but unclean [until sunset] so far as eating it is concerned."

[M]   He said to him, "The cited passage [Lev. 11:33] refers explicitly to utensils. Have you got the possibility of maintaining that, with respect to utensils, they may be clean so far as being touched is concerned and unclean so far as being eaten is concerned?!"

[N]   The Mishnah pericope now cited also supports the position of Rab: *Unconsecrated food in the first remove from the original source of uncleanness is unclean and imparts uncleanness [to food which it touches]. Unconsecrated food in the second remove is unfit [to be eaten by one who eats his unconsecrated food in cleanness], but it does not impart uncleanness at all. And unconsecrated food in the third remove [that is, which has touched unconsecrated food unclean in the second remove] may be eaten in a pottage of heave offering [M. Toh. 2:3].* [This is the view of Rab, that Aqiba's view is that there is a third remove to be taken into consideration for both heave offering and unconsecrated food. Why?]

[O]   Now, lo, it is prohibited to mix food in the third remove with heave offering, [and hence there is indeed a consideration of uncleanness affecting unconsecrated food in the third remove]. [If there is no such consideration, may not one mix the unconsecrated food in the third remove with heave offering?]

[P]   [No, this is not possible. For] cite what follows: *Heave offering in the first and in the second removes is unclean and renders other food unclean. Heave offering in the third remove is unfit and does not convey uncleanness. And heave offering at the fourth remove is eaten in a pottage of Holy Things [M. Toh. 2:4].* [Thus what is unclean at the third remove invalidates what it touches at the fourth, but it does not render it unclean so that what is at the fourth remove has an effect upon what it touches, that is, at the fifth remove.]

[Q]   Now if you reason [as you did above, then it must follow that] it is forbidden to treat [what is unclean in the fourth remove] as holy. Then you impute to Rab contradictory positions.

[R]   For R. Ba in the name of Rab [stated], "What is unclean in the third remove is affected by the original dead creeping thing's uncleanness. But as to what is affected in the fourth remove, it is indeed permitted to treat it as holy, [and it is not unclean at all].

[S]   "For the consideration of a fourth remove from the original source of uncleanness affects Holy Things only so far as the Most Holy Things of the sanctuary itself are concerned. [Hence the implication drawn just now contradicts Rab's position in the present matter.]"

[T]   Said R. Huna, "And are we not speaking here of heave offering [and not of Holy Things]? And as to heave offering, it is prohibited to treat it as subject to the laws governing Holy Things [which are more severe], so as not to cause any sort of mishandling of food in the status of heave offering. [Since the rules are less strict, if one treats heave offering by a more strict rule than is required, one will end up disposing of it, instead of eating it, when in fact it is valid and may be eaten. So there is no contradiction among Rab's several opinions.]"

[U]   And, [further,] cite what follows: *Holy Things in the first, second, and third removes are susceptible to uncleanness and impart uncleanness. Holy Things in the fourth remove are unfit* and *do not impart uncleanness. And Holy Things in the fifth remove are eaten in a pottage of Holy Things [M. Toh. 2:5].*

[V]   Now if you say this, then it is forbidden to treat as holy [what was touched that is unclean in the fourth remove]. [It cannot be eaten by itself.]

[W]   Now is there such a thing as the consideration of a fifth remove from the original source of uncleanness so far as Holy Things are concerned? [Certainly not.]

[X]   [It follows that the original, acute reading of the pericope vis-à-vis Rab is not possible. For] you must rule that there is no such thing [as a fifth remove in Holy Things], and here too there is no such thing [as a third remove, as reasoned above, N–Q]. [The entire argument is thus shown to lead to an absurd extreme and must be dropped.]

[II.A]   [That which has touched something unclean in the second remove is clean, for, in line with Lev. 11:33,] said R. Yohanan, "That which is in the third remove is third in contact with the dead creeping thing, [and it is not unclean, so] it is permitted to treat it as heave offering [that is, to declare that batch of food as heave offering for some larger batch of clean food]. [There is nothing unclean about it.]"

[B]   They asked before him: "[Is this statement of yours] even in accord with R. Aqiba [at M. 5:2B]?"

[C]   R. Yosé in the name of R. Hila, "And it even accords with the position of R. Aqiba." [Yosé-Hila maintain the position of Samuel, that at issue in Aqiba's saying is only food in the status of heave offering.]

[D]   "How so?

[E]   "A Tebul Yom is invalid [for eating heave offering, since he is in the second remove], and that which is in the second remove is invalid [for use as heave offering]. [That is, invalid but not unclean.]

[F]   "Just as a Tebul Yom does not invalidate unconsecrated food touched by him from being declared heave offering [for he does not impart uncleanness to that which he touches],

[G]   "so [whatever is] in the second remove [like the Tebul Yom] does not invalidate unconsecrated food [by rendering it unclean] from being declared heave offering."

[H]   [Taking the opposite line of thought, that Aqiba treats unconsecrated food as much as heave offering,] R. Yosé in the name
of R. Yohanan: "That which is unclean in the third remove is
unclean by reason of the contact with the dead creeping thing
[as much as that which is in the second remove from the original contact]. Consequently, it is permitted to declare food unclean in the third remove to be heave offering. It is [still]
forbidden to treat it as Holy Things, [for, in the case of other
food in the status of Holy Things, it will impart uncleanness
and so render such food invalid]. [But the uncleanness, so far
as heave offering is concerned, is imparted by food in the second remove to food in the third remove, at which point the
process ends for heave offering. The net effect is to extend the
process for heave offering into the third remove, rather than
into the second remove, as is the case for unconsecrated food.
This is in line with Rab's view of Aqiba's meaning.]"

[I]   R. Zeira raised the following question before R. Yosa, "It imparts uncleanness to food in the status of Holy Things, and do
you say this? [If the heave offering in the third remove can impart uncleanness to food in the status of Holy Things, then
how can you deem it clean when it is in the third remove?
Why stop here?]"

[J]   He said to him, "It is because of the more strict [procedures
attendant upon food in the status of Holy Things]."

[K]   Said R. Samuel bar R. Isaac, "The essence of the uncleanness
imputed to food in the status of Holy Things is [merely] by
reason of the more strict procedures attendant upon food in
that status. [That is, to protect such food in that status, uncleanness is imputed at a further remove from the original
source of uncleanness than the law would ordinarily require]."

[L]   [Along these same lines,] said R. Yosé, "And why does it impart uncleanness in the case of Holy Things? Because of the
more strict procedures attendant upon food in the status of
Holy Things [= I–J]."

[M]   [Reverting to the issue of the relationship of food in the status
of Holy Things to unconsecrated food (that is, in the third remove) clean,] said R. Yudan, "and even in accord with rabbis,
who maintain that there is no consideration of uncleanness at
the third remove in the case of unconsecrated food, why is it
said that such food [that is, in the third remove,] imparts un-

cleanness in the case of food in the status of Holy things [as at
M. Toh. 2:2–4]? It is again because of the more strict procedures [attendant upon food in the status of Holy Things]."

[N]   Said to him R. Yosé, "And do we really need to hear a teaching along this line from a great man such as yourself? [Yosé is
of the view that ordinary food which is prepared by the rules
governing preservation of the cleanness of Holy Things remains
in its status as ordinary food. It does not enter the status of
food in the status of Holy Things. Accordingly, the very consideration introduced at M is relevant to all potential circumstances. That is, there cannot be a case in which unconsecrated
food in the third remove affects food in the status of Holy
Things and so invalidates it. For all such food in any case will
be deemed null, clean to begin with, since unconsecrated food
leaves the ladder of uncleanness in the third and fourth removes from the original source of contamination.]"

[III.A]   [With reference to M. 5:2, Joshua's statement,] there [in Baby-
lonia] they say, "Since R. Joshua praised R. Aqiba, that is to
say that the practiced law accords with [Aqiba's] position."

[B]   Rabbis of Caesarea say, "He praised him for his exegetical
achievement. But for all practical purposes the law does not accord with his position."

[IV.A]   For R. Aha, R. Miasha in the name of R. Eleazar said, "Flogging is not administered to one [who brings] tithe [into contact
with food unclean in the second remove from the original
source of uncleanness] and who so puts it into the third remove
[from that original source]. And even in accord with the view
of R. Aqiba, flogging is not administered. [There is no consideration of a third remove from the original source of uncleanness, either for ordinary food or for tithe. One who is supposed
to eat his food in a state of cleanness—whether tithe or unconsecrated food—hence will not be flogged for eating food in the
third remove from the original source.]"

[B]   Why should this be so?

[C]   A Tebul Yoma [20b] has the power of invalidation [and he is in
the status of that which is in a second remove from the original
source of uncleanness],

[D]   and that which is in the second remove invalidates.

[E]   Just as a Tebul Yom who is in contact with unconsecrated food
has no effect upon it [in that the food need not await sunset to
be deemed clean again (Pené Moshe)],

[F]   so that which is unclean in the second remove which is in contact with unconsecrated food has no effect upon it.

[G]   Said R. Eleazar, "As we count [removes of uncleanness] in the
case of unconsecrated food, so we count removes of uncleanness in the case of tithe [as has just now been illustrated at E–
H]."

[H]   This is in line with that which R. Jonah, R. Imi said in the
name of R. Simeon b. Laqish, "In all other circumstances we
deal with unconsecrated food, but in the present context we
deal with tithe, [and that indicates, as Eleazar has just said,
that the two are subject to a single set of rules]."

[I]   Said R. Yosé, "And even with regard to [second tithe] which is
unclean in the first remove [from the original source of un-
cleanness] is not so clear[ly prohibited]. [If someone eats second tithe in the first remove, it is not so obvious that he should
be flogged. Why not?]

[J]   [" 'I have not eaten of the tithe while I was mourning or removed any of it while I was unclean' (Deut. 26:14).] 'I shall
not eat . . . ,' is not written, but rather, 'I did not eat . . . ,'
[and, as we shall now see, the difference matters]."

[K]   Said R. Abba Meri, "How do we know [that the statement before us is not deemed a negative commandment at all, on account of which one may be flogged]? For it is written, '. . .
according to all that thou hast commanded me' (Deut. 26:14),
as if it were not entirely clear. [That is to say, the confession
states that one will not have kept the commandment in its
proper way if he eats the second tithe in a state of uncleanness.
But there is no negative commandment in that regard. It is
simply part of the general advice on how to do things right,
and for violating such instructions one is not flogged.]"

[V.A]   R. Abbahu in the name of R. Mana, "On what account did
they rule, 'Unconsecrated food which is unclean in the second
remove imparts uncleanness to unconsecrated liquids'? [For we
know full well that unconsecrated food in the second remove
does not impart uncleanness to unconsecrated solid food in the
second remove at all. Yet in the case of liquids, the unconse-

crated solids in the second remove have that very effect; indeed, as a result the liquid is deemed unclean in the first remove. (Cf. M. Toh, 2:2ff.).]

[B] "It is on account of the hands, which are deemed unclean in the second remove by decree of the scribes. They do impart uncleanness to unconsecrated liquid [putting the liquid into the first remove].

[C] "[If that is so,] then that which is unconsecrated in the second remove in accord with the teaching of the Torah [that is, in line with Aqiba's reading of Lev. 11:33, any unconsecrated food in the second remove] all the more so [should have that same power to impart uncleanness to unconsecrated solid food in the second remove]!

[D] "[What follows assumes knowledge of M. Toh. 4:7D–J, as follows: *A doubt concerning liquids, in respect to contracting uncleanness—it is deemed unclean. A doubt concerning liquids, in respect to conveying uncleanness—it is deemed clean. A doubt concerning hands, either in respect to contracting uncleanness or in respect to conveying uncleanness, or in respect to being made clean—[in all these cases, matters of doubt are resolved as] clean.]* [Along these same lines, in accord with the proposition just now stated,] just as in the case of uncleanness imparted by the hands, a matter of doubt as to whether the hands have imparted uncleanness to other things is deemed to be clean,

[E] "so in the case of that which is unclean in the second remove [in general, as distinct from the hands], a doubt involving whether that which is unclean in the second remove has imparted uncleanness to other things is resolved as clean."

[F] R. Hanina objected to R. Mana, "Lo, if one eats unclean food and drinks unclean liquid, a matter of doubt concerning them which affects their having imparted uncleanness to other things is resolved as unclean. [This is a strict rule, in that a doubt concerning their secondary effects is resolved in a strict way. If we do not know, for instance, that the person who ate or drank these unclean things touched an object, we assume that he has.]

[G] "And as to liquids which exude from them, a matter of doubt affecting them, as to whether or not they have imparted uncleanness to other things, likewise is resolved as unclean. [Accordingly, in all these areas of doubt, which affect uncleanness imputed solely by decree of the scribes, we resolve doubt in a strict way.]

[H]   "And yet, that which is unclean in the second remove, which is a status imputed by the Torah [and not merely by scribes, in line with Aqiba's exegesis]—should a matter of doubt affecting it so far as it has imparted uncleanness to other things be deemed clean? [Surely not!]"

[I]   Said R. Mana before R. Haninah (Leiden MS and *editio princeps:* R. Haninah before R. Mana), "And are we not in fact dealing with heave offering [to which a more strict rule applies, and that accounts for the stringency outlined at F–H? But in the case of unconsecrated food, the lenient rule proposed by me, Mana, applies.]"

[J]   Said to him [R. Hanina], "And even if you maintain that we are dealing with heave offering, what difference does it make?

[K]   " 'It will be unclean . . . it will convey uncleanness' represents the teaching of Torah [cf. M. 5:2A] [for liquid]. [The power of liquid to impart uncleanness to food is based on the law of the Torah.] Is that not [Yosé's view, in line with] Aqiba? [But we hold that the reference to uncleanness is to their being unclean, not to their imparting uncleanness. So the Torah law is not involved. Consequently, the original question which I phrased at F–H indeed is valid. (For further discussion, cf. Pené Moshe.)]"

[VI.A]   There they have said [with reference to Haggai 2:11–14: "Thus says the Lord of hosts: Ask the priests to decide this question, 'If one carries holy flesh with the skirt of his garment and touches with his skirt bread, pottage, wine, oil, or any kind of food (in sequence), does it become holy?' The priests answered, 'No.' Then said Haggai, 'If one who is unclean by contact with a dead body touches any of these, does it become unclean?' The priests answered, 'It does become unclean.' Then Haggai said, 'So is it with this people . . . says the Lord . . . and so with every work of their hands; and what they offer there is unclean].' " Two questions did Haggai the prophet ask them:

[B]   In the case of one, they answered him properly, and in the case of the other, they did not answer him properly.

[C]   "The skirt" is in the first remove of uncleanness [having touched some source of uncleanness].

[D]   "The holy flesh" is in the second.

[E]   "The bread and pottage" are in the third remove.

[F]   "The wine, oil, and food" are in the fourth.

[G]   "Now," [he asked them,] "Is there such a thing as a fourth remove [from the original source of uncleanness] in regard to Holy Things?"

[H]   They answered him, "No."

[I]   They did not answer him properly, for there [most certainly] is a fourth remove in regard to Holy Things.

[J]   "Then said Haggai, 'If one who is unclean by contact with a dead body touches any of these, does it become unclean?' "

[K]   [That is to say,] if the skirt of his garment should be unclean with corpse uncleanness and touch any of these, will it impart uncleanness to them?

[L]   "The priests answered, 'It does become unclean.' "

[M]   [In so saying], they answered him [quite] correctly.

[N]   [But characterizing the former answer as wrong is not necessarily so.] For R. Jeremiah, R. Hiyya in the name of R. Yohanan said, "It was in early times, before [scribes] had decreed that we take account of a fourth remove [from the original source of uncleanness] in the matter of Holy Things, that he addressed his question to them. [Accordingly, they answered quite properly.]"

[O]   Then why does Haggai curse them [if they gave the right answer]?

[P]   He was in the position of someone looking for any excuse to curse his fellow.

[Q]   But why then did he include reference to their making the house of the Lord unclean if in fact the law was as they said it was, that he should say to them, "And what they offer there is unclean"?

[R]   It was in line with that which R. Simon bar Zebedi said, "They found the skull of Arnon the Jebusite buried under-

neath the altar [which meant that a principal source of uncleanness contaminated all the offerings made in the Temple]."

[S]   [Explaining the matter differently,] R. Aha in the name of R.
Abba bar Kahana: "They were expert in the laws of transferring uncleanness by shifting an object, but they were not expert in the laws of transferring uncleanness by *maddaf* [which
is the mode of uncleanness transferred by a *zab*, *zabah*, or
menstruating woman (Lev. 15), to objects used for lying or sitting (but not to food or drink) even without direct contact, located above their heads].

[T]   " 'If one carries holy flesh in the skirt of his garment . . .' He
asked them, 'Does one unclean with corpse uncleanness impart
uncleanness to an object merely by shifting it [without direct
contact with it]?'

[U]   " 'The priests said to him, 'No.'

[V]   "They answered him quite correctly, for one unclean with
corpse uncleanness does not impart uncleanness to an object
merely by shifting it [without actual contact with it].

[W]   "He asked them, 'Does one who is unclean with corpse uncleanness convey uncleanness by *maddaf* [as explained at S]?'

[X]   "The priests answered him, 'He does transmit uncleanness in
that way.'

[Y]   "In this regard they did not reply to him correctly. For one
unclean with corpse uncleanness does not impart uncleanness
through the mode of *maddaf* [as explained at S]."

[Z]   R. Tanhuma, R. Pinhas in the name of R. Levi: "It was concerning whether or not we take account of a fifth remove from
the original source of uncleanness in matters of Holy Things
that he asked them. [And the indication is as follows:]

[AA]   " 'If one carries holy flesh in the skirt of his garment . . .':

[BB]   " 'the skirt of his garment' is in the first remove.

[CC]   " 'holy flesh' is in the second remove.

[DD]   " 'bread and pottage' are in the third remove.

[EE]   " 'wine and oil' are in the fourth remove.

[FF]   " 'and food' is in the fifth.

[GG] " 'Now he asked them do we take account of a fifth remove in respect to Holy Things?'

[HH] " 'And the priests answered, 'No.'

[II] "They answered him quite correctly, for there is no consideration of a fifth remove in Holy Things."

[JJ] Then why does Haggai curse them [if they gave the right answer]?

[KK] He was in the position of someone looking for any excuse to curse his fellow.

[LL] But why then did he include reference to their making the house of the Lord unclean, if in fact the law was as they said it was, that he should say to them, "And what they offer there is unclean"?

[MM] It was in line with that which R. Simeon bar Zebedi said, "They found the skull of Arnon the Jebusite buried underneath the altar."

[VII.A] It was taught: **Said R. Yosé, "How do we know that that which is unclean by a source of uncleanness in the fourth remove [from the original source of uncleanness] in the case of Holy Things is invalid [= M. Hag. 3:2E–F]?**

[B] **"And it is reasonable.**

[C] **"Now if one who has not completed his atonement rites [by bringing the required offering, e.g., a *zab* (Lev. 15) or a woman after childbirth, Lev. 12] is not invalid in the case of heave offering but is invalid in the case of Holy Things,**

[D] **"that which is made unclean by a source of uncleanness in the fourth remove, which is invalid in the case of heave offering—is it not reasonable that it should invalidate [that which touches it, in the case of Holy Things]?**

[E] **"We have learned in Scripture [M. Sot. 5:2] that that which is made unclean by a source of uncleanness in the third remove from the original source of uncleanness invalidates, and in connection with that which is unclean in the fourth remove [we thus derive the same lesson] by an argument a fortiori [T. Hag. 3:18].**

[F]   Objected R. Yohanan: "Food which has been touched by a Tebul Yom [unclean in the second remove, we recall] will prove
the contrary.

[G]   "For it is invalid so far as being designated heave offering is
concerned [in line with Lev. 11:33],

[H]   "but it has no invalidating affect upon Holy Things [in the
fourth remove]. [That is: Just as the Tebul Yom invalidates in
the case of heave offering, so he invalidates in the case of Holy
Things. But he does not render the Holy Things unclean in
such wise that the Holy Things will then go and impart uncleanness. In this case, then, the argument a fortiori of Yosé
will not serve, as it does above, and so it is shown to be
invalid.]"

[I]   [Providing a second attack on Yosé's reasoning,] R. Hiyya in
the name of R. Yohanan, "The view of R. Yosé is in line with
the theory of R. Aqiba, his teacher.

[J]   "Just as R. Aqiba said, 'will be unclean' (Lev. 11:33, referring
to food) means 'will impart uncleanness' [in the third remove,
as at M. 5:2A], as a matter of the law of the Torah,

[K]   "so R. Yosé said, 'will be unclean' (Lev. 11:34, with reference
to liquid) means 'will impart uncleanness' as a matter of the
law of the Torah. [In this case, why not construct the same argument a fortiori to prove that we take account of a fourth remove in regard to food in the status of heave offering and deem
such food to be invalid? Now if a Tebul Yom, who is permitted to touch unconsecrated food, is invalid so far as heave offering is concerned, food in the third remove, which is invalid
so far as unconsecrated food is concerned (in line with the position of Aqiba at M. 5:2A, unconsecrated food in the third remove is invalid and may not be designated heave offering), all
the more so should be deemed to invalidate food in the fourth
remove for heave offering. This then is a further argument
against the reasoning of Yosé at A–E.]"

[L]   R. Abbahu in the name of R. Yosé bar Haninah: "R. Yosé has
no need for the argument a fortiori [to prove that that which is
in the fourth remove from the original source of uncleanness in
the case of Holy Things is invalid].

[M]   "R. Yosé [is perfectly able to prove the same thing] on the basis of the exegesis of [the following verse of] Scripture:

[N]   "['Flesh that touches any unclean thing shall not be eaten' (lev. 7:19).] 'Flesh that touches'—This refers to meat in the second remove of uncleanness which touched that which is unclean in the first remove of uncleanness.

[O]   " 'Any unclean thing'—This refers to meat in the third remove of uncleanness which touched that which was unclean in the second remove of uncleanness [as is clear in the sequence of the verse].

[P]   " 'Shall not be eaten'—That which is made unclean at the end is not to be eaten. [That is to say, what touches this meat in the third remove is itself in the fourth remove and is not to be eaten. That proves the proposition.]"

[VIII.A]   Up to this point we have dealt with food made unclean in the airspace of a clay utensil contaminated by a dead creeping thing [Lev. 11:33]. [That is, Aqiba's proof, based on Lev. 11:33, shows that food made unclean in the contained airspace of a clay utensil into which a dead creeping thing has fallen has the capacity to impart uncleanness to food which touches it.]

[B]   How do we know that food itself which has been made unclean by a dead creeping thing [has the power to impart uncleanness to other food]?

[C]   Now it is a matter of logic.

[D]   If utensils do not receive uncleanness when they are located in the contained airspace of a clay utensil which has been rendered unclean by a dead creeping thing—lo, such utensils impart uncleanness as does a dead creeping thing [so that food which touches them will be unclean]—

[E]   food itself, which is rendered unclean by a dead creeping thing, is it not a matter of logic that it should have the capacity to impart uncleanness as does a dead creeping thing to [other] food [with which it comes into contact]? [Surely that is obvious.]

[F]   Up to this point we have dealt with the matter in line with the theory of R. Aqiba [who regards the uncleanness imparted in the third remove as a matter of the law of the Torah].

[G]   But as to R. Ishmael [how does he prove that there is a third remove in regard to food which has been in contact with that which has been made unclean?]

[H]   It is taught by R. Ishmael: " 'Flesh that touches any unclean thing shall not be eaten.'

[I]   "[This refers to] food in the first remove, 'which touched any unclean thing.'

[J]   " 'It shall not be eaten' is meant to encompass that which is in the second remove.

[K]   "And as to the third remove, how do we prove that that is taken into account?

[L]   "It is a matter of logical inference.

[M]   "Now if a Tebul Yom does not invalidate in the case of unconsecrated food, lo, he has the power to invalidate in the case of heave offering [which he touches, so that said heave offering is deemed unclean and may not be eaten,]

[N]   "food unclean in the second remove, which indeed is invalid in the case of unconsecrated food [as at M. Toh. 2:3ff.]—is it not logical that it should have the power to invalidate in the case of heave offering?

[O]   "And as to a fourth remove in the case of Holy Things, how do we prove that proposition?

[P]   "Now it is a matter of logic.

[Q]   "If one who has not yet brought his offerings to complete the process of atonement is not invalid for eating heave offering, lo, he is invalid so far as Holy Things are concerned [Lev. 12, 15 indicate that until the offerings are brought to complete the process of atonement, the woman after childbirth and the *zab* and *zabah* are not permitted to eat Holy Things],

[R]   "that which is in the third remove from the original source of uncleanness, which indeed is invalid so far as heave offering is concerned—is it not logical that it should have the power to invalidate in the case of Holy Things [with which it comes into contact, hence, the fourth remove]?

[S]   "Lo we have learned from Scripture the law governing the uncleanness of invalidity of that which is in the first remove and the second remove from the original source of uncleanness, and from a logical process we have derived the same rule for that which is in the third remove, and as to that which is in the fourth remove, we have derived the same proposition from an argument a fortiori.

[T]   "[After we have] reasoned one law from the other [deriving the rule governing the third remove in the case of heave offering from the second remove in the case of the Tebul Yom, we derive yet another rule by means of an argument for that which is in the fourth remove, that it is invalid in the case of food in the status of Holy Things], so that all should be governed by the law,

[U]   "thus with the result that heave offering in the third remove, and Holy Things in the fourth remove, should be deemed invalid."

The Talmud's extensive and original inquiry into Aqiba's position at M. 5:2A–B plumbs the depths of the law. Unit **I** takes up the interpretation of precisely what Aqiba maintains. At issue, as we see, is whether we speak only of food in the status of heave offering, that is, consecrated food, or also of ordinary, unconsecrated food. Rab's position, that Aqiba refers to both, is the more complicated of the two. We turn to the comparison of Rab's opinions here and elsewhere. Unit **II** briefly takes up Samuel's view of Aqiba's meaning, then turns to Rab's once more. After the brief observation of unit **III**, discourse in unit **IV** broadens, while still focusing on the matter of the interpretation of Aqiba's position. Unit **V** concludes with a fresh discussion of essentially the same theme. At unit **VI**, we make use of the ideas rather than their sources or the authority behind them. Now at issue is how we deal with food in the several removes of uncleanness. Unit **VII** introduces a relevant pericope of the Tosefta, which alludes to the present passage of the Mishnah and presents an extensive analysis of the cited materials. The close relevance to the Mishnah is pointed out in context. Unit **VIII**, finally, presents Ishmael's proof for the same proposition as is held by Aqiba. So, throughout, the discussion is sustained, remains centered on a single unfolding theme, and asks the most fundamental questions of law and exegesis. It would be difficult to point to a finer intellectual achievement in this excellent tractate.

5:3 [Leiden MS and *editio princeps:* 5:5]

[A]   *On that day did R. Aqiba expound as follows: " 'And you shall measure without the city for the east side two thousand cubits . . .' (Num. 35:5). And another Scripture says, 'From the wall of the city and outward a thousand cubits round about' (Num. 35:4).*

[B]   *"It is not possible to state that the required measure is a thousand amahs, for two thousand amahs also have been specified.*

[C]   *"But it is not possible to state that the required measure is two thousand amahs, for one thousand amahs also have been specified.*

[D]   *"So how shall we rule?*

[E]   *"A thousand amahs form the outskirts, while two thousand amahs form the Sabbath limit."*

[F]   *R. Eliezer the son of R. Yosé the Galilean says, "A thousand amahs form the outskirts, and two thousand amahs [cover] the surrounding fields and vineyards."*

[I.A]   **R. Eleazar b. R. Yosé the Galilean says, "Two thousand amahs form the limit of the cities of the Levites. Subtract from them a thousand amahs for the outskirts, and you turn out to have a quarter for outskirts and the rest for fields and vineyards" [M. 5:3F] [T. Sot. 5:13].**

[B]   [As to the "quarter for outskirts" of Eleazar's saying,] R. Jeremiah, R. Samuel bar R. Isaac in the name of Rab: "A quarter of a thousand. [That is, we take a quarter out of the space on each side of the city. The city has a thousand *amahs* of outskirts. Hence each side contributes two hundred fifty to the thousand cubits of outskirts]."

[C]   Said R. Isaac, "[Following the reading of Qorban ha'edah:] Even if you say that we take a quarter from each side [as has just been said], it still adds up to a quarter. He who quadrates four storage houses requires sixteen."

[D]   R. Mana gives the measure in rectangles [bricks].

[E]   R. Abin does so in a belt [four cubits square].

[F]   R. Oshaiah does the same by marking out [the dimensions].

[**II**.A]   R. Yosé b. R. Bun said, "Fifty by fifty cubits is a *seah* area [the area in which one may scatter a *seah* of seed]. One hundred by one hundred cubits form an area of four *seahs*."

[B]   This is illustrated in the following case: The exilarch was assigned a tax of filling with wheat a room forty by forty cubits.

[C]   He came to R. Huna, who instructed him, "Go and make a deal with them. Let them assign you a room of twenty by twenty to be filled now, and one of twenty by twenty to be filled after a while, and you will save half [of the assigned tax, which you will not have to give at all, in line with the calculation of A]."

[**III**.A]   R. Ba in the name of R. Judah, R. Zeira in the name of R. Uqba: *They measure only with a rope fifty cubits long. [If one was measuring and reached a valley or a fence, he takes account only of the horizontal span and continues his measuring. If he came to a mountain he takes account only of the horizontal span and continues his measuring. And this is on condition that he does not go outside the Sabbath limit. If he cannot take account of the horizontal span, "In this case," said R. Dosetai b. R. Yannai in the name of R. Meir, "I heard that they treat hills as though they were pierced" (M. Erub. 5:4)].* [That is, if the other side of the valley lies outside of the Sabbath limit, we do not follow the stated procedure. If one cannot span the area, since it is longer than fifty cubits, then, Meir says, we calculate in such a way as to measure the horizontal distance as if it were a straight line.]

[B]   [In this connection,] said R. Zeira in the name of R. Hisdai, "They do not measure [with a rope] in the towns of the Levites [in the two thousand cubits of outskirts] or [20c] in the place in a ravine where a heifer is to be killed [that is, when determining which city must bring the heifer to be killed when a neglected corpse turns up, one does not make the measurement with a rope]."

[C]   Now this statement poses no problems to the one [Aqiba] who says that a thousand cubits form the outskirts, and two thousand cubits, the Sabbath limit. [That is, Aqiba can accept this statement of Hisdai's, they measure with the rope for that purpose, and in the case of the towns of the Levites, they do not take such a measurement.]

[D]   But in accord with the one [Eliezer] who said a thousand cubits
       form the outskirts, and two thousand cubits the area for fields
       and vineyards, [how will they derive the measurement for the
       Sabbath limit if they do not measure with a rope in the towns
       of the Levites?] For [in his view] have they not learned the
       Sabbath limits from [analogy to] the towns of the Levites?
       Shall we then say that for the principal purpose they do not
       take a measure [namely, for establishing the boundaries of the
       Levitical cities they do not measure with a rope,] while for the
       auxiliary purpose they do take measure [namely, for establish-
       ing the Sabbath limits]?

[IV.A] How do we know that they do not bury the dead in the Le-
        vites' cities?

[B]   R. Abbahu in the name of R. Yosé bar Haninah: " 'Their pas-
       ture lands shall be for their cattle and for their livestock and
       for all their beasts' (Num. 35:3)—they have been assigned for
       their cattle and beasts, and they have not been assigned for use
       as a burial ground."

       Unit I takes up the Tosefta's amplification of M. 5:3F, with
       special reference to the meaning of "a quarter" for outskirts.
       We should have half, not a quarter, and that is what occupies
       the Amoraic interpreters of the pericope of the Tosefta. B is
       the simplest explanation, "the quarter" means a quarter of a
       thousand, two hundred fifty on all sides, thus a thousand or
       half of the whole. For a full account of these materials, cf.
       Pené Moshe. Unit II simply illustrates the notion of how one
       deals with multiples of a cube. The relevance of unit III is at
       III.D, which criticizes the view of Eliezer in line with the cited
       pericope of M. Erub. 5:4. Unit IV is tacked on.

       5:4 [Leiden MS and *editio princeps:* 5:6]

[A]   *On that day did R. Aqiba expound as follows: "Then sang
       Moses and the children of Israel this song unto the Lord and
       spoke saying" (Ex. 15:1).*

[B]   *"Now Scripture hardly needs to add 'saying,'*

[C]   *"And why does Scripture state 'saying'?*

[D]   *"It thereby teaches that the Israelites responded word by word after Moses,*

[E]   *"as they do when they read the Hallel psalms.*

[F]   *"Therefore 'saying' is stated in this context."*

[G]   R. Nehemiah says, *"[They did so] as they do when they read the Shema, not as when they read the Hallel."*

[I.A]   [The following is in the Tosefta's version, which is fuller than that in the printed version of Yerushalmi]: **[How did they say that song?] Like a child who recites the Hallel in school.**

[B]   **And they answered him at each and every phrase [thus]:**

[C]   **Moses said, "I shall sing unto the Lord" (Ex. 15:1), and the Israelites answered after him, "I will sing unto the Lord" [T. Sot. 6:2C–E].**

[D]   **Moses said, "My strength and my song is the Lord" (Ex. 15:2), and the Israelites said, "My strength and my song is the Lord" [cf. M. 5:4A–F].**

[E]   **R. Eleazar b. R. Yosé the Galilean says, "They proclaimed the song like an adult who proclaims the Hallel in synagogue worship, responding to him with the foregoing phrase, as follows:**

[F]   **"Moses said, 'I will sing to the Lord' (Ex. 15:1), and the Israelites said, 'I will sing to the Lord.'**

[G]   **"Moses said, 'My strength and song is the Lord,' and the Israelites said, 'I will sing unto the Lord.'**

[H]   **"Moses said, 'The Lord is a man of war' (Ex. 15:3), and the Israelites said, "I will sing unto the Lord.' "**

[I]   [Yerushalmi lacks I–M:] **R. Nehemiah says, "[They proclaimed the song] like men who recite the Shema in the synagogue worship, as it is said, 'And they said, saying' (Ex. 15:1).**

[J]   **"This teaches that Moses would open first with a given matter, and the Israelites would respond to him and complete saying [the whole verse].**

[K]   **"Moses said, 'Then Moses sang,' and the Israelites said, 'I shall sing unto the Lord.'**

[L]   "Moses said, 'My strength and song is the Lord,' and the Israelites said, 'This is my God and I will glorify him.'

[M]   "Moses said, 'The Lord is a man of war,' and the Israelites said, 'The Lord is his name' " [M. 5:4G] [T. Sot. 6:3].

[N]   **R. Yosé the Galilean says, "When the Israelites came up out of the sea and saw their enemies strewn as corpses on the seashore, they all burst out into song—even a child lying on his mother's lap and an infant sucking at its mother's breast.**

[O]   **"When they saw the Presence of God, the babe raised his head and the infant took his mouth off his mother's teat and all responded in song, saying, 'This is my god and I will glorify him' " (Ex. 15:2).**

[P]   **R. Meir says, "Even foetuses in their mothers' wombs broke out into song, as it is said, 'Bless God in the great congregation, the Lord, O you who are of Israel's fountain' (Ps. 68:26).**

[Q]   **"And even an infant took his mother's teat out of his mouth and broke into song, as it is said, 'By the mouth of babes and infants thou has founded a bulwark, because of thy foes' " (Ps. 8:2) [T. Sot. 6:4].**

[R]   R. Nehemiah said, "When our forefathers came up out of the sea, they saw the corpses of sinful men, who had cruelly overseen their labor, and now all of them were corpses, scattered about on the seashore.

[S]   "They sought to break out into song, and the Holy Spirit rested upon them, so that even the least among all the Israelites could proclaim the song just like Moses.

[T]   "This is in line with that which is written, 'Then he remembered the days of old, of Moses his servant. Where is he who brought up out of the sea the shepherds of his flock? Where is he who put in the midst of them his Holy Spirit . . .?' (Is. 63:11).

[U]   " 'The shepherd of the flock' is not stated, but rather, 'The shepherd of *his* flock.'

[V]   "This teaches that he made them all into shepherds [just like Moses]."

[W]   Why [at the song of the sea] does Scripture say "saying"?

[Y]   It means "speaking to generations to come."

[Z]   [When they recited the song of the sea,] R. Abbahu in the name of R. Yosé b. R. Haninah [said,] "It is like a Scripture teacher [who teaches children in school]. [He quotes the beginning of a verse, and the children complete it.]

[AA] "Moses said, 'I shall sing.'

[BB] "And they said after him, 'I shall sing to the Lord, for he has triumphed gloriously; the horse and his rider he has thrown into the sea.'

[CC] "Moses said, 'The Lord is my strength and my song.'

[DD] "And they said after him, 'The Lord is my strength and my song, and he has become my salvation.' "

[II.A] It is written, "[Then sang Deborah and Barak the son of Abinoam on that day]: 'That the leaders took the lead in Israel, that the people offered themselves willingly' " (Judg. 5:1–2)—the heads of the people offered themselves willingly.

[B]   When the Holy One, blessed be he, does wonders for them, let them say the song [Ex. 15].

[C]   They objected: "Lo, there is the redemption from Egypt [when they said the song only after the redemption, not when it took place]."

[D]   It is different, for it is the beginning of their redemption.

[E]   They objected: "Lo, there is the redemption in the time of Mordecai and Esther."

[F]   It is different, for the Israelites were outside of the Holy Land.

[G]   There are those who wish to say, "Mordecai and Esther were saved from their enemies. They were not saved from the monarch [himself], [so there was no true redemption and freedom]."

The Talmud complements the Mishnah, first with relevant materials of the Tosefta, then with other pertinent sayings and tales.

5:5 [Leiden MS and *editio princeps:* 5:7]

[A]   *On that day did R. Joshua b. Hurqanos expound as follows:*
        "Job served the Holy One, blessed be he, only out of love,

[B]   *"since it is said, 'Though he slay me, yet will I wait for him'*
        (Job 13:15).

[C]   *"But still the matter is in doubt [as to whether it means] 'I will*
        wait for him' or 'I will not wait for him.'

[D]   *"Scripture states, "Until I die I will not put away mine integ-*
        rity from me' (Job 27:5).

[E]   *"This teaches that he did what he did out of love."*

[I.A]   It was taught in the name of R. Judah: " 'As God lives, who
        has taken away my right, and the Almighty, who has made my
        soul bitter' (Job 27:2).

[B]   "For a man takes a vow by the life of a king only if he loves
        him."

[C]   In the name of R. Nathan they said, " 'This will be my salva-
        tion, that a godless man shall not come before him' (Job
        13:16).

[D]   "One verse of Scripture says, 'And you shall love the Lord
        your God [with all your heart, and with all your soul, and with
        all your might]' (Deut. 6:5).

[E]   "And another verse of Scripture says, 'You shall fear the Lord
        your God; you shall serve him, [and swear by his name]'
        (Deut. 6:13).

[F]   "Do [his will] out of love, do his will out of fear.

[G]   " 'Do [his will] out of love,' so that if you should come to hate,
        you will know that you love him, and one who loves cannot
        hate.

[H]   " 'Do his will out of fear,' so that if you come to rebel against
        him, [you will know that] one who fears does not rebel."

[II.A] There are seven types of Pharisees: the shoulder-Pharisee; the
        wait-a-while Pharisee; the bookkeeping Pharisee; the niggardly
        Pharisee; the show-me-what-I-did-wrong Pharisee; the Phari-
        see-out-of-fear; and the Pharisee-out-of-love.

[B]   "The shoulder-Pharisee" carries the religious deeds he has done on his shoulder [for all to see].

[C]   "The wait-a-while Pharisee"—"Wait a minute, so I can go off and do a religious deed."

[D]   "The bookkeeping Pharisee"—He does one deed for which he is liable and one deed which is a religious duty, and then he balances one off against the other.

[E]   "The niggardly Pharisee"—"Who will show me how I can save so that I can do a religious deed."

[F]   "The show-me-what-I-did-wrong Pharisee"—"Show me what sin I have done, and I will do an equivalent religious duty."

[G]   "A Pharisee-out-of-fear," like Job.

[H]   "A Pharisee-out-of-love," like Abraham.

[I]   And the only one of them all who is truly beloved is the Pharisee-out-of-love, like Abraham.

[**III**.A]   Abraham made the impulse to do evil into good.

[B]   What is the Scriptural basis for that statement?

[C]   "And thou didst find his heart faithful before thee, [and didst make with him the covenant to give to his descendants the land of the Canaanite, the Hittite, the Amorite, the Perizzite, the Jebusite, and the Girgashite]" (Neh. 9:8).

[D]   Said R. Aha, "He made an agreement with it: '[And thou didst find his heart faithful before thee,] and didst make with him the covenant [to give to his descendants the land of the Canaanite, the Hittite, the Amorite, the Perizzite, the Jebusite, and the Girgashite]' (Neh. 9:8)."

[E]   But David was unable to overcome it, so he had to kill it in his heart.

[F]   What is the Scriptural basis for that statement?

[G]   "[For I am poor and needy,] and my heart is stricken within me" (Ps. 109:22).

[**IV**.A]   R. Aqiba was on trial before Tonosteropos the Wicked. The time for reciting the *Shema* came. He began to recite it and smiled.

[B] [The wicked one] said to him, "Old man, old man! You are either a wizard or you have contempt for pain [that you smile]."

[C] He said to him, "May the soul of that man perish. I am no wizard, nor do I have contempt for pain.

[D] "But for my whole life I have been reciting this verse: 'And you shall love the Lord your God with all your heart, with all your soul, and with all your might' (Deut. 5:6).

[E] "I loved God with all my heart, and I loved him with all my might.

[F] "But 'with all my soul' until now was not demanded of me.

[G] "And now that the time has come for me to love him with all my soul, as the time for reciting the *Shema* has arrived, I smile that the occasion has come to carry out the verse at that very moment at which I recite the Scripture."

[H] Nehemiah Imsoni, who served R. Aqiba for twenty-two years, would say, "[When we see in Scripture the words] *et* [the object marker] and *gam* ['also'], [they serve as exegetical tools for] encompassing an unstated subject.

[I] "[When we see the words] *akh* and *rak* ['only'], [they serve to] limit [and exclude].

[J] He said to him, "What is the meaning of that which is written, 'You shall fear [+ *et*] the Lord your God' " (Deut. 6:13).

[K] He said to him, "Him and his Torah [shall you fear]."

Unit **I** takes up the themes of the Mishnah. Unit **II** intersects at **II**.G, and, as we see in a moment, also serves M. 5:6. Units **III** and **IV** relate to the Mishnah as does unit **I**.

5:6 [Leiden MS and *editio princeps*: 5:8]

[A] *Said R. Joshua, "Who will remove the dirt from your eyes, Rabban Yohanan b. Zakkai. For you used to expound for your entire life that Job served the Omnipresent only out of awe,*

[B] *"since it is said, 'The man was perfect and upright and one who feared God and avoided evil' (Job 1:8).*

[C]   *"And now has not Joshua, the disciple of your disciple, taught that he did what he did out of love?"*

[I.A]   When did Job live?

[B]   R. Simeon b. Laqish in the name of Bar Qappara: "In the days of Abraham, our father, did he live.

[C]   "This is in line with that which is written, 'There was a man in the land of Uz, whose name was Job, [and that man was blameless and upright, one who feared God, and turned away from evil]' (Job 1:1).

[D]   "And it is written, '[Now after these things it was told to Abraham, Behold, Milcah also has borne children to your brother Nahor:] Uz the firstborn, [Buz his brother, Kemuel the father of Amram, Chesed, Hazo, Pildash, Jidlaph, and Bethuel]' " (Gen. 22:20–21).

[E]   R. Abba said, "It was in the days of our father, Jacob, and his wife was Dinah.

[F]   "This is in line with that which is written, '[But he said to her,] You speak as one of the foolish women would speak' (Job 2:10).

[G]   "And it is written, '[The sons of Jacob came in from the field when they heard of it; and the men were indignant and very angry,] because he had wrought folly in Israel [by laying with Jacob's daughter, for such a thing ought not to be done]' " (Gen. 34:7).

[H]   R. Levi said, "It was in the time of the tribes that he lived.

[I]   "That is in line with that which is written, '[I will show you, hear me; and what I have seen I will declare,] what wise men have told, and their fathers have not hidden' " (Job 15:17–18).

[J]   R. Yosé b. Halafta said, "He was among those who went down to Egypt, and when they came up, he died."

[K]   "It may be compared to a shepherd, to whose flock a wolf came and joined up. What did he do? He set the bellwether against him.

[L]   "That is in line with the following verse of Scripture, 'God gives me up to the ungodly, and casts me into the hands of the wicked' " (Job 16:11).

[M]   R. Ishmael taught, "Job was one of the servants of Pharaoh. He was one of the great members of his retinue.

[N]   "That is in line with the following verse of Scripture: 'Then he who feared the word of the Lord among the servants of Pharaoh made his slaves and his cattle flee into the houses' (Exod. 9:20).

[O]   "And concerning him it is written, 'And the Lord said to Satan, Have you considered my servant Job, [that there is none like him on the earth,] a blameless and upright man, who fears God and turns away from evil?' " (Job 1:8).

[P]   R. Yosé bar Judah says, "He was in the time in which the judges ruled Israel.

[Q]   "That is indicated in the following verse of Scripture: 'Behold, all of you have seen it yourselves; why then have you become so vain?' (Job 27:12).

[R]   "You have seen the deeds of my generation.

[S]   "For they collected tithes at the threshing floors: '[Rejoice not, O Israel? Exult not like the peoples; for you have played the harlot, forsaking your God.] You have loved a harlot's hire upon all [20d] the threshing floors' " (Hos. 9:1).

[T]   R. Samuel bar Nahman in the name of R. Jonathan: "He lived in the time of the kingdom of the Sabeans, for it is said, 'And the Sabeans fell upon them and took them, [and slew the servants with the edge of the sword; and I alone escaped to tell you]' " (Job 1:15).

[U]   R. Nathan said, "He lived in the time of the Chaldeans, for it is said, '[While he was yet speaking, there came another, and said,] The Chaldeans formed three companies, [and made a raid upon the camels and took them, and slew the servants with the edge of the sword; and I alone have escaped to tell you]' " (Job 1:17).

[V]   R. Joshua b. Qorha said, "He lived in the days of Ahasueros, for it is said, '[Then the king's servants said,] Let beautiful young virgins be sought out for the king' (Esther 2:2).

[W]   "And it is written, 'And in all the land there were no women so fair as Job's daughters; [and their father gave them inheritance among their brothers]' " (Job 42:15).

[X]   R. Joshua b. Levi said, "He was among those who came up from the Exile."

[Y]   R. Yohanan said, "He was among those who came up from the Exile, but he was an Israelite."

[Z]   On that account, R. Yohanan derived from his behavior rules governing conduct in the time of mourning.

[AA]   "Then Job arose, and rent his robe, [and shaved his head, and fell upon the ground, and worshipped]" (Job 1:20).

[BB]   R. Judah b. Pazzi in the name of R. Yohanan, "On the basis of the cited verse we learn that a mourner has to tear his garment while standing up."

[CC]   R. Hiyya taught, "In my realm [?] there was a righteous gentile [such as Job, who was not an Israelite], and I paid him his wage, and I dismissed him from my realm."

[DD]   R. Simeon b. Laqish said, "Job never existed and never will exist."

[EE]   The opinions attributed to R. Simeon b. Laqish are at variance with one another.

[FF]   There R. Simeon b. Laqish said in the name of Bar Qappara, "He lived in the time of Abraham, our father," and here has he said this?

[GG]   But he really did exist, while the sufferings ascribed to him never really took place.

[HH]   And why were these sufferings ascribed to him? It is to indicate that if such sufferings had come to him, he would have been able to endure them.

[II.A] R. Aqiba interpreted the following verse: "Then Elihu the son of Barachel the Buzite, of the family of Ram, became angry" (Job 32:2).

[B]   [Aqiba said,] "Elihu is Balaam the son of Barachel, who came to curse Israel but blessed them."

[C]   "Nevertheless the Lord your God would not hearken to Balaam [the Buzite]" (Deut. 23:5).

[D]   [He was called] "the Buzite," for his prophecy was despised (BZZ).

[E]   "[The oracle of him who hears the words of God, who sees the vision of the Almighty] falling down, but having his eyes uncovered" (Num. 24:4).

[F]   "[And Balaam took up his discourse, and said,] 'From Aram Balak has brought me, [the king of Moab from the eastern mountains]' " (Num. 23:7).

[G]   Said R. Eleazar b. Azariah, "If [Job] really was the same as Balaam, then the Omnipresent hid that fact, and if he really was not Balaam, then in time to come he is going to have quite a dispute with you.

[H]   "But Elihu is the same as Isaac b. Barachel—a son whom God blessed,

[I]   "as it is said, '[And Isaac sowed in the land, and reaped in the same year a hundredfold.] The Lord blessed him, [and the man became very rich]' (Gen. 26:12–13).

[J]   " 'The Buzite'—for he despised all houses of idolatry,

[K]   "when he was bound on the altar.

[L]   " 'Of the family of Ram'—he was a son of Abram."

[**III**.A]   Moses wrote five books of the Torah, and then he went back and wrote the pericope of Balak and Balaam, and, [at the end], he wrote the book of Job.

[B]   "[There was a man in the land of Uz, whose name was Job;] and that man was blameless and upright, one who feared God, and turned away from evil" (Job 1:1).

[C]   Said R. Tahalipa of Caesarea, "For he was a forgiving person."

[D]   Said to him R. Zeira, "One who is not a forgiving person cannot be a truly suitable person.

[E]   "But he forgave him who cursed him."

The Talmud presents an anthology of materials on Job and ignores the specific allegation of the Mishnah.

6 Yerushalmi Sotah
Chapter Six

6:1

[A]   *He who expresses jealousy to his wife,*

[B]   *but she [then] goes aside in secret,*

[C]   *"even if he hears [that she has done so] from a bird flying by—*

[D]   *"he puts her away, but pays off her marriage contract," the words of R. Eliezer.*

[E]   *R. Joshua says, "[He does so] only if the women who spin their yarn by moonlight trade stories about her."*

[I.A]   R. Yohanan in the name of R. Yannai: "All [of the laws in] this chapter [at M. 6:2A–B, apply to a case in which] the husband has given a warning [that is, expressed jealousy], saying to her, 'Do not go in private with Mr. So-and-so.' Then after he expressed jealousy to her, she went in private with him."

[B]   R. Simeon b. Laqish said, "[The rules apply] even if she did not go in private with him."

[C]   Said R. Zeira in the presence of R. Yosa, "It is not that R. Simeon b. Laqish differs [from R. Yohanan].

[D]   "But he is of the opinion of that Tanna who imposes a lenient ruling with regard to witnesses to the woman's actually going in private with the named man. [He concurs with Eliezer, M. 1:1, who maintains that the husband may impose the ordeal of drinking the water on the testimony of only a single witness that the woman has gone in private with the named man. Along these same lines, even if he heard from a bird flying overhead that she has gone in private with the named man, he must divorce her, but he pays off her marriage contract. But if there is no evidence at all that she has gone aside, he may not divorce her.]"

[E]   We have learned in the Mishnah pericope that there is a dispute [of Eliezer and Joshua].

[F]   There are Tannaim who repeat the law of the Mishnah pericope without dispute at all [omitting at D "the words of R. Eliezer"].

[G]   Said R. Zeira in the presence of R. Mana, "It is not in regard to what R. Eliezer said that R. Joshua takes issue. [Each one said what he said, not in the context of a dispute at all.]

[H]   "But it is on account of that which we have learned, *R. Joshua says, "He does so only if the women who spin their yarn by moonlight trade stories about her [M. 6:1E].* [The use of the language 'only if' implies that there is a dispute, and from Joshua's viewpoint it is insufficient to hear the news from a bird flying by.]"

[I]   R. Abba Mari raised the question there: Said R. Hezekiah, R. Abbahu in the name of R. Eleazar, "In every setting in which Rabbi taught [the law in the form of a] dispute and then went and repeated it without assigning it to a named authority, the law is in accord with the version not in the name of a specific authority. And yet do you say this [that here, Rabbi gave the law in accord with Eliezer's view, F–H, without noting his name, which means the law follows Eliezer]? [It surely should follow Joshua!]"

[II.A]   We learn that the word [used at M. 6:1E, women who spin their yarn,] is MWṢRWT.

[B]   There are Tannaim who repeat the word as MWZRWT.

[C]   The authority who repeats the word as MWṢRWT speaks of those who spin wool.

[D]   The own who repeats the word as MWZRWT speaks of those who work in flax.

[III.A]   How shall we interpret the passage [M. 6:1E]?

[B]   If we speak of those who have heard but do not know from whom they have heard it, then their testimony is in the status of that of a bird flying by.

[C]   If we speak of those who have heard and do know from whom they have heard it, then it is hearsay evidence [which is totally valid here].

[D]   But thus must we interpret the matter: "It was Mr. So-and-so who heard from Mr. So-and-so, and Mr. Such-and-such who heard from Mr. Such-and-such," that is to say, a rumor without foundation. [Even such testimony is taken into account to require the husband to divorce his wife.]

The interest of unit **I** is in determining whether or not there is a dispute in the Mishnah. If we deem the saying of Eliezer to be unattributed, **I.F–G**, then it must follow that the law accords with him. This elicits a statement of surprise. Unit **II** clarifies the Mishnah's exact choice of words. Unit **III** interprets the sort of testimony to which the Mishnah makes reference. In all the Talmud focuses upon the close exegesis of the Mishnah.

6:2

[A]   *[If] one witness said, "I saw that she was made unclean,"*

[B]   *she would not undergo the ordeal of drinking the bitter water.*

[C]   *And not only so, but even if it was a slave boy or a slave girl, lo, even these are believed to invalidate her [from receiving payment of] her marriage contract.*

[D]   *As to her mother-in-law and the daughter of her mother-in-law, her co-wife, and the husband's brother's wife, and the daughter of her husband,*

[E]   *lo, these are believed [cf. M. Yeb. 15:4]—*

[F]   *not to invalidate her from receiving payment of her marriage contract, but that she should not undergo the ordeal of drinking the bitter water.*

[I.A]   "And there is no witness against her . . ." (Num. 5:13).

[B]   I know only that reference is to a valid witness.

[C]   How do I know that this encompasses even a slave boy, even a slave girl [in line with M. 6:2C]?

[D]   Scripture explicitly states 'no witness'— of any character what-
       soever [would be acceptable to invalidate her from receiving
       her marriage settlement]. [There being no witness of any sort,
       the ordeal is imposed.]

[E]   Now in accord with the position of R. Ishmael, [how do we
       explain matters]?

[F]   For R. Ishmael said, "In every place in Scripture in which it is
       said 'witness' [21a] without further specification, lo, subsumed
       in such a reference is the requirement that there be two wit-
       nesses, unless Scripture makes it explicit that it speaks of a sin-
       gle witness."

[G]   There indeed is found [a teaching indicating that even in the
       matter of the woman's being made unclean, two witnesses are
       required], for it was taught: R. Ishmael says, "Two witnesses
       [are required even here]."

[II.A] The Mishnah comes from the time before R. Aqiba conceded
       the position of R. Tarfon [in the following discourse].

[B]   It has been taught: R. Tarfon says, "A single witness is be-
       lieved for purposes of declaring the woman unclean, but a sin-
       gle witness is not believed for purposes of depriving the woman
       of payment of her marriage settlement [vs. M. 6:2C]."

[C]   R. Aqiba says, "Just as a single witness is believed to declare
       the woman unclean, so a single witness is believed to deprive
       the woman of payment of her marriage settlement [in accord
       with M. 6:2C]."

[D]   Said to him R. Tarfon, "Where do we find a case in which the
       testimony of a single witness in a monetary case is worth a
       thing?"

[E]   Said to him R. Aqiba, "And where do we find a case in which
       the testimony of a single witness in marital matters is worth a
       thing?

[F]   "But just as a single witness is believed to declare the woman
       unclean, so a single witness is believed to deprive the woman of
       payment of her marriage settlement."

[G]   R. Aqiba reverted and taught the law in accord with the posi-
       tion of R. Tarfon. [Consequently, before this reversion, the law
       of the Mishnah was that a single witness is accepted to declare
       the woman unclean, as at M. 6:2A–B, so she does not undergo

the ordeal. The husband divorces her and does not pay off her marriage settlement (= M. 6:2C).]

[III.A] R. Bun bar Hiyya raised the following question: "Her mother-in-law said, 'I saw her, that she was made unclean,' [in which case, we know, M. 6:2D–F, she is believed to the degree that the wife now does not undergo the ordeal of drinking the bitter water, but she does get her marriage settlement]—

[B] "[Leiden MS and *editio princeps* lack:] and another party came and said, 'I saw her, that she was made unclean'—[what is the law]? [Does this other party's testimony serve to deprive the woman of her marriage contract, since in any event she is not going to undergo the ordeal?]

[C] "Why has this one come to give testimony? If it is to deal with the husband's administering the water ordeal, it already has been established [by the mother-in-law's testimony] that she is not to undergo the ordeal.

[D] "But the valid witness came to give testimony only in order to deprive her of payment of her marriage settlement.

[E] "[But] a single witness does not cause a monetary loss."

[F] [Along these same lines,] R. Yosé raised the following question:

[G] "[If] the husband heard from a bird passing by 'I saw her, that she was made unclean,' now you rule that she should not drink the water.

[H] "But if then another party came and said, 'I saw her, that she was made unclean'—[what is the law]?

[I] "Why has this one come to give testimony? If it is to deal with the husband's administering the water ordeal, it already has been established [by the bird's testimony] that she is not to undergo the ordeal.

[J] "But [the valid witness] came to give testimony only in order to deprive her of payment of her marriage settlement.

[K] "[But] a single witness does not cause a monetary loss."

[L] [Along the lines of these two identical questions, we turn to a parallel case of the effect of a single witness's testimony.] It derives from that which R. Yosé said, "[If a witness came and said,] 'Mr. So-and-so ate forbidden fat, and I gave him warning not to do so,' the accused is not flogged [on the evidence of one witness].

[M]   "But if a single party warned him that it was forbidden fat, and two witnesses warned him not to eat it, then he is flogged.

[N]   "And is not the principal part of the testimony against him that of a single witness? [And such testimony is accepted in matters of prohibitions. A single witness is treated like two here, and likewise the accused wife now loses her marriage settlement. This parallel then answers A–E, F–K.]"

[O]   On the basis of what R. Judah maintains, [we answer the same questions,] for R. Judah says, "[If a single witness came along and said,] 'Mr. So-and-so, a Nazirite, has become unclean, and I gave him warning about it,' the accused is not flogged.

[P]   "If a single party said to him, 'You are a Nazir,' and he obeyed the laws of the Nazirite on the basis of his statement, and then he drank wine or contracted corpse uncleanness, and two witnesses warned him not to do so, he then will be flogged.

[Q]   "And is not the principal part of the testimony against him that of a single witness [to the effect that he is a Nazirite to begin with]?"

[R]   [The answer to A–E, F–K, furthermore,] is on the basis of that which R. Mana said, "[If a single witness came and said,] 'Mrs. So-and-so, wife of a priest, has gone and had sexual relations with another man, and then her husband had sexual relations with her, and her husband is a priest, and I warned him about it,' the husband is not flogged.

[S]   "If she went in private according to the testimony of two witnesses, and one of them said, 'I saw her, that she was made unclean, and then her husband, a priest, had sexual relations with her, despite the warning of two witnesses,' the husband is flogged.

[T]   "Now is not the principal part of the testimony against her that of a single witness?"

Unit **I** asks whether Ishmael can accord with the Mishnah's teaching that a single witness is acceptable. Indeed, he does not. Unit **II** then compares the Mishnah's view with the dispute between Aqiba and Tarfon and harmonizes the Mishnah

with Aqiba's view by assigning its formulation to the time before Aqiba accepted Tarfon's opinion. At unit **III** a secondary
question, made possible by unit **II**'s discussion (cf. Pené
Moshe), is raised. If the woman is exempted from the ordeal
and is to be divorced on the basis of her mother-in-law's testimony, and then another witness comes along—we have the sequence of M. 6:2D–F and then M. 6:2A–C—what is the law?
The question is amply spelled out twice, and then the answer is
amply supplied, no fewer than three times. It is that the effect
of the single valid witness is to deprive her of receiving her
marriage settlement, since she already has been exempted on
the basis of other evidence from undergoing the rite. The force
of the analogies is explained at N.

6:3

[A] *For logic might dictate as follows [vis-à-vis M. 6:2A–B]: Now,
if, in the case of the first kind of testimony [that she has been
warned not to get involved with such-and-such a man], which
does not impose upon her a permanent prohibition [but only
until she has undergone the ordeal of the bitter water], [the ac-
cusation] is not sustained by less than two witnesses,*

[B] *in the case of the second kind of testimony [that she has indeed
been made unclean], which does impose upon her a permanent
prohibition [against remaining wed to her husband], surely [the
accusation] should not be sustained by less than two witnesses.*

[C] *But Scripture says, "And there is no witness against her"
(Num. 5:13)—[meaning,] any sort of testimony which there is
against her [will suffice].*

[D] *On these grounds, we may now construct an argument from
the less to the greater with reference to the first kind of
testimony:*

[E] *Now if the second kind of testimony, which imposes upon her
a permanent prohibition, lo, is sustained by a single witness,
the first kind of testimony, which does not impose upon her a
permanent prohibition, surely should be sustained by means of
a single witness.*

[F] *But Scripture says, "Because he has found some unseemly matter in her" (Deut. 24:1), and elsewhere it says, "At the mouth*

*of two witnesses shall be a matter be established" (Deut.
19:15)— just as "matter" spoken of there requires two witnesses, so "matter" spoken of here requires two witnesses.*

[I.A]   "The former testimony" concerns going aside in secret.

[B]   "The latter testimony" refers to the act of sexual relations.

[C]   The Mishnah pericope follows the view of R. Joshua, for R.
Joshua has said, *"When he expresses jealousy, he warns her
with two witnesses present, and he imposes the rite of drinking
the water upon her on the evidence of two witnesses"* [M. 1:1]
[= M. 6:3A–C].

[D]   Said R. Mana, "And even in accord with the other Tanna [Eli-
ezer], the cited pericope is perfectly in order.

[E]   "For it has been taught:

[F]   **"R. Yosé b. R. Judah says in the name of R. Eleazar, 'He
expresses jealousy to her at the evidence of a single witness
or on the basis of his own testimony.**

[G]   **" 'But he imposes the requirement to undergo the ordeal on
the evidence of two witnesses' " [Y. Sot. T: 1 IV.A, T. Sot.
1:1]. [So the argument a fortiori derives from M. 6:3 D–F.]**

M. 6:3 then goes through the exercise of claiming that the
propositions of M. 6:2 can be proved only through exegesis of
Scripture, since simple logic will have yielded a contrary and
false result. A–B take up M. 6:2A–B: a single witness is sufficient to free the woman from the ordeal of drinking the bitter
water, if such a single witness testifies that the woman has in
fact been made unclean. A single witness suffices that the
woman has gone alone with the man. A–B then propose that if
at that testimony, two witnesses are required (M. 1:1, Joshua),
then we surely should have two witnesses to testify that the
woman has actually become unclean. C then follows. D–F reverse the argument. If a single witness is valid to prove the
woman has been made unclean (and thus loses her marriage
contract), then surely a single witness should suffice to testify
that she has gone alone with the man, so D–E. But Scripture
insists that two witnesses must be present to testify that she has
gone alone with the man. The Talmud then makes explicit the

fact that the Mishnah's arguments serve, successively, Joshua
and Eliezer.

6:4

[A]   *[If] one witness says, "She was made unclean," and one witness says, "She was not made unclean,"*

[B]   *[if] one woman says, "She was made unclean," and one woman
says, "She was not made unclean,"*

[C]   *she would undergo the ordeal of drinking the bitter water.*

[D]   *[If] one witness says, "She was made unclean," and two witnesses say, "She was not made unclean," she would undergo
the ordeal of drinking the bitter water.*

[E]   *[If] two say, "She was made unclean," and one says, "She was
not made unclean," she would not undergo the ordeal of drinking the bitter water.*

[I.A]   Giddul bar Minyamin in the name of Rab: "In any case in
which [sages] have declared the testimony of a woman to be as
valid as that as a man, the testimony of a man serves to discredit that of a woman, and the testimony of a woman serves to
discredit that of a man."

[B]   [If that is so, then let the Tanna of M. 6:4A] teach [the law as
follows]: "[If] one [male] witness said, 'She has been made unclean,' and a woman said, "She has not been made unclean,'

[C]   "[or] a woman said, 'She has been made unclean,' and a [male]
witness said, 'She has not been made unclean,' [and that would
have indicated the point made by Rab at A].

[D]   Along these same lines did the house of Rabbi [teach the law].

[II.A]   It was taught in the name of R. Nehemiah, "They follow the
majority of the [available] testimony."

[B]   What would be a practical illustration of that proposition?

[C]   In the case in which two women testify [in one wise], and one
woman [testifies in another], they have treated such a case as
one in which there are two witnesses against one witness.

[D]   That rule which you have stated applies to a case in which
there was one woman against two women.

[E]   But if they were a hundred women and a single male witness, all the women are deemed equivalent to a single male witness.

[III.A]   R. Ada bar Ahvah said, "A single witness is believed so as to declare her unclean.

[B]   "A single witness is not believed so as to deprive the woman of the right to collect her marriage settlement."

[C]   Said R. Hisda, "What is the reason that they have ruled, 'A single witness is believed to declare [the accused wife] unclean'? It is because there is some foundation for the matter" [cf. Y. 6:2 II].

[IV.A]   [With reference to M. 6:4A, C, if one witness says she was made unclean and one says she was not made unclean, she would drink the water, there is a version that she would not drink the water. It is on the basis of that version that the following is stated:] Simeon bar Ba in the name of R. Yohanan: "Here she would not drink the water, but in the case of a neglected corpse, they would certainly break the neck of a heifer [at M. Sot. 9:7, where there is contradictory testimony about whether or not the murderer was seen]."

[V.A]   Rab said, "She would drink the water."

[B]   The Mishnah's formulation is at variance with the position of Rab: *If one witness says "She was made unclean," and two witnesses say, "She was not made unclean," she would undergo the ordeal of drinking the bitter water [M. 6:4D].*

[C]   Lo, [it follows that] if one witness [contradicted another], then she would not drink the water.

[D]   [Rab would] interpret the rule to apply to one who was [ordinarily] invalid to give testimony [in which the two who testified that she not made unclean are unfit to testify in an ordinary case, while the one who says she was made unclean was a suitable witness. Now a valid witness weighs as much as the two invalid ones [= I.A], so, in the state of doubt, she does drink the water.]

[E]   Now if we deal with those invalid to testify, then note what is said at the latter part of the Mishnah's statement: *If two say, "She was made unclean, and one says, "She was not made unclean," she would not undergo the ordeal of drinking the bitter water [M. 6:4E].*

[F]   Lo, here we have a case in which one witness contradicts an-
       other, and in such a case, she would not drink the bitter water.

[G]   Accordingly, how could Rab maintain that she would indeed
       drink the water?

[H]   R. Yohanan said, "She would not drink the water."

[I]   The Mishnah is at variance with the position of R. Yohanan: *If
       two say, "She was made unclean," and one witness says, "She
       was not made unclean," she did not drink the water.*

[J]   Lo, in the case of one [witness's word] against that of another,
       she indeed would drink the water.

[K]   [Yohanan] would interpret the rule to apply to a case involving
       witnesses ordinarily invalid to give testimony.

[L]   If we deal with those invalid to testify, then note what is said
       at the opening part of the Mishnah's statement: *If one witness
       says, "She was made unclean," and two witnesses say, "She
       was not made unclean," she would undergo the ordeal of drink-
       ing the bitter water [M. 6:4D].*

[M]   Lo, if it were a case in which one witness contradicts another,
       she would drink the water.

[N]   [Accordingly], how can R. Yohanan maintain that she did not
       drink?

[O]   They say in the name of R. Samuel, "The [whole pericope of]
       Mishnah treats a case in which those who give testimony are
       ordinarily invalid to do so, [and we follow the majority, which
       ever way]."

[VI.A] They say in the name of R. Samuel, "The Mishnah [at M.
       6:4D–E] speaks of a case of another act of going aside."

[B]   R. Zeira raised the question before R. Mana, "What is the
       meaning of this statement, 'The Mishnah speaks of a case of
       another going aside in secret'?"

[C]   He said to him, "Thus did R. Yohanan state in the name of R.
       Yannai, 'This entire chapter deals with a case in which the hus-
       band had expressed jealousy to the wife, and then she had gone
       aside.' [The point is that the testimony that the woman has
       gone aside with the named man must fall within an interval
       close to the husband's original expression of jealousy. But if the
       husband expresses jealousy about a given man, and nothing

happens and then, later on, a witness testifies that the wife went aside with him, that is deemed null.]

[D]   "If she went aside on the basis of the testimony of two witnesses,

[E]   "and one witness said, 'I saw her, that she was made unclean during the interval of privacy with the named man,'

[F]   "what we have here is evidence for her having gone aside in secret, and we also have here evidence that she was made unclean. [She does not drink.]

[G]   "If the evidence was that it was after the time of going aside in secret, we have evidence of her having gone aside in secret, but we have no evidence of her having been made unclean [she does not drink]."

[H]   [Following Pené Moshe's reading:] If there were three witnesses,

[I]   one of them says, "I saw her, that she was made unclean after an interval sufficient for her to have gone aside [with the originally named man]," we have evidence of her having gone aside, but we do not have here evidence of her having been made unclean [so she drinks] [= M. 6:4D].

[J]   If one of them said, "I saw her, that she was made unclean during an interval sufficient for her to have gone aside [with the named man]," here we have evidence that she has gone aside and that she was made unclean, [so she does not drink] [= M. 6:4E].

[VII.A]   If there were three witnesses,

[B]   one of them says, "I saw her, that she was not made unclean during an interval sufficient for her to have gone aside [with the named man]," [and the others know nothing on that score]—

[C]   how do you treat such a case?

[D]   Is it a case in which part of the testimony has been nullified, in consequence of which all of it is treated as null?

[E]   Or do we maintain that the testimony may be confirmed by the other parties?

[F]   Said R. Aba Meri, "While in general you maintain in the case of testimony, part of which has been nullified, that the whole of it is null,

[G]   "here you must agree that the testimony is to be confirmed by the remainder of the witnesses,

[H]   "because there is a basis for the matter."

We now qualify M. 6:1–2, which specify the sorts of testimony that indicate the woman does not undergo the ordeal of drinking the bitter water. We have conflicting reports, A, B. In either case, the woman is not proved to be unclean and therefore goes through the ordeal, because the single witness who would suffice (M. 6:2–3) is cancelled out by another witness. D of course follows. E then completes the matter. If we have two witnesses that the woman has become unclean, then we invoke the conception of M. 6:1–3. The main question of interest to the Talmud is how to deal with conflicting testimony. From beginning to end that is the dominant theme, although unit **VII** is clearest on the point. Unit **I** clarifies the matter of the effect of women's testimony. Unit **II** deals with essentially the same matter, since its point is **II.E**. Unit **III** does not belong here; it has been extensively treated above. Unit **IV** likewise is out of place, and it is curiously undeveloped. It is at unit **V** and beyond that the discussion becomes sustained. Unit **V** presents two exercises, each of which proves that the Mishnah contains internal contradictions. Unit **VI** then introduces the concept that the testimony about the woman's actually having had sexual relations with the named man must be temporally contiguous with the husband's warning. That conception is read into the rules of the Mishnah, as indicated. There are textual problems in the printed version, not fully solved here. I translate Pené Moshe's picture of the matter. Unit **VII** is distinct from what precedes. It phrases and answers its question with great clarity.

7 Yerushalmi Sotah
Chapter Seven

7:1

[21b/A] *These are said in any language: the pericope of the accused wife (Num. 5:19–22), the confession of the tithe (Deut. 26:13– 15), the recital of the Shema (Deut. 6:4–9), and the prayer, the oath of testimony, and the oath concerning a bailment.*

[I.A] It is written, "And the priest shall say to the woman" (Num. 5:19)—

[B] "In any language which she understands," the words of R. Josiah.

[C] Said to him R. Jonathan, "If she does not understand, then why should she say after him, 'Amen'? [So B is obvious.]

[D] "But the meaning of the verse just now cited is that he should not speak to her through an interpreter."

[II.A] R. Yohanan in the name of R. Eleazar b. R. Simeon, "We find that the Omnipresent never spoke with any woman except for Sarah alone."

[B] But [this cannot be, for] lo, it is written, "To the woman he said, 'I will greatly multiply your pain in childbearing' " (Gen. 3:16).

[C] Said R. Jacob of Kefar Hanin, "It was through an [angelic] interpreter."

[D] And lo, it is written, "And the Lord said to her, 'Two nations are in your womb' " (Gen. 25:23).

[E] Said R. Ba bar Kahana, "The word came to her."

175

[F]   Said R. Biri, "How many circles around circles did the Lord draw in order to listen to the conversation of that righteous woman?

[G]   "He said, 'No, but you did laugh' " (Gen. 18:15).

[III.A]   *The confession in respect to the tithe [M. 7:1A].*

[B]   As it is written, "And you shall respond and say before the Lord your God" (Deut. 26:5).

[IV.A]   *The recitation of the Shema, as it is written, "And you shall talk of them . . ." (Deut. 6:7).*

[B]   **Rabbi says, "I say, 'The recitation of the Shema is said only in the Holy Language.' "**

[C]   What is the Scriptural basis for that view?

[D]   **"And these words which I command you . . ." (Deut. 6:6) [T. Sot. 7:7].**

[E]   R. Levi Bar Haitah [?] went to Caesarea. He heard them read the *Shema* in Greek. He wanted to stop them from doing so. R. Yosé heard and was angered. He said, "Should I say, 'He who does not know how to read them in Assyrian letters [of Hebrew] should not read them at all'?

[F]   "Rather one fulfills his obligation in any language which he knows."

[G]   R. Berekhiah replied, "Lo, the Scroll of Esther, if one knew how to read it in either Assyrian letters [of Hebrew] or in everyday speech, he carries out his obligation to read it only in Assyrian letters."

[H]   [Rejecting G,] said R. Mana, "As to the Scroll of Esther, if one knew how to read it in Assyrian letters and in everyday speech, he fulfills his obligation to read it only in Assyrian.

[I]   "[If he knew how to read it only] in everyday speech, he fulfills his obligation to read it [even] in everyday language.

[J]   "And so one carries out his obligation to read it in any language which he knows."

[V.A]   *And as to the prayer:* [He may say it in whatever language he knows,] so that he may know how to beseech [God] for what he needs.

[B]   As to the grace after meals, [he may say it in whatever language he knows,] so that he may know to whom he says the blessing.

[VI.A]   *As to the oath of testimony and the oath concerning a bailment:* One administers the oath to a person in his own language.

[B]   If one administered the oath not in one's own language, and the person said, "Amen," lo, these are exempt [from the penalty for having taken a false oath].

[C]   This is in line with the following tradition:

[D]   **"An oath administered by the judges accords with the stipulations which are in our heart, not with the stipulations which are in your heart" [T. Sot. 7:3].**

[E]   Said R. Judah, "It is assumed that it is in accord with the stipulations which are in our heart that he administers the oath.

[F]   "And why does one stipulate with him?"

[G]   "It is because of uninformed people.

[H]   "So that they may not say, 'There are stipulations which apply to oaths.' "

[I]   R. Hananiah taught before R. Mana, "And lo, it is written, 'Nor is it with you only that I make this sworn covenant, but with him who is not here with us this day as well as with him who stands here with us this day' (Deut. 29:14–15).

[J]   "What does this statement imply?"

[K]   He said to him, "As to the generations [21c] which follow us, there can be no stipulation in their heart. [In oaths taken in the future, stipulations will be null]" [T. Sot. 7:5].

The Talmud stays fairly close to the exegetical requirements of the Mishnah. Only unit **II** is tacked on, for obvious reasons. Units **I, III, IV, V,** and **VI** take up the Mishnah's materials, and, in the indicated cases, there is some secondary development of the topic.

7:2

[A]   *And these are said [only] in the Holy Language: the verses of the first fruits (Deut. 26:3–10), the rite of halisah (Deut. 25:7, 9), blessings and curses (Deut. 27:15–26), the blessing of the priests (Num. 6:24–26), the blessing of a high priest [on the Day of Atonement], the pericope of the king (Deut. 17:14–20), the pericope of the heifer whose neck is to be broken (Deut. 21:7f), and [the message of] the anointed for battle when he speaks to the people (Deut. 20:2–7).*

[B]   *"The verses of the first fruits" (M. 7:2A1]—how so?*

[C]   *"And you will answer and say before the Lord thy God (Deut. 26:5)."*

[D]   *And later on it says, "And the Levites will answer and say" (Deut. 27:14).*

[E]   *Just as "answering" which is said in that later passage is to be said in the Holy Language, so "answering" which is said here [in reference to the first fruits] to be said in the Holy Language.*

[F]   *"The rite of halisah" [M. 7:2A]—how so?*

[G]   *"And she will answer and say" (Deut. 25:9)."*

[H]   *And later on it says, "And the Levites will answer and say" (Deut. 27:14).*

[I]   *Just as later on "answering" is to be said in the Holy Language, so here "answering" is to be said in the Holy Language.*

[J]   *R. Judah says, " 'And she will answer and say, Thus'—[so it is not valid] unless she says precisely these words."*

[I.A]   It was taught in the name of R. Judah, "In any place in Scripture [not merely those cited in the Mishnah] in which the language of 'answering' and 'saying' is used, it must be in the Holy Language [= M. 7:3D–E, F–I].

[B]   "If [also] it says, 'Thus and so,' lo, it must be in the Holy Language."

[C]   Said R. Eleazar, "The generative analogy for them all is as follows: 'Moses spoke, and God answered him in thunder' " (Ex. 19:19).

[D]   R. Haggai objected [to Judah's statement at A], "And is it not written, 'Then Laban and Bethuel answered' (Gen. 24:50)?

[E]   "If you say it was in respect only to 'answering,' but not to 'saying,' has it not also been stated, 'And they said' (Gen. 24:50)?

[F]   "If you say that it was in respect only to 'saying,' not to 'answering,' has it not been said, 'The thing comes from the Lord; we cannot speak to you bad or good' (Gen. 24:50)?

[G]   "And if you say that, indeed, all of this was said in the Holy Language, and is it not written, 'And Laban called the place, Yaggar Sahaduta [in Aramaic]' (Gen. 31:47)?

[H]   "And if you explain that that was because it was prior to the giving of the Torah, lo, there is the pericope of the confession for tithe. Lo, it comes from the time after the giving of the Torah, and it may be said in any language at all."

[I]   R. Samuel bar Nahman in the name of R. Yohanan: "It is so that the Sursi language [Aramaic] should not be cheap in your eyes.

[J]   "For in the Torah, Prophets, and Writings, that language is to be found.

[K]   "In the Torah: it is written, 'And Laban called it, Yagar Sahaduta' (Gen. 31:47).

[L]   "In the Prophets it is written, 'Thus will you say to them' [in Aramaic] (Jer. 10:11).

[M]   "And in the Writings, it is written, 'And the Chaldeans spoke to the king [in Aramaic]' " (Dan. 2:4).

[II.A]   Said R. Jonathan of Bet Gubrin, "Four languages are appropriately used in the world, and these are they: everyday speech [Greek] for song; Latin for war; Sursi [Aramaic] for wailing; Hebrew for [clear] speech."

[B]   And there are those who say, "Also Assyrian, for writing."

[C]   Assyrian is a mode of writing, but it is not a mode of speech.

[D]   Hebrew is a mode of speech, but it is not a mode of writing.

[E]   They selected for themselves Assyrian writing and Hebrew speech.

[F]   And why is it called Assyrian ('SWRY)?

[G]   For it is particularly felicitous (M'WSR) in its mode of writing.

[H]   Said R. Levi, "It is because they brought it with them from Assyria."

[III.A]   It is written, "And the Levites shall declare to all the men of Israel with a high voice (QWL RM)" (Deut. 27:14).

[B]   With the voice of the Most High (RM).

[C]   This teaches that the Holy One, blessed be he, joined his voice to theirs.

[D]   Another matter: "The high voice"—the most elevated of all voices.

[E]   Said R. Isaac, "Not too soft and not too loud, but in the middle."

Unit **I** complements the Mishnah as indicated. Unit **II** is thematically relevant, and unit **III** takes up a verse cited in the Mishnah.

7:3

[A]   *"Blessings and curses" [M. 7:2A]—how so?*

[B]   *When Israel came across the Jordan and arrived before Mount Gerizim and before Mount Ebal in Samaria, near Shechem, beside the oak of Moreh,—*

[C]   *as it is written, "Are not they beyond the Jordan . . ." (Deut. 11:30) and elsewhere it says, "And Abram passed through the land to the place of Shechem to the oak of Moreh" (Gen. 12:6)—just as the oak of Moreh spoken of there is at Shechem, so the oak of Moreh spoken of here is at Shechem—)*

[I.A]   Are they not beyond the Jordan [that is,] from the Jordan and beyond, west of the road, toward the going down of the sun, [that is,] the place where the sun sets, in the land of the Canaanites, who live in the Arabah, over against Gilgal, beside the oak of Moreh?" (Deut. 11:30).

[B]   "This refers to Mount Gerizim and Mount Ebal in Samaria," the words of R. Judah.

[C]   R. Eliezer says, "This does not refer to Mount Gerizim and Mount Ebal in Samaria.

[D]   "For it is said, 'Are they not beyond the Jordan, [that is,] from the Jordan and beyond, west of the road, toward the going down of the sun, [that is,] the place where the sun sets.'

[E]   " 'In the land of Canaanites'—this refers to the Hivites.

[F]   " 'Who live in the Arabah'—this is the area among the hills [where the Hivites live].

[G]   " 'Over against Gilgal'—this does not refer to Gilgal

[H]   " 'Beside the oak of Moreh'—this does not refer to the oak of Moreh."

[I]   How does R. Eliezer then deal with the reference to Mount Gerizim and Mount Ebal?

[J]   They made two heaps of stones and named them Mount Gerizim and Mount Ebal.

[K]   In the view of R. Judah, they traversed a hundred and twenty *mil* on that day.

[L]   In the opinion of R. Eliezer they did not move from where they were.

[II.A]   It was taught: R. Eliezer b. Jacob says, "The verse of Scripture comes only to lay out the road for them and to indicate that they should go on the road and not across the fields,

[B]   "in a settled area and not in the wilderness,

[C]   "in the Arabah and not in the mountains."

[III.A]   Said R. Eleazar b. R. Simeon, "I stated to Samaritan scribes, 'You have forged your own Torah, and it has done you no good.

[B]   " 'For you have written in your Torah, '. . . near the oak of Moreh, Shechem.'

[C]   " 'And is it not known that this is Shechem? But [you forge your Torah] for you do not know how to provide an exegesis through analogy, and we do know how to provide an exegesis by analogy.

[D]   " 'Here it is stated, 'Oak of Moreh,' and elsewhere it is stated, 'Oak of Moreh.'

[E]   *"Just as 'the oak of Moreh' spoken of there is at Shechem, so 'the oak of Moreh' spoken of here is at Shechem [M. 7:3C].* [Hence you did not need to forge your Torah's text.]"

[**IV**.A] And in accord with the view of R. Ishmael [they did not come to Shechem until after the land was divided, so he would concur with Judah].

[B]   For R. Ishmael said, "All those occasions for coming [into the land] which are mentioned in the Torah refer to events which took place after fourteen years, seven years in which they conquered the land, and seven years in which they divided it up."

[C]   And along these same lines, the blessings and the curses were stated only after fourteen years.

[D]   R. Hananiah objected in the presence of R. Mana, "And has it not been written, 'And on the day when you pass over the Jordan to the land which the Lord your God gives you, you shall set up large stones, [and cover them with plaster]'?" (Deut. 27:2).

[E]   He said to him, "They set up the stones right away. But as to the blessings and the curses, they actually stated them only after fourteen years."

The Talmud presents an anthology of materials on the verse critical to the Mishnah, Deut. 11:30. Only unit **III** clearly relates to and augments the Mishnah.

7:4

[A]   *Six tribes went up to the top of Mount Gerizim, and six tribes went up to the top of Mount Ebal.*

[B]   *And the priests and Levites and ark of the covenant stood at the bottom, in the middle [between two mountains].*

[C]   *The priests surround the ark, and the Levites [surround] the priests, and all Israel are round about, since it says, "And all Israel and their elders and officers and judges stood on this side of the ark and on that . . ." (Joshua 8:33).*

[D]   *They turned their faces toward Mount Gerizim and began with the blessing:*

[E]   *"Blessed is the man who does not make a graven or molten image."*

[F]   *And these and those answer, "Amen."*

[G]   *They turned their faces toward Mount Ebal and began with the curse:*

[H]   *"Cursed is the man who makes a graven or molten image"* *(Deut. 27:15).*

[I]   *And these and those answer, "Amen."*

[J]   *[And this procedure they follow] until they complete the blessings and the curses.*

[I.A]   It was taught [in the Tosefta's version]: **How did the Israelites say the blessings and the curses?**

[B]   **Six tribes went up to the top of Mount Gerizim, and six tribes went up to the top of Mount Ebal. And the priests and the Levites and the ark of the covenant stood at the bottom in the middle [M. Sot. 7:4A–B].**

   The priests surround the ark, and the Levites [surround] the priests and all Israel are round about, since it says, "And all Israel and their elders and officers and judges stood on this side of the ark and on that" (Joshua 8:33) [M. Sot. 7:4A–C].

[C]   **What is the meaning of the Scripture, "Half of them in front of Mount Gerizim and half of them in front of Mount Ebal" (Joshua 8:33)?**

[D]   **This teaches that the part which was before Mount Gerizim was greater than that before Mount Ebal, since the part of the tribe of Levi was below.**

[E]   **[Yerushalmi begins here:] R. Eliezer b. Jacob [Yerushalmi: Rabbi] says, "You cannot say that Levi was below, for it already has been said that Levi was above, and you cannot say that Levi was above, for already has it been stated that Levi was below.**

   "On this basis you must say that the elders of the priesthood and the Levites were below, but the rest of the tribe was above."

[F]   **Rabbi [Yerushalmi: R. Simeon] says, "Those who were suitable for service stood below, and those who were not suitable for service stood above" [T. Sot. 8:9].**

[G]   R. Simeon says, " 'Simeon and Levi' (Deut. 27:12)—Just as all of the tribe of Simeon was up above, so all of the tribe of Levi was up above."

[H]   How does this Tanna interpret the statement "before the Levitical priests," [which indicates that they were down below]?

[I]   It is in accord with that which R. Joshua b. Levi said, "In twenty-four places in Scripture the priests are called Levites, and this is one of them.

[J]   " 'But the Levitical priests, the sons of Zadok, [who kept charge of my sanctuary when the people of Israel went astray from me, shall come near to me to minister to me; and they shall attend on me to offer me the fat and the blood, says the Lord God' " (Ezek. 44:15)].

[II.A]   Is it possible to suppose that those who were on Mount Gerizim were the ones to say the blessings, and those on Mount Ebal were the ones to say the curses?

[B]   Scripture states, "[And afterward he read all of the words of the law,] the blessings and the curses, [according to all that is written in the book of the law]" (Joshua 8:34).

[C]   The meaning is that both this group and that group said both the blessings and the curses.

[D]   Is it possible to suppose that after they said the blessings, they said the curses?

[E]   Scripture states, "[And when all these things come upon you,] the blessings and the curses, [which I have set before you, and you call them to mind among all the nations where the Lord your God has driven you]" (Deut. 30:1).

[F]   Is it possible to suppose that those who were on Mount Gerizim were to answer "Amen" after the blessings, and those who were on Mount Ebal were to answer "Amen" after the curses?

[G]   Scripture says, "['Cursed be the man who makes a graven or molten image, an abomination to the Lord, a thing made by the hands of a craftsman, and sets it up in secret.'] And all the people shall answer and say 'Amen' " (Deut. 27:15). These and those would say "Amen" after the blessings and after the curses.

[H]   How so?

[I]   When they would say the blessings, they would turn toward Mount Gerizim.

[J]   When they would say the curses, they would turn toward Mount Ebal.

[III.A]   A blessing was in general, and a blessing was in particular, so too, a curse was in general, and a curse was in particular [thus four].

[B]   There were sixteen covenants for each item: "To learn, to teach, to keep, to do," [that is, four for each item, times four for the two blessings and the two curses, sixteen in all].

[C]   It was thus, too, at Mount Sinai, and also at the Plains of Moab [thus forty-eight].

[D]   R. Simeon would remove from the list the covenants at Mount Gerizim and Mount Ebal and introduced in their stead that of the Tent of Meeting.

[E]   **And so did R. Simeon say, "There is no teaching of the Torah on account of which 576 covenants were not made:**

[F]   **"Twelve at the blessing, 12 at the curse, 12 at the general statement, 12 at the particularization thereof—lo, 48 covenants; 'To study and to teach, to guard and to do'—lo, 192 covenants;**

[G]   **"and so at Mount Sinai, so on the Plains of Moab—lo, 576 covenants."**

[H]   **R. Simeon b. Judah of Kefar Akko says in the name of R. Simeon, "They are 603,550."**

[I]   **Rabbi says, "In accord with the statement of R. Simeon b. Judah of Kefar Emum in the name of R. Simeon, 'There is no matter in the Torah on account of which [there was no covenant] 48 times, 603,550 for each time' " [= T. Sot. 8:10–11] [21d].**

[J]   [As to A, above,] up to this point, we have dealt with matters subject to both general and particular [statements].

[K]   As to matters which are given as generalizations but not expressed in particular terms, [what is there to say]?

[L]   He said to him, "Thus did R. Yohanan say in the name of R. Simeon, 'Whatever matter was included within the generalization and then singled out and made particular has been singled out to teach a lesson.

[M]   " 'It was not to teach a lesson in its own regard that it is singled out, but rather to teach a lesson regarding the generalization of which it was a part that it was singled out.' "

[N]   He said to him, "Was it not in regard to teaching a lesson about a single matter [that Yohanan made this statement]? Did it apply to teaching about two matters? But [in the passage under discussion,] we are dealing with an item singled out in regard to two different matters [or more]."

[O]   Said R. Tanhuma, "Since at the end it is written, 'Amen,' it is as if the whole of it is deemed a single matter."

[IV.A]   It is written, "Cursed be he who does not support the words of this Torah . . ." (Deut. 27:26).

[B]   Now does the Torah fall down [that someone has to hold it up]?

[C]   Simeon b. Yaqim says, "This refers to the leader of the prayers, indicating that he has to stand [when he says the prayers for the congregation]."

[D]   R. Simeon b. Halafta says, "This refers to [supporting] the court below [reading: Bet Din] on earth."

[E]   For R. Huna, R. Judah in the name of Samuel said, "In regard to this statement, Josiah tore his garments and said, 'It is my duty to hold up [the Torah and support those who study it].' "

[F]   R. Aha in the name of R. Tanhum b. R. Hiyya: "If one has learned, taught, kept, and carried out [the Torah], and he has ample means in his possession to strengthen the Torah and he did not do so, lo, such a one still is in the category of those who are cursed." [The meaning of 'strengthen' here is to support the masters of Torah.]

[G]   R. Jeremiah in the name of R. Hiyya bar Ba, "[If] one did not learn, teach, keep, and carry out [the teachings of the Torah], but did not have ample means to strengthen [the masters of the

Torah] [but nonetheless he did strengthen them, so Pené Moshe] lo, such a one falls into the category of those who are blessed."

[H]   And R. Hannah, R. Jeremiah in the name of R. Hiyya: "The Holy One, blessed be he, is going to prepare a protection for those who carry out religious duties [of support for masters of Torah] through the protection afforded to the masters of Torah [themselves].

[I]   "What is the Scriptural basis for that statement? 'For the protection of wisdom is like the protection of money' (Qoh. 7:12).

[J]   "And it says, '[The Torah] is a tree of life to those who lay hold of it; those who hold it fast are called happy' " (Prov. 3:18).

[V.A]   ["And all Israel . . . with their elders, officers, and judges, stook on opposite sides of the ark before the Levitical priests who carried the ark of the covenant of the Lord, half of them in front of Mount Gerizim, and half of them in front of Mount Ebal . . ." (Joshua 11:33).] What is the meaning of that which Scripture states, "Half of them"?

[B]   It teaches that the minority was on Mount Gerizim, and the majority on Mount Ebal.

[C]   And why [was the larger number on Mount Ebal]?

[D]   For the whole tribe of Levi was not located there, but if the whole tribe of Levi had been located there, they would have been equal [in numbers on both sides].

[E]   R. Samuel bar Nahman in the name of R. Jonathan: "If the entire tribe of Levi had been there, they still would not have been equal in numbers.

[F]   "And why [is that so]? For out of the tribe of Simeon, twenty-four thousand had already fallen at Shittim."

[G]   Said R. Yosé b. R. Bun, "If the entire tribe of Levi had been there, they indeed would have been equal in numbers.

[H]   "And why [is that so]? For out of the tribes of Reuben and Gad only forty thousand armed soldiers came."

[I]   Kahana said, "Just as they were divided here, so they were divided at the beginning of the second book of the Pentateuch [Ex. 1:1–5]."

[J]   There are Tannaim who teach: "Just as they were divided here, so they were divided by divisions: the sons of Leah on one side, the sons of Rachel on the other side, and the sons of the handmaidens in the middle."

[K]   Said R. Mattenaiah, "The Scriptural basis for the view of that Tanna is as follows: 'Hear this, O house of Jacob, who are called by the name of Israel' (Is. 48:1).

[L]   "Just as, when one joins beams, the thick side of one is set next to the thin side of another, and the thick side of one is set by the thin side of the other, [so the tribes are laid out so that they come out even]."

[M]   There are Tannaim who teach: "Just as they are divided here, so they are divided in their rows in the stones on the priestly breastplate [Ex. 28:21]."

[N]   Their rows [are to be such] that there will be twenty-five [letters] on one side, and twenty-five on the other.

[O]   And are not all the letters of the tribes put together only forty-nine [not fifty]?

[P]   Said R. Yohanan, "The name of Benjamin [normally written BNYMN] is written fully [BNYMYN] in the story of his birth."

[Q]   Said R. Judah bar Zabeda, "The name of Joseph [YWSP] is written fully, 'He made it a decree in Joseph [YHWSP]' " (Ps. 81:5).

[R]   But are they not [when spelled out by tribes] indeed twenty-three letters on one side, and twenty-seven letters on the other?

[S]   Said R. Yohanan, "Benjamin was at the breaking point: 'Ben . . .' on one side, and '. . . jamin' on the other."

[T]   Said R. Zebida, "And that is so. It is written, 'Their six names' [at Ex. 28:21, meaning, fully spelled out]? No. It is written, '*of* their names' (Ex. 28:21), meaning, part of their names, and not the whole of their names."

[U]   The former ones are written at the right hand of the high priest, which is at the left hand of the one who reads them.

[V]   The latter ones are written at the left hand of the high priest, which is at the right hand of the reader.

[W]   The former ones are not written down in order [of birth], since Judah is the royal tribe [and comes first].

[X]   The latter ones are written down in order [of birth].

Discussion focuses upon the division of the Israelite tribes, which is the theme introduced in the Mishnah. Unit **I**, given in the Tosefta's somewhat fuller version, produces a significant amplification of the Mishnah. Unit **II** carries forward that same theme. I cannot claim to see the point of the discussion of unit **III**. Unit **IV** continues the interest of the Mishnah in the blessings and the curses, and unit **V**, in the division of the tribes.

7:5

[A]   *And afterward they brought stones and built an altar and plastered it with plaster.*

[B]   *And they wrote on it all the words of the Torah in seventy languages,*

[C]   *as it is written, "Very plainly" (Deut. 27:8).*

[D]   *And they took the stones and came and spent the night in their own place (Joshua 4:8).*

[I.A]   [In line with M. 7:5D and against the view of M. 7:5A that they wrote the words of the Torah on the stones of the altar,] it was taught: "[The words of the Torah] were written on the stones of the lodging place [on the other side of the Jordan; Joshua 4:3, 8]," the words of R. Judah.

[B]   R. Yosé says, "They were written on the stones of the altar itself."

[C]   The one who says that the words of the Torah were written on the lodging [that is, in a stationary place, may well understand the following]:

[D]   Every day the nations of the world send their scribes and copy out the Torah, which is written in seventy languages.

[E]   But he who said that the words of the Torah were written on the stones of the altar—[how can he explain that fact]? For is it not so that they were used only for a moment and then hidden away?

[F]   [From his viewpoint,] it is [merely] another miracle.

[G]   [That is to say,] the Holy One, blessed be he, gave insight into the heart of every nation, so that they copied out the words of the Torah which were written in seventy languages.

[H]   In the view of him who said, they were written on the stones of the lodging, the following verse poses no problems: "and plaster them with plaster" (Deut. 27:2).

[I]   But as to him who said that they were written on the stones of the altar, how does he explain this requirement, "and plaster them with plaster"?

[J]   It was to be between one stone and the next.

[K]   R. Samuel bar Nahmani in the name of R. Yohanan: " 'And peoples will be as if burned to lime' " (Is. 33:12).

[L]   On account of plaster [that is, the writing on the plaster,] the verdict for them was death [for they had access to the Torah and declined to obey it].

[M]   R. Abba bar Kahana in the name of R. Yohanan, " '[For the nation and kingdom that will not serve you shall perish;] those nations shall be utterly laid to waste (HRWB YHRBW)' (Is. 60:12)—From Horeb the verdict concerning them was the death penalty."

[N]   **You turn out to say, There are the three sets of stones:**

[O]   **Stones of the lodging, stones which Joshua laid down under the feet of the priests, and the resting stations which Moses put up for them [T. Sot. 8:6].**

[P]   Said R. Haninah, "It is clear to us that there are four kinds of stones." [The stones of the lodging and those of the altar are different and counted separately, vs. O.]

[Q]   Said R. Simon bar Zebid, "And that is so. If you say that the stones of the lodging were [the same as those of the altar, then they] were used for a moment and then were put away [= E].

[R]   "If you say that the stones [of the lodging were the ones] which Joshua put under the feet of the priests, [that is not so, for] they sank down into the water.

[S]   "If you say that [they were] the stations which Moses set up for them, [those stones] already were taken with them into the land.

[T]   "But so we must interpret the matter: [The altar was made] of stones which Joshua set up for them at the Jordan [and not stones used for any other purpose]."

[II.A]   **It was taught: R. Judah says, "R. Halafta, Eleazar b. Matia, and Hananiah b. Kinai stood on those very stones and estimated that each one weighted forty seahs" [T. Sot. 8:6D–E].**

[B]   On this basis you may reckon how much there is in a grape cluster.

[C]   It is written, "[And Joshua said to them, 'Pass on before the Ark of the Lord your God into the midst of the Jordan,] and take up each of you a stone upon his shoulder, [according to the number of the tribes of the people of Israel]' " (Joshua 4:5).

[D]   Not of so much weight is a load which one lifts straight away from the ground to his shoulder as the load which one lifts from the ground to the knees, and from the knees to the shoulder.

[E]   Not of so much weight is that which one lifts from the ground to his knees and from the knees to the shoulder, as the load which another party places on oneself, [since the other will put on a heavier load than the load one may lift only by himself].

[F]   Not of so much weight is the load which another party places on oneself as the load which is lifted by two people.

[III.A]   It is written: "[Now therefore take twelve men from the tribes of Israel,] from each tribe a man" (Joshua 3:12). [At issue in what follows is whether the repeated language, "twelve men . . . from each . . . a man" means to encompass more than twelve, that is, twenty-four.]

[B]   In the opinion of R. Aqiba [Leiden MS and *editio princeps:* Simeon], who says that the purpose of the repetition is to encompass [more than the stated twelve], there will be twenty-four: sixteen for the grape cluster, and eight for the figs, pomegranates, and baggage train.

[C]   In the opinion of R. Ishmael [Leiden MS and *editio princeps:* Aqiba], who says that the purpose of the repetition is not to encompass [more than the stated twelve], there will be twelve only: eight for the grape cluster, and four for the figs, pomegranates, and baggage train [Leiden MS and *editio princeps:* reverse order of B, C].

[D]   In the opinion of R. Ishmael [who said they were twelve, they carried the grape cluster through] a pair of balancing poles.

[E]   In the opinion of R. Aqiba, [they did so through] a couple of pairs of balancing poles.

[IV.A]   It is written: "The waters coming down from above stood and rose in a heap far off at Adam, the city that is beside Zarathan, [and those flowing down toward the sea of the Arabah, the Salt Sea, were wholly cut off; and the people passed over opposite Jericho]" (Joshua 3:16).

[B]   Said R. Yohanan, "Adam was a city, and Zarathan was a city."

[C]   They were twelve *mil*s apart.

[D]   This teaches that the water rose in a heap up to the side of Zarathan.

[E]   **Now which is faster, water or man? Water is faster than man. You know that that is the case. So this teaches that the water was rising up in heaps, wave upon wave [ever higher] [T. Sot. 8:3].**

[F]   R. Levi said, "[The water reached] to the heart of the firmament."

[G]   There they say, "[The water reached] to Babylonia."

[H]   Here it is said, "Far off" (Joshua 3:16), and there it is said, "[Then Isaiah the prophet came to King Hezekiah, and said to him, 'What did these men say? And whence did they come to you?' And Hezekiah said,] 'They have come from a far country, from Babylon'" (2 Kings 20:14).

[22a/I]   It was taught: **R. Eleazar b. R. Simeon says, "[In the Tosefta's version:] And is man swifter, or is water swifter? You have to say that water is swifter than man. This teaches that the waters were continually driven backward and] heaped higher and higher, stacks by stacks, three hundred mils until all the kings of the nations of the world saw them" [T. Sot. 8:3].**

[J]   This is in line with that which is written, "When the kings of the Amorites that were beyond the Jordan to the west, and all the kings of the Canaanites that were by the sea, heard that the Lord had dried up the waters of the Jordan for the people of Israel until they had crossed over, [their heart melted, and there was no longer any spirit in them, because of the people of Israel]" (Joshua 5:1).

[V.A] Said R. Simeon b. Laqish, "At the Jordan they took upon themselves responsibility for hidden [sins, as well as revealed ones].

[B]   "Said to them Joshua, 'If you do not accept upon yourselves responsibility for the hidden things, the water will come and drown you.' "

[C]   Said R. Simon B. Zabeda, "Well said. You know that that statement is true, for lo, Achan sinned [in secret], and the majority of the Sanhedrin fell at Ai [on account of his sin]."

[D]   Said R. Levi, "In Yavneh the strap was untied. An echo went forth and said, 'You have no more need to get involved in hidden [sins or to make inquiry about them].' "

Unit **I** takes up an issue tangential to the Mishnah. This produces sizable discussion on the various heaps of stones mentioned in the narratives. Unit **II** continues this same theme. Units **III**, **IV**, and **V** intersect with the matter. The whole seems organized, at best, as a thematic anthology.

7:6

[A]   *"The blessing of the priests"* [M. 7:2A]—*how so?*

[B]   *In the provinces they say it as three blessings, and in the sanctuary, as one blessing.*

[C]   *In the sanctuary one says the Name as it is written, but in the provinces, with a euphemism.*

[D]   *In the provinces the priests raise their hands as high as their shoulders, but in the sanctuary, they raise them over their heads,*

[E]   *except for the high priest, who does not raise his hands over the frontlet.*

[F]   *R. Judah says, "Also the high priest raises his hands over the frontlet,*

[G]   *"since it is said, 'And Aaron lifted up his hands toward the people and blessed them' " (Lev. 9:22).*

[H]   *"The blessing of the high priest" [M. 7:2A]—how so?*

[I]   *The minister of the assembly takes a scroll of the Torah and gives it to the head of the assembly, and the head of the assembly gives it to the prefect, and the prefect gives it to the high priest.*

[J]   *And the high priest stands and receives it and reads in it: "After the death . . ." (Lev. 16:1ff.) and "How be it on the tenth day" (Num. 29:7–11).*

[K]   *Then he rolls up the Torah and holds it at his breast and says, "More than I have read for you is written here."*

[L]   *"And on the tenth . . ." which is in the book of Numbers (Num. 29:7–11) did he read by heart.*

[M]   *And afterward he says eight blessings: . . . for the Torah, . . . for the Temple service, . . . for the Thanksgiving, . . . for the forgiveness of sins, . . . for the sanctuary, . . . for Israel, . . . for the priests, and the rest of the prayer.*

[I.A]   [With regard to the priests who had to raise their hands above their heads throughout the blessings,] R. Hisda said, "It was very painful for them."

[II.A]   In every place people go to the Torah. But here [at M. 7:6I] you say that they bring the Torah to them.

[B]   But because they are important men, the Torah is exalted through them.

[C]   But lo, over there [in Babylonia] they bring the Torah to the exilarch, [who is not esteemed]?

[D]   Said R. Yosé b. R. Bun, "Because the ancestry of David is imputed to him, they treat him in accord with the custom applicable to their ancestors [in the house of David]."

[**III**.A]   [With reference to M. 7:6J,] there we have learned: *They may leave out verses in the Prophets, but not in the Torah [M. Meg. 4:4].*

[B]   They leave out verses in a prophetic reading, but they do not read out verses [in skipping] from one prophet to another.

[C]   But in the case of one of the twelve minor prophets, it is permitted.

[D]   But they do not leave out verses in the Torah.

[E]   R. Jeremiah in the name of R. Simeon b. Laqish, "The reason is that they may not roll up [or unroll] the scroll of the Torah in public [and thus inflict discomfort on the people by making them wait for the reading]."

[F]   R. Yosé raised the question: "Take note: What if it was a brief pericope [to be skipped]? [There would be little bother. E's reason therefore is unacceptable.]

[G]   "But it is so that the Israelites may hear the Torah read in its proper order [and so understand its teachings in context]."

[H]   And lo, we have learned, *". . . and reads in it, 'After the death,' and 'How be it on the tenth day' "* [M. 7:6J]?

[I]   That case is different, for the stated readings follow the order of the rite for the Day [of Atonement].

[J]   You will note that it is the case [that a different rule prevails here], for R. Simeon b. Laqish said, "In every place the reader of the Torah does not read from memory, while he here [M. 7:6L] reads from memory."

[K]   R. Yosé gave instructions to Bar Ulla, the preceptor of the synagogue of the Babylonians [in his town], "On the day on which you bring out only one Torah, roll it up behind the veil [so as not to bother the community]. If it is a day on which you bring out two scrolls, you should take out one and put it back [and then take out the other]."

[**IV**.A]   *And afterward he says eight blessings [M. 7:6M].*

[B]   *For the Torah:* ". . . who has chosen the Torah."

[C]   *for the Temple service:* ". . . for you alone in reverence do we serve."

[D]   *For the Thanksgiving:* ". . . to whom it is good to give thanks."

[E]   *For the forgiveness of sin:* ". . . who forgives the sins of his people Israel in mercy."

[F]   *For the sanctuary:* ". . . who has chosen the sanctuary." And R. Idi said, ". . . who dwells in Zion."

[G]   *For Israel:* ". . . who has chosen Israel."

[H]   *For the priests:* ". . . who has chosen the priests."

[I]   *And for the rest of the prayer:* ". . . with supplication and beseeching for your people Israel need to be saved before you. Blessed are you, Lord, who hears prayer."

The Talmud systematically comments on M. 7:6H–M.

7:7

[A]   *"The pericope of the king"* [M. 7:2A]—how so?

[B]   *At the end of the first festival day of the Festival [of Sukkot],*

[C]   *on the eighth year, [that is] at the end of the seventh year,*

[D]   *they make him a platform of wood, set in the courtyard.*

[E]   *And he sits on it,*

[F]   *as it is said, "At the end of every seven years in the set time" (Deut. 31:10).*

[G]   *The minister of the assembly takes a scroll of the Torah and hands it to the head of the assembly, and the head of the assembly hands it to the prefect, and the prefect hands it to the high priest, and the high priest hands it to the king, and the king stands and receives it.*

[H]   *But he reads sitting down.*

[I]   *Agrippa the king stood up and received it and read it standing up, and sages praised him on that account.*

[J]   *And when he came to the verse "You may not put a foreigner over you, who is not your brother" (Deut. 17:15), his tears ran down from his eyes.*

[K]   *They said to him, "Do not be afraid, Agrippa, you are our brother, you are our brother!"*

[I.A] [Regarding M. 7:7H,] did not R. Hiyya teach, "The right to sit down in the courtyard was accorded only to kings of the house of David"?

[B]   And R. Ami in the name of R. Simeon b. Laqish said, "Even the kings of the house of David did not have the right to sit down in the courtyard."

[C]   Interpret the matter to speak of a case in which one leaned against the wall as if to sit down.

[D]   And lo, it is written, "And King David went in and sat before the Lord" (2 Sam. 7:18), [so why should the king not sit, vs. A–C]?

[E]   Said R. Aibu bar Nigri, "He sat down in prayer."

[F]   There we have learned: *When the first group went out, they sat on the Temple Mount [if the fourteenth of Nisan coincided with the Sabbath], the second on the Rampart, and the third in its place [in the courtyard] [M. Pes. 5:10].*

[G]   It remained standing in its place.

[H]   R. Nahman in the name of R. Mana, "What then is the meaning of that which we have learned, *It sat in its place?* It stood in its place."

[II.A] It was taught: R. Haninah b. Gamaliel says, "Many corpses fell on that day on which they flattered him [Agrippa]"

The Talmud analyzes the rule of M. 7:7H.

7:8

[A]   *He reads from the beginning of "These are the words" (Deut. 1:1) to "Hear O Israel" (Deut. 6:4), "And it will come to pass, if you harken" (Deut. 11:13), and "You shall surely tithe" (Deut. 14:22), and "When you have made an end of tithing" (Deut. 26:12–15), and the pericope of the king [Deut. 17:14–20], and the blessings and the curses [Deut. 27:15–26], and he completes the whole pericope.*

[B]   *With the same blessings with which the high priest blesses them [M. 7:7F], the king blesses them.*

[C]   *But he says the blessing for the festivals instead of the blessing for the forgiveness of sin.*

[I.A]   Said R. Abbahu, "And why do they read, 'You shall surely tithe,' and 'When you have made an end of tithing'?

[B]   "On account of the fact that the Israelites have gone from the seventh year [during which there is no requirement to tithe], to the eighth year [when it again is required to tithe], it is so that the people should not forget about tithing."

[II.A]   R. Haggai raised the question before R. Yosé, "And is it not necessary to say the prayer of Separation [between the sanctity of the seventh year and the new year which is now begun]?"

[B]   He said to him, "They already stated such a prayer of Separation at the New Year itself [when the seventh year came to an end]."

Unit **I** explains the selection of the cited verses of Scripture, and unit **II** asks about the omission of a prayer one might expect to find.

8:1

[22b/A] *The anointed for battle, when he speaks to the people, in the Holy Language did he speak,*

[B] *as it is said, "And it shall come to pass when you draw near to the battle, that the priest shall approach [this is the priest anointed for battle] and shall speak to the people [in the Holy Language] and shall say to them, 'Hear, O Israel, you draw near to battle this day' " (Deut. 20:2–3)—*

[C] *"against your enemies" (Deut. 20:3)—and not against your brothers,*

[D] *not Judah against Simeon, nor Simeon against Benjamin.*

[E] *For if you fall into their [Israelites'] hand, they will have mercy for you.*

[I.A] The anointed for battle—why [does he speak in the Holy Language]?

[B] Because it is written, "shall speak" (Deut. 20:2).

[C] But lo, there is the case of the recitation of the *Shema,* in which regard, lo, it is written, "And you shall speak of them" (Deut. 6:7), and it [the *Shema*] may be recited in any language.

[D] But the reason is that it is written [in regard to the speech of the anointed for battle], "Saying" (Deut. 20:2).

[E] Now lo, there is the pericope of the confession in regard to tithes [cited above, in which regard, lo, "speaking" is mentioned. Yet it may be said in any language [just like the *Shema*].

199

[F]   Said R. Haggai, "In the present context, 'drawing near' is
       mentioned. And yet in another context, 'drawing near' appears
       as follows: 'And the priests, the sons of Levi, shall draw near
       . . .' (Deut. 21:5). Just as 'drawing near' stated in that latter
       context requires use of the Holy Language, so here it requires
       use of the Holy Language."

[G]   Up to this point [the answer has been supplied] in accord with
       the principle of R. Aqiba, who maintains that when language is
       repeated, it is for the purpose of encompassing yet another
       matter.

[H]   But in accord with the view of R. Ishmael, who says that when
       language is repeated, it is merely a stylistic trait [bearing no ex-
       egetical consequences, how is the matter to be explained]?

[I]   Said R. Hiyya bar Abba, "Here, the language of 'drawing near'
       is used. And in yet another context, 'drawing near' appears as
       follows: 'Moses drew near to the thick darkness where God
       was' (Ex. 20:21). Just as 'drawing near' stated in the latter con-
       text requires use of the Holy Language, so here it requires use
       of the Holy Language."

[II.A] [At issue in what follows is the logical sequence of verses.
       Deut. 20:9 states, "When the officers have made an end of
       speaking to the people, then commanders shall be appointed at
       the head of the people." Logically, the commanders should be
       appointed, then they should speak.] Is it not logical that [first
       comes], "Commanders shall be appointed at the head of the
       people," and then, "The priest shall draw near and speak to
       the people" (Deut. 20:3)?

[B]   The one who arrays them for battle [does so] and then he ad-
       dresses them.

[C]   [It must follow that] the Scripture does not follow [chronologi-
       cal] order [in this matter].

[III.A] At the frontier you must say, the officer listens to what the
       priest says and he repeats it in all the languages [spoken by the
       troops]. But in the battle lines [the priest speaks, without hav-
       ing his message repeated, because the troops are busy] provid-
       ing water and food for themselves and repairing the lines of
       communication.

[B]   R. Haggai raised the question, "Just as you maintain that at
       the frontier the officer listens to what the priest says and re-

peats it in all the languages [spoken by the troops], why should
you not say that also in the battle lines the same procedure is
followed?"

[C]   R. Hiyya bar Ada objected, "Is it not logical that first comes,
'When the officers have made an end of speaking to the people'
(Deut. 20:9), then follows, 'The priest shall draw near and
speak to the people' (Deut. 20:2)?"

[D]   He said to him, "Scripture does not follow [chronological or-
der], and consequently one may not draw any conclusions from
the order which it does follow."

Unit I takes up the basic proposition that Hebrew is used. Unit
II points out that the verses under discussion do not follow the
logical order of the events they describe. Unit III then builds
on that same proposition. Only unit I closely relates to the
Mishnah.

8:2

[A]   *As it is said, "And the men which have been called by name*
rose up and took the captives and with the spoil clothed all that
were naked among them and arrayed them and put shoes on
their feet and gave them food to eat and something to drink and
carried all the feeble of them upon asses and brought them to
Jericho, the city of palm trees, unto their brethren. Then they
returned to Samaria" (2 Chron. 28:15).

[B]   *"Against your enemies" do you go forth.*

[C]   *For if you fall into their hand, they will not have mercy upon*
you.

[I.A]   [The cited verse provides an example of the mercy of the Israelites for the Judeans. What is striking is that some of the
chiefs of the Ephraimites stood up against the troops coming
back with the captives and protested. In this regard,] said R.
Yohanan, "Whoever is not like these [chiefs of the Ephraimites,] who had the means to object [to the sinful act, and to
make their objection stick,] should not object."

[B]   R. Aha in the name of R. Yohanan: "Just as it is a religious
duty to speak out in a case in which what one says will be car-

ried out, so it is a religious duty not to speak out in a case in which what one says will not be carried out."

[C]   Said R. Eleazar, "Just as it is prohibited to declare what is unclean to be clean, so it is prohibited to declare what is clean to be unclean."

[D]   R. Ba bar Jacob in the name of R. Yohanan, "If a case of law comes to hand, in which you do not know whether [to declare something unclean and so to order it to be] burned or whether to hold the item in suspense, under all circumstances you should choose the alternative of burning more than that of holding the matter in suspense.

[E]   "For there is no offering in the Torah more beloved than the offering of bullocks which are to be burned and goats which are to be burned, and, it is clear, they are disposed of by burning up."

[F]   R. Yosé raised the question, "Do they learn the rule governing a matter the religious duty of which is not in so doing, from a matter the religious duty of which indeed is in so doing? [That is, the religious duty concerning the bullocks and goats is to burn them up. But no religious duty attends upon burning up what is not definitely unclean.]"

The main point is that one should not take up futile causes; let people sin unknowingly, rather than telling them they sin, if they will not listen. This has nothing to do with the Mishnah.

8:3

[A]   *"Let not your heart be faint, fear not, nor tremble, neither be afraid" (Deut. 20:3).*

[B]   *"Let not your heart be faint" on account of the neighing of the horses and the flashing of the swords.*

[C]   *"Fear not" at the clashing of shields and the rushing of the tramping shoes.*

[D]   *"Nor tremble" at the sound of the trumpets.*

[E]   *"Neither be afraid" at the sound of the shouting.*

[F]   *"For the Lord your God is with you" (Deut. 20:4)—*

[G]   *they come with the power of mortal man, but you come with the power of the Omnipresent.*

[H]   *The Philistines came with the power of Goliath. What was his end? In the end he fell by the sword, and they fell with him.*

[I]   *The Ammonites came with the power of Shobach (2 Sam. 10:16]. What was his end? In the end he fell by the sword, and they fell with him.*

[J]   *But you are not thus: "For the Lord your God is he who goes with you to fight for you"*

[K]   *(—this is the camp of the ark).*

[I.A] It is written, "Out of the brightness before him there broke through his clouds hailstones and coals of fire. [The Lord also thundered in the heavens, and the Most High uttered his voice, hailstones and coals of fire]" (Ps. 18:12–13).

[B]   [Following the text and translation of Lauterbach, *Mekhilta* 1. 212–13:] "His thick clouds" as against their squadrons.

[C]   "Hailstones" as against their catapults.

[D]   "Coals" as against their missiles.

[E]   "Fire" as against their naphtha.

[F]   "The Lord also thundered in the heavens" as against the clasping of their shields and the noise of their trampling shoes.

[G]   [Yerushalmi, Leiden MS, and *editio princeps* lack:] "And the Most High uttered his voice," as against their whetting the swords.

[H]   "And he sent out his arrows, and scattered them" (Ps. 18:14) as against their arrows.

[I]   "And he shot forth lightnings, and routed them" (Ps. 18:14). This teaches that the arrows would scatter them.

[J]   Said R. Ba bar Kahana, "This teaches that they would form units, and the arrows scattered them, and the lightning would make them huddle together again."

[K]   "Lightning," as against their swords.

[L]   "He routed them." He routed them and confused them and threw down their signals.

[M]   Rabbi says, "The word 'routed them' means only pestilence, along the lines of the following: 'And shall discomfort them with great pestilence until they are destroyed' " (Deut. 7:23).

[II.A]   "[For the Lord your God is he that goes with you, to fight for you against your enemies,] to give you the victory" (Deut. 20:4).

[B]   *This is the camp of the ark [M. 8:3J–K].*

[C]   And some say, "This refers to the Name which is placed in the ark."

[D]   For it has been taught [following Tosefta's version]: **R. Judah b. Laqish says, "There were two arks with Israel in the wilderness; one which went out with them to battle, and one which stayed with them in the camp.**

[E]   **"In the one which went out with them to battle there was a scroll of the Torah, as it is said, 'And the ark of the covenant of the Lord went before them three days' journey' (Num. 10:33).**

[F]   **"And this one which stayed with them in the camp, this is the one in which were the tablets and the sherds of the tablets, as it is said, 'Neither the ark of the covenant of the Lord, nor Moses, departed out of the camp' " (Num. 14:44) [T. Sot. 7:18].**

[G]   And rabbis say, "There was only one. It went forth to battle one time, in the days of [22c] Eli, [and] it was captured."

[H]   The following verse of Scripture supports the position of rabbis: "[And the Philistines said,] 'Woe to us! For nothing like this has happened before. Woe to us! Who can deliver us from the power of these mighty gods?' " (1 Sam. 4:7–8).

[I]   This was something they had never seen in their entire lives.

[J]   The following verse of Scripture supports the position of R. Judah b. Laqish: "And Saul said to Ahijah, 'Bring hither the ark of God.' [For the ark of God went at that time with the people of Israel]" (1 Sam. 14:18).

[K]   Now was the ark not in Qiriat Yearim? [Yes! Thus there must have been two arks.]

[L]   How do the rabbis interpret the verse just now cited?

[M]   They say that Saul said, "Bring me the frontlet."

[N]   A [further] verse of Scripture supports the position of R. Judah b. Laqish: "Uriah said to David, 'The ark, Israel, and Judah dwell in booths; . . . shall I then go into my house . . . ?' " (2 Sam. 11:11).

[O]   Now was the ark not in Zion [normally]? [Hence it had been taken into battle.]

[P]   How do the rabbis interpret the verse just now cited?

[Q]   [The ark was kept] in a booth which was covered over but used only temporarily, for the Temple had not yet been built at that time.

[III.A]   [Following the Tosefta's version:] **The bottle containing the manna, the flask of the anointing oil, the staff of Aaron, with its almonds and blossoms, and the chest sent as a gift when the Philistines return the Glory of Eli the God of Israel—all of them are in the house of the Most Holy of Holies.**

[B]   **When the ark was stored away, they were stored away with it [T. Yom. 2:15].**

[C]   Who stored it away?

[D]   It was Josiah. When he saw that it was written, "The Lord will bring you and your king . . . to a nation that neither you nor your fathers have known" (Deut. 28:36), [he decided to do so].

[E]   This is in line with the following verse of Scripture: "And he said to the Levites who taught all Israel and who were holy to the Lord, 'Put the holy ark in the house which Solomon the son of David, king of Israel, built; you need no longer carry it upon your shoulders' " (2 Chron. 35:3).

[F]   He said, "If it goes into exile with you to Babylonia, you are not going to bring it back to its place. But: 'Now serve the Lord your God and his people Israel' " (2 Chron. 35:3).

[G]   The flask of anointing oil: "Take the finest spices: of liquid myrrh five hundred shekels, and of sweet-smelling cinnamon half as much, that is, two hundred and fifty, and of aromatic cane two hundred and fifty, and of cassia five hundred, according to the shekel of the sanctuary, and of olive oil a *hin*" (Ex. 30:23–24).

[H]   The *hin* contains twelve *logs* of liquid measure.

[I]   "In this [oil] they seethed the roots," the words of R. Meir.

[J]   R. Judah says, "One would seethe them in water and then put oil on them. When the water would absorb the scent, one would then remove them, as the perfumers do."

[K]   This is in line with that which is written, "And you shall make of these a sacred anointing oil, blended as by the perfumer; a holy anointing oil it shall be" (Ex. 30:25).

[L]   ["It will be"]—this refers for all generations to come (cf. Ex. 30:37).

[M]   It was taught: R. Judah b. R. Ilai says, "With the anointing oil which Moses made in the wilderness miracles were done from beginning to end [Y. Hor. 3:2 **X**.N–JJ = M–R, **IV**.A–U].

[N]   "For at the outset there were only twelve *log*s, as it is said, '. . . and of olive oil, a *hin*' (Ex. 30:24).

[O]   "Now if there was not sufficient oil for putting oil on the wood, how much the more so [that the oil was insufficient for much else]!

[P]   "And yet the fire fed on it, the wood fed on it, the pot fed on it,

[Q]   "with it were anointed the tabernacle and all its utensils, the table and all its utensils, the lampstand and all its utensils;

[R]   "with it were anointed Aaron and his sons for all the seven days of consecration;

[S]   "from it were anointed high priests and kings. [And yet it sufficed (see **IV**.D)!]"

[**IV**.A]   A king [anointed] at the outset [of a dynasty] requires anointing. But the son of an anointed king does not, for it is said, "Arise, anoint him; for this is he" (1 Sam. 16:12).

[B]   This one requires anointing. But his son does not require anointing.

[C]   But a high priest who is son of a high priest requires anointing, even down to the tenth successive generation.

[D]   Now the whole [of the twelve *hin* of oil] will remain for the age to come, for it is said, "It will be holy anointing oil for all your generations" (Ex. 30:31).

[E]   They anoint kings only over a spring, as it is said, "Cause Solomon my son to ride on my own mule, and bring him down to Gihon; and let Zadok the priest and Nathan the prophet there anoint him king over Israel" (1 Kings 1:33–34).

[F]   They anoint a king who is son of a king only on account of dissension.

[G]   Why was Solomon anointed at all? Because of the struggle with Adonijah; Joash, because of Athaliah; Jehu, because of Joram.

[H]   Now is it not written, "Rise, anoint him; for this is he" (1 Sam. 16:12)?

[I]   This one requires anointing, but the kings of Israel do not require anointing.

[J]   But Jehoahaz, because of Jehoiakim, his brother, who was two years older than he, [was anointed].

[K]   Now did not Josiah hide [the anointing oil away; so where did they get it]?

[L]   You must say, they anointed him with oil from a balsam tree.

[M]   They anoint kings only from a horn. Saul and Jehu, who were anointed from a cruse, had a transient reign. David and Solomon, who were anointed from a horn, had an enduring reign.

[N]   They do not anoint priests as kings.

[O]   R. Judah of Ein-Todros: "This is on account of the verse which states, 'The sceptre shall not depart from Judah' " (Gen. 49:10).

[P]   Said R. Hiyya b. Adda, " '[That he may not turn aside from the commandment . . . ,] so that he may continue long in his kingdom, he and his children, in Israel' (Deut. 17:20). What is written thereafter? 'The Levitical priests, that is, all the tribe of Levi, shall have no portion or inheritance with Israel' " (Deut. 18:1).

[Q]   Said R. Yohanan: "Johanan is the same as Jehoahaz."

[R]   And is it not written, "The sons of Josiah, Johanan the first-born" (1 Chron. 3:15)—first born to rule?

[S] And is it not written, "The second Jehoiakim, the third Zedekiah, the fourth Shallum"? Zedekiah was third for the throne, and fourth in order of birth.

[T] He was called Zedekiah, because he accepted the righteousness of the harsh decree.

[U] Shallum was so called for in his time the household of David fulfilled its time.

[V] His name was not really Shallum, nor was it Zedekiah, but it was Mattaniah,

[W] as it is written, "And the king of Babylonia made Mattaniah, Jehoiachin's uncle, king in his stead, and changed his name to Zedekiah" (2 Kings 24:17).

[V.A] Said R. Yohanan, "The ark was made in accord with the measure of a cubit of six handbreadths."

[B] Who taught that it was a cubit of six handbreadths?

[C] It is R. Meir.

[D] For we have learned: *R. Meir says, "All the cubit measures were middle sized [except for the golden altar, the horns, the circuit, and the base of the altar]" [M. Kel. 17:10A].*

[E] In the view of R. Meir, who has said that the ark was made in accord with a cubic measure of six handbreadths, the length of the ark was fifteen, as it is written, "They shall make an ark of acacia wood; two cubits and a half shall be its length, a cubit and a half its breadth, and a cubit and a half its height" (Ex. 25:10).

[F] Thus a cubit is six, another cubit is six, and half a cubit is three.

[G] And there were four tables of the law in it, two broken ones, two unbroken ones.

[H] This is in line with that which is written, "[And I will write on the tables the words that were on the first tables] which you broke, and you shall put them [the broken tables] in the ark" (Deut. 10:2).

[I] And each of the tablets of the law was six handbreadths long, and three wide.

[J]   Place the tablets breadthwise along the length of the ark, and there will then remain three handbreadths. Assign half a handbreadth to each wall, and two handbreadths will remain for the scroll of the Torah.

[K]   Allow the surplus of three handbreadths [over the space occupied by the tablets] for the balcony.

[L]   The breadth of the ark is nine handbreadths, as it is written, "A cubit and a half its breadth" (Ex. 25:10).

[M]   Now there were four tablets in it, two broken and two unbroken, as it is written, ". . . which you broke, and you shall put them in the ark" (Deut. 10:2).

[N]   Each of the tablets was six handbreadths long.

[O]   Place the tablets lengthwise across the breadth of the ark.

[P]   Three handbreadths will then remain, half a handbreadth on each side, for handling the tablets.

[Q]   The place in which they deposit the scroll of the Torah is two cubits.

[R]   R. Simeon b. Laqish said, "The ark was made in accord with a cubit of five handbreadths."

[S]   What Tanna maintains that it was one of five handbreadths?

[T]   It was R. Judah.

[U]   For we have learned there: *R. Judah says, "The cubit of the Temple building was six handbreadths, and of utensils, five"* [M. Kel. 17:10B].

[V]   Now the ark is a utensil.

[W]   In accord with the view of R. Judah, who has said that the ark was made in accord with a cubit of the measure of five handbreadths, the ark was twelve and a half handbreadths,

[X]   for it is written, "They shall make an ark . . . two cubits and a half shall be its length, a cubit and a half its breadth, and a cubit and a half its height" (Ex. 25:10).

[Y]   A cubit is five, another cubit is five, and half a cubit is two and a half.

[Z]   Now four tablets were in it, two broken, and two unbroken, as it is written, ". . . which you broke, and you shall put them in the ark" (Deut. 10:2).

[AA]   Each of the tables of the law was six handbreadths long and three wide.

[BB]   Place the tablets breadthwise along the long side of the ark, and there then will remain a half handbreadth, a finger's breadth for the wall on one side, and a finger's breadth for the wall on the other side.

[CC]   Now the breadth of the ark was seven handbreadths and a half, as it is written, "A cubit and half its breadth" (Ex. 25:10).

[DD]   A cubit is five handbreadths, and half a cubit is two and a half.

[22d/   Now there were four tablets in it, two broken and two un-
EE]   broken, as it is written, ". . . which you broke, and you shall put them in the ark" (Deut. 10:2).

[FF]   Each of the tablets was six handbreadths long and three broad.

[GG]   Place the tablets lengthwise across the breadth of the ark.

[HH]   There will then remain a handbreadth and a half, a finger breadth for the wall on this side, and a finger breadth for the wall on that side.

[II]   Then there will be half a handbreadth on this side, and half a handbreadth on that side, for handling.

[VI.A] How did Bezallel make the ark?

[B]   R. Haninah said, "He made three boxes, two of gold, one of wood. He put the one of gold into one of wood, and the one of wood into the other one of gold, and he covered it over.

[C]   "This is in line with that which is written, 'And you shall over-lay it with pure gold, within and without you shall overlay it, and you shall make upon it a molding of gold round about' " (Ex. 25:11).

[D]   Why does Scripture say, "You will overlay it"?

[E]   It encompasses the upper lip.

[F]   R. Simeon b. Laqish said, "He made a single box and covered it over."

[G]   This is in line with that which is written, "And you shall overlay it with pure gold, within and without you shall overlay it."

[H]   Why does Scripture say, "You will overlay it"?

[I]   R. Pinhas says, "To encompass the space between the boards."

[VII.A]   How were the tablets laid out?

[B]   R. Hananiah b. Gamaliel says, "Five commandments were on
one side, and five on the other tablet."

[C]   Rabbis say, "Ten were on one tablet, and ten were on the
other."

[D]   This is in line with that which is written, "And he declared to
you his covenant, which he commanded you to perform, that
is, the ten commandments; and he wrote them upon two tables
of stone" (Deut. 4:13).

[E]   "Ten on this tablet, ten on that one."

[F]   R. Simeon b. Yohai says, "There were twenty on this tablet
and twenty on that one."

[G]   This is in line with that which is written, "And he declared to
you his covenant which he commanded you to perform, that is,
the tens of commandments,"—twenty on this tablet and twenty
on that one.

[H]   R. Simai says, "There were forty on this tablet and forty on
that one.

[I]   "They corresponded to one another as a tetragon [four-sided
figure]."

[J]   Hananiah, nephew of R. Joshua, says, "Between each one of
the commandments were its details and refinements.

[K]   " '[His arms are rounded gold, set with jewels. His body is
ivory work,] encrusted with sapphires' (Song of Sol. 5:14)—

[L]   "Like the great sea."

[M]   R. Simeon b. Laqish, when he would reach this verse, would
say, "Well did you teach me, Hananiah, nephew of R. Joshua.

[N]   "Just as in the great sea, between one great wave and another
are small swells, so between each commandment were the details and refinements of the Torah [written out]."

[**VIII**.A] Said R. Tanhuma, "I raised the question before R. Pinhas, 'The law should be in accord with the view of R. Judah, and not in accord with the view of R. Meir.'

[B] "What is the Scriptural basis for the position of R. Judah? 'Take this book of the law, and put it by the side of the ark of the covenant of the Lord your God, that it may be there for a witness against you' (Deut. 31:26).

[C] "In the opinion of R. Judah, who said this, where was the scroll of the Torah? It was set in a kind of chest, which they made for it outside [of the ark], and there the scroll of the Torah was kept. [So he can make sense of the verse.]"

[D] "What is the Scriptural basis for the position of R. Meir?

[E] " 'And you shall put the mercy seat on the top of the ark; and in the ark you shall put the testimony that I shall give you' (Ex. 25:21).

[F] "In the view of [read:] R. Judah, who maintains that considerations of temporal sequence do not apply in the Torah, [the verse cited by Meir poses no problems]. Why not?

[G] " 'And in the ark you shall put the testimony that I shall give you' (Ex. 25:21).

[H] "And afterward: 'And you shall put the mercy seat on the top of the ark' (Ex. 25:21). [Judah can interpret this language in accord with his position (Qorban ha'edah).]"

[**IX**.A] R. Pinhas in the name of R. Simeon b. Laqish, "The Torah which the Holy One, blessed be he, gave—the hide on which it is written is white fire.

[B] "The letters with which it is engraved are black fire.

[C] "It is fire, surrounded with fire, engraved out of fire, and set in fire.

[D] " 'With flaming fire at his right hand' " (Deut. 33:2).

The general theme of the Mishnah, that God is with the Israelite forces, accounts for the inclusion of unit **I**. Unit **II** takes up the Mishnah's language, pursuing its own interests. Unit **III** (**IX**) then moves off in a quite new direction, sharing with the Mishnah the topic of the ark, but nothing else. Once more the

Talmud presents what is essentially an anthology on a single theme, spun out every which way.

8:4

[A] *"And the officers shall speak to the people, saying, 'What man is there who has built a new house and has not dedicated it? Let him go and return to his house' "* (Deut. 20:5).

[B] *All the same are the ones who build a new house, a house for straw, a house for cattle, a house for wood, and a house for storage.*

[C] *All the same are the ones who build it, who purchase it, who inherit it, and to whom it is given as a gift.*

[I.A] "Who has built a house."

[B] I know that the law encompasses only one who has built a house.

[C] If he *purchased it, inherited it, or was given it as a gift* [M. 8:4C], how do I know [that the same law applies]?

[D] Scripture says "The man . . . who is the man. . . ."

[E] How do I know that the same law applies to a building *a house for straw, cattle, wood, or storage [M. 8:4B]?*

[F] Scripture says, "Who has built," that is, a building of any sort.

[G] Is it possible to suppose that the law applies to him who builds *a gate house, portico, or porch,* so that he should go home [cf. M. 8:7B]?

[H] Scripture says, "A house."

[I] Just as a house is characterized by the fact that it serves as a dwelling place, so these are excluded, for they do not serve as a dwelling place.

[II.A] This further excludes a house which is not four cubits square [at the very least].

[B] For it has been taught: A house which is not four cubits square is exempt from the requirements of having a parapet and from having a *mezuzah,*

[C]   from being covered by the intermingling of ownership of houses in a courtyard for purposes of permitting carrying in the courtyard on the Sabbath,

[D]   and [for the purpose of tithe, entry into such a house does not constitute] the beginning of liability of food to the separation of tithes [since it is not regarded as a normal dwelling place, entry into which subjects agricultural produce to the obligation for separation of tithes].

[E]   And they do not assign four cubits [of free use to the owner] at its doorway.

[F]   And they do not treat it as joined to a city [for purposes of measuring Sabbath limits].

[G]   And he who vows against making use of a house is permitted to dwell in such a place.

[H]   And ownership of it does not permanently fall to the holder in the Jubilee year.

[I]   And it is not subject to uncleanness by reason of a *nega* [such as is described at Lev. 14].

[J]   And the owner of such a house does not return to it, [if he just built it, by reason of the draft exemption].

[III.A]   Why does Scripture say, "who has built"?

[B]   It means to exclude one whose house fell down and who then rebuilt it.

[C]   Said R. Yosé, "Along these same lines, he who remarries a woman whom he has divorced likewise does not go home [as exempt from battle]."

[IV.A]   Is it possible to suppose that he who builds a house outside of the land should go back [in time of war]?

[B]   Scripture says, "And has not dedicated it."

[C]   The one who is subject to the religious requirement of dedicating the house is subject to the law, excluding this one, who is not subject to the religious duty of dedicating the house.

[V.A]   If one has built a house and rented it out to others, and the latter paid the rent in advance, lo, this is as if he has dedicated it, [and he stays in the battle line].

[B]   If the tenant paid the rent after twelve months, the owner is in the status of one who has not dedicated the house.

[C]   If one built a house and locked it up as a storage unit for his possessions, if in the house were possessions which one usually leaves unguarded, it is as if he has dedicated the house [and is now deemed to dwell therein], and if not, it is not as if he has dedicated the house.

Unit **I** goes over the Scriptural foundations for the Mishnah's law. Unit **II** intersects the theme at **II.J**, but its interest is in the house of less than minimal dimensions. Unit **III** then reverts to the exercise of unit **I**, and so does unit **IV**. Units **IV** and **V** clarify the matter of dedicating the house, which expands on an item only tangential to the Mishnah.

8:5

[A]   *"And who is the man who has planted a vineyard and has not used the fruit thereof?" (Deut. 20:6)—*

[B]   *All the same are the ones who plant a vineyard and who plant five fruit trees,*

[C]   *and even if they are of five different kinds.*

[D]   *And all the same are the ones who plant such a tree, who sink them into the ground, and who graft them.*

[E]   *And all the same are the ones who buy a vineyard, and who inherit it, and to whom it is given as a gift.*

[**I**.A]   "Who has planted."

[B]   I know only that the law applies to one who has planted the vineyard.

[C]   If he bought it, inherited it, or received it as a gift [M. 8:5E], how do I know [that the law applies to him too]?

[D]   Scripture says, "The man . . . who is the man."

[E]   How do I know that the law applies to one who plants five trees, *fruit trees, even of five different kinds* [M. 8:5C]?

[F]   Scripture says, "Who has planted . . ."—any sort of planting [being taken into consideration].

[G]   Is it possible to suppose that if one has planted four fruit trees or five unproductive trees, he should go home?

[H]   Scripture says, "A vineyard."

[I]   Just as a vineyard is defined by the characteristic of being made up of five vines, so this one is excluded, which is not made up of five vines.

[II.A]   Now as to wine straight from the vat, that is, sharp wine—they prepare a symbolic meal for the intermingling of the Sabbath boundaries with it;

[B]   and they prepare a symbolic meal for joining ownership for an alleyway with it;

[C]   and they bless over it [for the sanctification of the Sabbath];

[D]   and they call one to share in the grace after meals over it;

[E]   and they say the prayers of sanctification for a bride over it;

[F]   and they say the blessing of comfort to a mourner over it;

[G]   and it is sold in a shop as wine;

[H]   and he who sells wine to his fellow without further specification as to its character may not sell him sharp wine;

[I]   and it is prohibited to give instruction or to release vows if one has drunk that sort of wine [which is inebriating];

[J]   but as to entering the sanctuary, the only prohibition is that one may not serve at the altar [if one has drunk that kind of wine].

[K]   And as to the wine to be drunk by the son deemed to be a rebellious and incorrigible son, it is necessary to inquire whether or not this kind of wine serves [to incur liability].

[III.A]   Is it possible to suppose that he who plants a vineyard outside of the land should return [home as exempt from battle]?

[B]   Scripture says, "And has not used the fruit thereof."

[C]   One who is under the religious obligation to use the fruit thereof is liable, excluding this one, who is not under the religious requirement to use the fruit thereof.

[**IV**.A]   It was taught [in the Tosefta's version]: **All the same are the one who plants a vineyard and the one who plants five fruit trees of five different kinds, even in five distinct rows—lo, such a one goes home [M. 8:5B–C].**

[B]   **R. Eliezer b. Jacob says, "I find implied in this Scripture only one who has planted a vineyard"** [T. Sot. 7:18].

[C]   And along these same lines: implied in this Scripture is only one who has planted.

[D]   It was taught: "And has not eaten the fruit thereof . . . ," thus excluding the one who sinks a root into the ground or grafts a root [who has already eaten the produce of that plant, and who therefore does not qualify for the exemption].

[E]   Said R. Yohanan, "That statement represents the view of R. Eliezer b. Jacob [at B, C]."

[F]   Said R. Hisda, "It represents the opinion of all parties."

[G]   [The cited teaching, C, declaring that it is forbidden to go home if one has sunk a root or grafted a branch] applies to the case of his having grafted a branch of a fruit onto another sort of tree, in which case the produce will be subject to a transgression.

[H]   How shall we interpret the matter [of a dispute as to being permitted grafting]?

[I]   If it applies to a case in which one has grafted a branch of one sort of fruit tree onto a fruit tree of another species, the produce will be subject to transgression.

[J]   And if he grafted a branch of a fruit tree onto an unproductive tree, of the same species, then it is in the status of one who plants a tree at the outset [in which case the man does go home].

[K]   But we must interpret the dispute to concern a case in which one has grafted a branch of a black fig tree onto a white fig tree.

[**V**.A]   When does he make use of the fruit [deeming the tree to be beyond the prohibited years when its fruit may not be utilized, that is, when it is the fourth year]? [At issue is the interpretation of the following verses: "When you come into the land and plant all kinds of trees for food, then you shall count their fruit as forbidden to you. . . . And in the fourth year all their fruit shall be holy . . . but in the fifth year you may eat of their fruit" (Lev. 19:23–25).]

[B]   In the fourth year and in the fifth? [That is, the produce is forbidden for three years. In the fourth year the produce is in the status of fourth-year fruit, which must be eaten in Jerusalem in accord with the laws governing second tithe. Now the issue is when we deem the produce to be routinely utilized? Is it in the fourth year, or the fifth?]

[C]   It is reasonable to suppose that it is in the fifth year.

[D]   But in the fourth year, one is liable to make up the value of the produce of the tree [if one makes use of it, and one must spend the money one sets aside in that connection in Jerusalem].

[E]   And rabbis of Caesarea say, "It is reasonable to suppose that it is only in the fourth year.

[F]   "For it is written, 'And in the fourth year all their fruit shall be holy, an offering of praise to the Lord' " (Lev. 19:24).

Unit **I** presents an account of the Scriptural basis for the Mishnah's law. I cannot account for the inclusion of unit **II**, except as a parallel to Y. 8:4 **II**. Unit **III** runs parallel to Y. 8:4 **IV**. Unit **IV** introduces a relevant passage of the Tosefta and compares its views to those of the Mishnah. Unit **V** is completely out of place here, except for its interest in the point at which one is permitted to use the fruit of a tree one has planted.

8:6

[A]   *"And who is the man who has betrothed a wife" (Deut 20:7)—*

[B]   *All the same are the one who betroth a virgin and who betroth a widow—*

[C]   *and even a childless brother's widow who awaits the levir.*

[D]   *And even if one heard during the battle that his brother had died,*

[E]   *he returns and comes along home.*

[F]   *All these listen to the words of the priest concerning the arrangements of battle and go home.*

[G]   *And they provide water and food and keep the roads in good repair.*

[I.A]   "Who has betrothed a wife"—

[B]   I know only that that applies to a virgin male who marries a virgin female.

[C]   How do I know that it applies to a virgin male who marries a widow?

[D]   A widower who married a virgin?

[E]   Scripture says, "A woman"—of any sort.

[F]   Why does Scripture say, "New" (Deut. 20:5)?

[G]   It is to exclude one who takes back a woman whom he has previously divorced [cf. Y. 8:4 III.C].

[H]   Said R. Yosé, "That is to say [23c], He who marries a woman incapable of producing offspring, since it is not a religious duty to dwell with her, may not go back."

[II.A] **[All the same are he who betroths and he who enters into levirate marriage],** *and even if there is a woman awaiting levirate marriage with one of five brothers [M. 8:6B–D];* **and even if there are five brothers who heard that their brother had died in battle, all of them return and come home [T. Sot. 7:19].**

[B]   And along these same lines, may we say that even if there is a new house, not dedicated, belonging to five brothers, [all five should go home]?

[C]   There not each one of the five is able to live therein [but only one of them], while here, in the case of the childless widow, any one of the brothers is suitable to enter into levirate marriage with her.

[D]   [The case of the Mishnah's law, therefore is not parallel.]

[III.A] If one has betrothed a woman for an interval of twelve months, and the time has run out [so that he is to marry her] while he is in battle, he picks himself up and goes along home.

Once again, unit **I** provides the analysis of the Scriptural foundations for the Mishnah's law. Unit **II** takes up the conundrum of the Mishnah. Unit **III** augments the rule.

8:7

[A]   *And these are the ones who do not return home.*

[B]   *He who builds a gatehouse, a portico, or a porch;*

[C]   *He who plants only four fruit trees or five barren trees;*

[D]   *he who remarries a woman whom he has divorced,*

[E]   *or [he who marries] a widow in the case of a high priest, a divorcée or a woman who has undergone the rite of halisah in the case of an ordinary priest, or a mamzeret or a Netinah in the case of an Israelite, or an Israelite girl in the case of a mamzer or a Netin—*

[F]   *such a one does not go home.*

[G]   *R. Judah says, "Also: He who builds his house on its original foundation does not go home."*

[H]   *R. Eleazar says, "Also: He who builds a house of bricks in the Sharon does not go home."*

[I.A]   It was taught: **[(If) his house fell down and he built it up again, lo, this one goes home].**

[B]   **R. Judah says, "If he did something new in connection with the house, he goes home, but if not, he does not go home"** [cf. M. 8:7G] [T. Sot. 7:18H].

[C]   [If] he merely plastered the house with mortar or opened new windows in its walls, he does not go home.

[D]   [If] it was a large house, and he made it a small one,

[E]   [if] it was one and he subdivided it into two, [he goes home].

[II.A]   It was taught: **R. Eliezer says, "The men of the Sharon did not go home to their houses, because they do something new to their houses once a week"** [M. 8:7H] [T. Sot. 7:18I].

[B]   So too did the high priest pray for them on the Day of Atonement, that their houses should not be turned into their graves.

The Talmud merely cites and glosses the Tosefta relevant to the Mishnah.

8:8

[A] *And these are the ones who [to begin with] do not move from their place:*

[B] *He who has [just now] built a house and dedicated it, who has planted a vineyard and used its fruits, who has married the girl whom he has betrothed, or who has consummated the marriage of his childless brother's widow,*

[C] *since it is said, "He shall be free for his house one year" (Deut. 24:5)—*

[D] *"For his house"—this is his house.*

[E] *"Will be"—this refers to his vineyard.*

[F] *"And shall cheer his wife"—this applies to his own wife.*

[G] *"Whom he has acquired"—to include even his childless brother's widow.*

[H] *These do not [even] have to provide water and food and see to the repair of the road.*

[I.A] [In the Tosefta's version:] **I know only that the law applies to one who builds his house but has not dedicated it, planted a vineyard but has not eaten the fruit, betrothed a wife but has not taken her.**

[B] **How do we know that if one has built a house and dedicated it, but has not lived in it twelve months [M. 8:8B], planted a vineyard and eaten its fruit, but has not had the use of it for twelve months, betrothed a wife and taken her, but has not dwelt with her for twelve months—how do we know that these do not move from their place [M. 8:8A]?**

[C] **Scripture says, "When a man is newly married, he shall not go out with the army or be charged with any business; he shall be free at home one year, to be happy with his wife whom he has taken" (Deut. 24:5).**

[D]   **This matter was covered by the general principle, and why has it been explicitly stated? To allow for the imposition of an analogy on its basis, so teaching you:**

[E]   **Now just as this one is distinguished in having betrothed a wife and taken her but not having lived with her for twelve months, that he does not move from his place, so all of them are subject to the same rule [T. Sot. 7:20].**

[II.A] It was taught: **All those concerning whom they have said, They do not go forth at all, for example, he who has built a house and dedicated it but has not lived in it for twelve months, planted a vineyard and eaten the fruit but not made use of it for twelve months, betrothed a wife and taken her in marriage and has not remained with her twelve months [M. 8:8B]—**

[B]   **these do not pay their share of the taxes of the town, and do not provide water and food for the battle,**

[C]   **and do not repair the roads [M. 8:8H] [T. Sot. 7:24].**

[D]   For it has been said, "[When a man is newly married, he shall not go out with the army] or be charged with any business" (Deut. 24:5)—

[E]   This one is not to be charged with any business, but others may be charged with communal duties.

The Talmud again utilizes relevant materials of the Tosefta. I give the Tosefta's version for both units.

8:9

[A]   *"And the officers shall speak further unto the people, [and they shall say, What man is there who is fearful and fainthearted]? Let him return to his home" (Deut. 20:8).*

[B]   *R. Aqiba says, " 'Fearful and fainthearted'—just as it implies:*

[C]   *"He cannot stand in the battle ranks or see a drawn sword."*

[D]   *R. Yosé the Galilean says, " 'Fearful and fainthearted'—this is one who trembles on account of the transgressions which are in his hand.*

[E]   *"Therefore the Torah has connected all of these, 'so that he re-turns home because of them [and will not be publicly shamed].' "*

[F]   *R. Yosé says, "As to a widow married to a high priest, a divor-cée or woman who has undergone the rite of halisah to an ordi-nary priest, a mamzer girl or a Netinah girl married to an Israelite, an Israelite girl to a mamzer or a Netin—lo, these are the ones who are 'fearful and fainthearted.' "*

[I.A]   It is written, "And the officers shall speak further. . . ."

[B]   This means only that they add [to what already has been said, but do not contribute their own fresh ideas], like a man who says, "I add to what my master has stated [along the lines of what he has said]."

[C]   [At issue in what follows is the relationship between the mes-sage of the officers to the people, "What man is there that has built a new house . . ." (Deut. 20:5), and "The officers shall speak further to the people and say, 'What man is there that is fearful and fainthearted?' " (Deut. 20:8). Now the dispute is whether both Deut. 20:5 and Deut. 20:8 belong to the original message of the officers, or whether the former is one message, the latter a separate and distinct one given by different authori-ties.] It was taught: The latter message is of the character of an addition. [Now this statement requires explanation.]

[D]   Said R. Yosé: "There are two Tannaim [who disagree on this matter].

[E]   "One who said '[It is like a man who says,] 'I add to what my master has said' maintains that both the former message and the latter message are one and the same. The master has said them both. [The officers then simply repeat them and clarify them for the people.]

[F]   "The one who said 'The latter message derives from what is added' holds that the former message did the master state, and the latter message was said by the officer but not by the master."

[G]   Said R. Mana, "It is the view of one Tanna only. As to the former message, the master said it, and as to the latter, the of-ficer said it, and his master did not say it."

[H]   The Tannaitic teaching [which follows] is at variance with the position of R. Yosé: "One hears the pericope from the priest [in the Holy Language] and repeats it to the people in any language. [This indicates that what the officers say is precisely what they have heard from the high priest]."

[I]   The end of the same passage is at variance with R. Mana, "Yet a further message did he add." [This explicitly rejects G.]

[J]   If you say so, then there is no disagreement even with the position of R. Yosé, for it is taught: "As to the former message, the officer repeats it in line with what his master has said. As to the latter message, the officer said it, and his master did not say it [= F]"

[II.A]   It was taught: All parties have to bring proof for their claim, except this one. For testimony in support of his position is right there with him [in the evidence of his fright].

[B]   Now this view is in accord with him who said that [one should go home if] *he cannot stand in the battle ranks or see a drawn sword [M. 8:9C].*

[C]   But in accord with him who says that he is afraid by reason of the sins which he has committed [which he believes will be his downfall], he surely has to bring proof for his claim.

[D]   *Therefore the Torah has connected all of these, so that he returns home because of them [M. 8:9E],*

[E]   and will not be required to publicize his sins.

[F]   And this accords with that which R. Levi said in the name of R. Simeon b. Laqish: " 'In the place in which the burnt offering is killed the sin offering is to be killed' (Lev. 6:25).

[G]   "This is so as not to publicize [the shame of] sinners."

Unit **I** takes up the question of the relationship between the several verses of Scripture, cited in the Mishnah. The problem is the interpretation of Scripture, not of the Mishnah. Unit **II** goes over the ground of M. 8:9B–E.

8:10

[A] *"And it shall be when the officers have made an end of speaking to the people that they shall appoint captains of hosts at the head of the people (Deut. 20:9), and at the rear of the people.*

[B] *They station warriors at their head and others behind them, and iron axes are in their hand.*

[C] *And whoever wants to retreat—he has the power to break his legs.*

[D] *For the start of defeat is falling back,*

[E] *as it is written, "Israel fled before the Philistines, and there was also a great slaughter among the people" (1 Sam. 4:17).*

[F] *And further it is written, "And the men of Israel fled from before the Philistines and fell down slain" (1 Sam. 31:1).*

[G] *Under what circumstances [do the foregoing rules apply]?*

[H] *In the case of an optional war.*

[I] *But in the case of a war subject to religious requirement, everyone goes forth to battle—*

[J] *even a bridegroom from his chamber, and a bride from her marriage canopy.*

[K] *Said R. Judah, "Under what circumstances [do the foregoing rules apply]? In the case of a war subject to religious requirement.*

[L] *"But in the case of an obligatory war, everyone goes forth to battle—*

[M] *"even a bridegroom from his chamber, and a bride from her marriage canopy."*

[I.A] It is written, "And it shall be when the officers have made an end of speaking to the people that they shall appoint captains of hosts at the head of the people" (Deut. 20:9).

[B] I know only that that applies to the head of the people.

[C] How do I know that the same applies at the rear of the people [M. 8:10A]?

[D] Scripture says, ". . . and they shall be appointed" [with the "and" encompassing yet another set of officers].

[E]   Up to this point the proposition has been proved in accord with [the exegetical approach of] R. Aqiba.

[F]   [How is it shown through the exegetical approach] of R. Ishmael?

[G]   R. Ishmael accords with the view of R. Meir, for R. Meir called the end of a rope the head of the rope.

[H]   Said R. Meir, "It is written, 'The wise man has his eyes in his head, but the fool walks in darkness' " (Qoh. 2:14).

[I]   Said R. Abba Mari, "As to a wise man, while he is at the beginning of a matter he knows what will be at the end of it."

[II.A]   "Raiders shall raid Gad, but he shall raid at their heels" (Gen. 49:19).

[B]   Raiders will come and raid him, and he will raid them.

[C]   That is the meaning of the Mishnah, *For the start of defeat is falling back [M. 8:10D].*

[III.A]   R. Yohanan said, "It is the implications of language which is at issue [between M. 8:10G–J and K–M]:

[B]   **"R. Judah did call an optional war, a war subject to religious duty.**

[C]   *"But in the case of an obligatory war, everyone goes forth,*

[D]   *"even a bridegroom from his chamber and a bride from her canopy" [M. 8:10K–M] [T. Sot. 7:24].*

[E]   Said R. Hisda, "There is a dispute between them.

[F]   "Rabbis say that a war which is a religious duty is such as a war fought by David.

[G]   "A war which is obligatory is the war fought by Joshua.

[H]   "R. Judah would call an optional war such as one in which we go forth against the enemy.

[I]   "He would regard a war of obligation as one in which the enemy makes war on us."

[IV.A]   It is written, "Then King Asa made a proclamation to all Judah, none was exempt" (1 Kings 15:22).

[B]   What is the meaning of "None was exempt"?

[C]   R. Simon and rabbis—

[D]   R. Simon says, "One is not exempt to remain at home even for one moment [e.g., a husband must leave his marriage chamber]."

[E]   Rabbis say, "None was deemed a great man, son of a great man [and hence exempt from the draft]."

Unit **I** once more lays forth the Scriptural foundations for the Mishnah's rule. Unit **II** makes the point illustrative of M. 8:10D, unit **III** proceeds to explain M. 8:10G–M. Only unit **IV** is outside of the Mishnah's program.

9 Yerushalmi Sotah
Chapter Nine

9:1

[23b/A] *The rite of the heifer whose neck is to be broken is said in the Holy Language.*

[B] *since it is said, "If one be found slain in the land lying in the field . . .*

[C] *"then your elders and your judges shall come forth" (Deut. 21:1–2).*

[D] *Three from the high court in Jerusalem went forth.*

[E] *R. Judah says, "Five, since it is said, 'Your elders'—thus two, and 'your judges,' thus two, and there is no such thing as a court made up of an even number of judges, so they add to their number yet one more."*

[I.A] [The verse cited at M. 9:1B–C] is not reasonably chosen, for [the proof text can]not [be other than Deut. 21:7] "They shall answer and say."

[B] [That is so, but the reason the Mishnah has cited the verses it has is] to begin [its citation] at the beginning of the entire passage.

[II.A] "If anyone is found slain" (Deut. 21:1)—not at a time at which corpses are commonplace [that is, at a time of war].

[B] "If anyone is found slain"—and not that one should go about searching for [a corpse].

[C] "If anyone is found slain"—the language of "finding" in all instances applies only when there are witnesses present.

228

[D] "And it is not known who killed him" (Deut. 21:1)—lo, if it is known who killed him, even a slave boy or a slave girl [testifying on that matter], then they would not break the neck of the heifer.

[E] And yet you say this [that there must be witnesses, that is, C]?

[F] [No, there is no difficulty.] Here [where there are no witnesses, we speak of] the slayer, but there [where we require witnesses] it is in the case of the slain. [If there is any sort of testimony about the identity of the killer, then there is no rite. But there must be witnesses who will observe the finding of the corpse, to indicate that the conditions of finding the corpse are such as to require the rite of breaking the heifer's neck.]

[G] And as to that which you have said, "Even a slave boy or even a slave girl [may give testimony], so that they do not carry out the rite of breaking the heifer's neck," that applies in a case in which [otherwise invalid witnesses] say, "If we should see [the murderer] we should recognize [and identify] him."

[H] But in the case of those who say, "If we should see the murderer, we should not recognize and identify him," they would in any event carry out the rite of breaking the heifer's neck.

[I] [Leiden MS and *editio princeps* omit:] In the case of a court which saw the murder [and] said, "If we should see him [the murderer], we should not recognize him," they [still] do not carry out the rite of breaking the neck,"

[J] for it is written, "Neither did our eyes see it shed" (Deut. 21:7).

[K] That is to say, lo, [if] the court has seen [the murder] under any circumstances, [they do not carry out the rite].

[III.A] As to a court which witnesses the act of slaying,

[B] there are Tannaim who repeat, "Let two of them stand and testify before the others."

[C] And there are Tannaim who teach: "Let all of them stand and give testimony before a court in some other location."

[D] R. Judah b. Pazzi in the name of R. Zeira, "Just as they differed in this matter, so they differed concerning giving testimony as to the appearance of the new moon."

[E]   R. Judah bar Pazzi in the name of R. Zeira: " 'Slain'—and not writhing."

[F]   If they saw him [23c] gasping here, and came later on and did not find him at all, I say that a miracle has been done for him, and he lived.

[G]   If they saw him writhing here and came and found him dead in some other place,

[H]   in such a case they measure from the place at which he was found [and not at which he was seen writhing].

[IV.A] "In the land which the Lord your God gives you to possess" (Deut. 21:1)—excluding foreign countries.

[B]   "To possess"—excluding Jerusalem, which belongs to all the tribes.

[C]   And in accord with R. Ishmael, for R. Ishmael has said, "All references to 'coming' which are stated in the Torah refer to the time fourteen years after they were stated, seven years for the conquest, seven years for the division of the land," [how was the law carried out in the interval?]

[D]   Said R. Pinhas b. R. Bun, "It is said, 'All those fourteen years, they would mark off the places [in which the slain were found].' "

[V.A]   It has been taught: **How did they do it for him?**

[B]   **The agents of the court go forth and take markers, and they dig a hole and bury him, and they mark off his place, until they come to the high court in the hewn-stone chamber, and then they measure out [T. Sot. 9:1E–F].**

[C]   How do we know that they mark off [graves to indicate the presence of a corpse]?

[D]   R. Berekiah and R. Jacob bar Bat Jacob in the name of R. Honiah of Bart Hauran, R. Yosé said it [in the name of] R. Jacob bar Aha in the name of R. Honia of Bart Hauran, R. Hezekiah, R. Uzziel son of R. Honia of Bart Hauran in the name of R. Honayya of Bart Hauran: " 'Unclean, unclean,' shall he cry out' (Lev. 13:45)—it is so that the uncleanness [present] will call out to you and tell you, 'Keep away.' "

[E]   R. Ila in the name of R. Samuel bar Nahman: "['They will set apart men to pass through the land continually and bury those

remaining upon the face of the land, so as to cleanse it. . . .]
And when these pass through the land and any one sees a
man's bone, then he shall set up a sign by it . . .' (Ezek.
39:14–15).

[F]   "On the basis of [the reference of this passage to 'bone,'] we
learn that they mark out bones when they are found.

[G]   "On the basis of [the reference to] 'man's,' we learn that they
mark out the place in which the backbone and skull are found.

[H]   "On the basis of [the reference to] 'set up,' we learn that they
mark the spot by plastering a stone permanently thereon.

[I]   "If, in any case, you say that it is with a stone not plastered
down, it may well roll away and impart uncleanness to some
other place.

[J]   "[On the basis of the reference to] 'by it,' we learn that it is to
be set up in a clean place [in which no bone is found].

[K]   "On the basis of [the reference to] 'sign,' we learn that they
mark such a place."

[L]   If one came across a marked stone, even though that is not
how they make a permanent mark,—if one overshadows such a
stone, he is unclean. I maintain that there was a corpse buried
thereunder. [Even though the stone is to be set up not over,
but at the side of, the corpse, it is entirely possible that that is
not what was done. Accordingly, we take account of the possibility that the stone was directly over the corpse.]

[M]   [If] there were two [such stones, however], he who overshadows them is clean. [If he overshadows the ground] between
them, he is unclean.

[N]   If one was ploughing between the stones, lo, they were treated
as individual markers. [The ground] between them is clean,
but [the ground] round about each of them is unclean.

[VI.A]   It was taught: They do not make a marker on account of coming across flesh. For the flesh may be consumed [in the passage
of time, as it rots].

[B]   R. Yusta bar Shunam raised the question before R. Mana, "[If
the flesh should turn up not rotted,] will it not then result in
retroactively imparting uncleanness to clean things?"

[C]   He replied to him, "It is better that people should stumble on that account for a brief while [until the flesh rots], and not stumble on that account forever [on account of the permanent marker of uncleanness]."

[VIII.A]   There we have learned: *"The laying of hands on a community sacrifice by elders, and the breaking of the heifer's neck, are to be done by three judges,"* the words of R. Simeon.

[B]   *R. Judah says, "By five" [M. San. 1:3A–B].*

[C]   What is the Scriptural basis for the position of R. Simeon?

[D]   ["And the elders of the congregation shall lay their hands upon the head of the bull . . ." (Lev. 4:15).] "Shall lay" means two do it.

[E]   A court cannot be made up of an even number of judges, so they add one more to their number, lo, three.

[F]   What is the Scriptural basis for the position of R. Judah?

[G]   "Shall lay" means two do it, "elders" means two more, and since a court cannot be made up of an even number of judges, they add one more to their number, lo, five.

[H]   And as to the Scriptural basis for the position of R. Judah in the case of the heifer?

[I]   *"Your elders"—two, and "Your judges" two, and there is no such thing as a court made up of an even number of judges, so they add to their number yet one more [M. 9:1E].* Lo, this makes five.

[J]   Said Rabbi, "The opinion of R. Simeon is preferable in the case of the laying of hands, and the opinion of R. Judah in the case of the heifer.

[K]   "The opinion of R. Simeon in the case of the laying on of hands is preferable, for he does not resort to an exegesis of the words 'and they shall lay hands.'

[L]   "And the opinion of R. Judah is preferable in the case of the heifer, because he does not resort to an exegesis of the words 'and they shall go forth.' "

[M]   If you say that the opinion of R. Judah is preferable in the case of the heifer, he does resort to an exegesis of the words "and lay their hands," and also, "and they will go forth."

[N] Accordingly, you rule, "And they will go forth" requires two. "Your elders" requires two. "Your judges" requires two. A court cannot have an even number of judges, so they add to them one more, so there are to be seven.

[O] How does R. Simeon [Leiden MS and *editio princeps:* rabbis] interpret the language, "Your elders . . . your judges"?

[P] They are to be your elders who are your judges.

[Q] It was taught: R. Eliezer b. Jacob says, " 'Your elders'—this refers to the high court. 'And your judges'—this refers to the king and high priest."

The bulk of the Talmudic discussion of this unit of the Mishnah is devoted to the exegesis of the relevant verses of Scripture. Unit **I** presents an important, if obvious, clarification. Unit **II** then takes up the principal verse and analyzes its language. Unit **III** is inserted because of **II.I–K**. Unit **IV** continues the exegesis of the relevant verses. Unit **V** provides an exegesis of Scripture to support the Tosefta's basic rule and then presents an elaborate account of Ezek. 39:14. Unit **VI** concludes the discussion of marking out the corpse, which unit **V** introduced. Unit **VII** proceeds to the exegetical basis for M. 9:1D–E.

9:2

[A] *[If] it was found hidden under a heap or hanging from a tree or floating on the surface of water, they did not break the neck of a heifer,*

[B] *since it is said, "On the ground" (Deut. 21:1)—not hidden under a pile of rock.*

[C] *"Lying"—not hung on a tree.*

[D] *"In the field"—not floating on the water.*

[E] *[If] it was found near the frontier, near a town which had a gentile majority, or near a town which had no court, they did not break a heifer's neck.*

[F] *They measure only from a town which has a court.*

[G] '   "[If] it was found exactly between two such towns, then the two of them bring two heifers," the words of R. Eliezer.

[H]   And sages say, "One town brings a heifer, and two towns do not bring two heifers."

[I]   And Jerusalem does not have to bring a heifer whose neck is to be broken.

[I.A]   [In the Tosefta's version: It was taught,] **R. Eleazar says, "In the case of all of them, if there was a corpse, they would go through the rite of breaking the heifer's neck [even if it was found hidden in a pile of rocks or hanging from a tree]." [Yerushalmi, Leiden MS, and editio princeps: If it was found strangled or hanging from a tree, they would not go through the rite.]**

[B]   **Said to him R. Yosé b. R. Judah, "[If] it was only strangled and lying in a field, did they break a heifer's neck? On this account it is said, 'Slain.' If so, why is it said, 'Lying'? But even if it was slain and hanging in a tree, they did not break a heifer's neck" [M. 9:2D] [T. Sot. 9:1B–C].**

[II.A]   R. Yosé b. R. Bun taught in the name of R. Yohanan, "If [the victim] was found standing over his bed, with a knife plunged into his heart, they do not go through the rite."

[B]   R. Simeon b. Yohai taught: "They would go through the rite. [He will fall in a moment and there is no reason to exclude a corpse found in such condition.]"

[C]   As to this teaching of R. Simeon b. Yohai, [we do not know] who those are who taught thus [in his name].

[D]   For R. Yohanan said, "As to these sayings of R. Simeon b. Yohai, [we do not know] who those are who taught them in this wise. They are singletons, and we do not rely upon them." [Following Qorban ha'edah's interpretation.]

[III.A]   If the slain was found at the entrance to a town [where there can be no doubt as to the nearest place], they nonetheless measure, so as to carry out in this regard the religious duty of engaging in the act of measuring.

[IV.A]   Rab went down [to Babylonia]. He announced, "I am the Ben Azzai of this place [and so am able to take on all inquiries]."

[B] One old man came along and asked him, "Two corpses, one on top of the other. . . . [From which one does one measure to the nearest town?]"

[C] Rab thought that the issue was whether or not they carry out the rite of breaking the heifer's neck at all.

[D] He said to him, "They do not carry out the rite of breaking the heifer's neck. [By the way, they also do not measure from either corpse.]"

[E] He said to him, "Why?"

[F] He said to him, "In regard to the lower corpse, [they do not carry out the rite] because it is deemed to be buried [M. 9:2B], and in regard to the upper corpse, [they do not carry out the rite] because it is deemed to be floating [not lying square on the ground in the field, M. 9:2D]."

[G] When he came up here, he came before Rabbi. He said to him, "He answered you quite properly.

[H] " 'When anyone is found slain'—not when [two] are found.

[I] "It is not reasonable that that should not be the conclusion.

[J] " 'On the ground'—not floating in the water.

[K] " 'In the field'—not hidden under a pile of rock."

[L] And the House of Rabbi taught the matter in exactly this way.

[V.A] The opinions imputed to rabbis are at variance with one another.

[B] [At issue is the following passage: *Whatever is buried in the ground, like arum, garlic, and onions, R. Judah says, "It is not deemed a Forgotten Sheaf." And sages say, "It is deemed a Forgotten Sheaf"* [M. Pe. 6:10]. Sages maintain that "in the field" (Deut. 24:19) in the relevant passage encompasses that which was hidden in the ground.]

[C] There [at the present pericope of the Mishnah] they say [that the reference "on the ground"] excludes what is hidden [under a pile of rock, hence what is buried in the ground] [= M. 9:2B].

[D] And here they maintain [that the same language serves] to encompass what is hidden in the ground [at M. Pe. 6:10].

[E]   [The basis for sages' view is the exegesis of the following verse: "When you reap your harvest in your field, and have forgotten a sheaf in the field" (Deut. 24:19)]. There, "your field" speaks of what is out in the open, thus excluding that which was buried.

[F]   "And your crop" speaks of what is out in the open, excluding what is buried.

[G]   Now we have two exclusionary clauses, and they serve to encompass what is hidden in the field [like a double negative].

[H]   But here, "in the ground" [= M. 9:2B] means to exclude what is floating on the surface of the water.

[VI.A]   If the corpse was found *near the frontier [M. 9:2E]*, I say that the Saracens killed him.

[B]   If it was found *near a town in which gentiles live*, I say that gentiles killed him.

[C]   *Or near a town which had no court, they did not break a heifer's neck. They measure only from a town which has a court [M. 9:2E–F].* This is in line with that which is written, "Our hands did not shed this blood, neither did our eyes see it shed" (Deut. 21:7).

[VII.A]   What is the Scriptural basis for the position of rabbis [at M. 9:2I]?

[B]   "And the elders of the city which is nearest to the slain man . . ." (Deut. 21:2).

[C]   And what is the Scriptural basis for the position of R. Eliezer?

[D]   "And they shall measure the distance to the cities which are around him that is slain" (Deut. 21:2).

[VIII.A]   What is the status as to cities of refuge [in regard to bringing the heifer]?

[B]   If you say that they were handed over in order to be divided up [for the Levites, like the rest of the land], then they too will bring a heifer whose neck is to be broken.

[C]   If you say that they were handed over as dwelling places [like Jerusalem], they do not bring a heifer whose neck is to be broken.

After citing the Tosefta, the Talmud proceeds to a series of clarifications of the law, none of them connected with the operative verses. Units **II**, **III**, and **IV** take up rather small complications. Unit **V** serves M. Pe. 6:10, as is clear. Unit **VI** cites and lightly glosses the Mishnah by giving reasons for its rules. Unit **VII** gives a Scriptural basis for the Mishnah's dispute, as indicated. Unit **VIII** raises a question more suited to Y. Mak. 2:7 **I**, on which it depends.

9:3

[A]   *From what point did they measure?*

[B]   *R. Eliezer says, "From his navel."*

[C]   *R. Aqiba says, "From his nose."*

[D]   *R. Eliezer b. Jacob says, "From the place at which he was turned into a corpse—from his neck."*

[**I**.A]   *From what point did they measure?*

[B]   *R. Eliezer says, "From his navel*—the place where the embryo is found."

[C]   *R. Aqiba says, "From his nose*—the place of recognition. [That is, people are recognized by the character of their noses.]"

[D]   And this is in line with that which R. Judah said in the name of Rab: " 'The point of recognition of their faces witnesses against them' (Is. 3:9, RSV: 'Their partiality . . .'). This refers to their noses."

[E]   Said R. Hiyya bar Ba, "Whoever wants not to be recognized should put a rag over his nose, and he will not be recognized."

[F]   This is in line with what happened in the times of Arseines the king. The residents of Sepphoris rebelled. So they put rags over their noses so as not to be recognized. In the end they were informed against, and they were all captured forthwith.

[G]   *R. Eliezer b. Jacob says, "From the place at which he was turned into a corpse—from his neck."*

[H]   What is the Scriptural basis for this position?

[I]   R. Simon in the name of R. Joshua, "To be laid on the necks of the wicked who are to be slain" (Ez. 21:29).

The Talmud cites and glosses the Mishnah.

9:4

[A]   *"[If] its head is found in one place and its body in another place, they bring the head to the body," the words of R. Eliezer.*

[B]   *R. Aqiba says, "They bring the body to the head."*

[I.A]   Said R. Eleazar, "The dispute has to do with the burial place."

[B]   R. Samuel in the name of R. Jonathan, "The dispute concerns a case in which the head was above and the body below.

[C]   "But if the head was below and the body was above, all parties concur that they bring the head to the body."

[D]   If the ground was sloping in all directions, I say that the head went down one side and the body went down the other side.

[E]   Or this head has no body, and this body has no head.

[F]   If the ground was flat [23d], in any place in which it is to be expected that the parts have scattered, I maintain that it is a single body [from which the parts have come, and the dispute of the Mishnah follows].

[G]   If it is not [so arrayed that it would be expected for the head and body to be scattered in this wise,] then I maintain that this head has no body, and that body has no head, [and we can do nothing].

The Talmud contributes to the Mishnah an explanation of what can possibly be at issue.

9:5

[A]   *The elders of Jerusalem took their leave and went away.*

[B]   *The elders of that town bring "a heifer from the herd with which labor had not been done and which had not drawn the yoke" (Deut. 21:3).*

[C]   *But a blemish does not invalidate it.*

[D]   *They brought it down into a rugged valley (and "rugged" is meant literally, hard, but even if it is not rugged, it is valid).*

[E]   *And they break its neck with a hatchet from behind.*

[F]   *And the place [where it is buried] is prohibited for sowing and for tilling, but permitted for the combing out of flax and for quarrying stones.*

[I.A]   ["And the elders . . . shall take a heifer which has never been worked and which has not pulled on the yoke" (Deut 21:3).] "Which has never been worked"—knowingly.

[B]   "And which has not pulled on the yoke"—whether knowingly or unknowingly.

[C]   R. Jonah interpreted the statement " 'which has never been worked' knowingly 'and which has not pulled on the yoke' whether knowingly or unknowingly" to apply to a case in which the beast has pulled on the yoke. [That is, to be invalidated, the beast must have borne part of the weight of the yoke.]

[D]   R. Yosé interpreted the Tannaitic statement: " 'Knowingly'— even if it has not drawn on the yoke. And 'unknowingly'—if it has drawn on the yoke. [If the owner has knowingly put the yoke onto the heifer, even if it has not drawn on it, it is invalid. If without the owner's knowledge, the yoke happened to come upon the heifer, it remains valid, unless the heifer should draw on the yoke.]"

[E]   [The dispute of Jonah and Yosé runs along familiar lines. For] the opinion of R. Jonah is in line with that of R. Ishmael, and that of R. Yosé accords with rabbis.

[F]   The opinion of R. Jonah accords with R. Ishmael.

[G]   For R. Ishmael has said, "The case of any statement which was covered by a general rule [and thus did not need to be repeated], and yet was singled out of the general rule [to be made explicit], is so treated in order to teach an interpretation of the general rule, and lo, it represents a new point.

[H]   "Accordingly, it was necessary to state, 'Which has never worked' knowingly; 'And which has not pulled on the yoke' whether knowingly or unknowingly—if the beast has actually pulled on the yoke. [That is, the only source of invalidation will be when the beast actually pulls on the yoke. But if there is no actual act of labor, the heifer remains valid.]"

[I]   And the view of R. Yosé accords with that of the rabbis.

[J]   For the rabbis say, "Lo, it remains part of the general statement [of which it forms an integral element], and lo, it serves to provide a new point pertinent to the whole of its context.

[K]   "Accordingly, it was necessary to state, 'If [it was worked] knowingly, [then it is invalid], even if it did not draw on the yoke.

[L]   " 'If [it was worked] unknowingly, [then it is not invalid] unless it actually draws on the yoke.' "

[II.A]   And how much should the beast have drawn on the yoke [for it to be deemed invalid]?

[B]   Rabbi says, "The length of the yoke."

[C]   R. Yosé b. R. Judah says, "Three fingerbreadths."

[D]   R. Simon in the name of R. Yosé b. Nehorai: "The girth of the yoke breadthwise."

[III.A]   R. Bun bar Hiyya raised the question before R. Zeira: " 'With which labor had not been done' is a general rule. 'And which had not drawn the yoke' is a particularization thereof. We have then a generalization and a particularization [which is deemed to be limiting]. Thus the general rule contains only what is expressed by the particularization thereof. [Accordingly, the only sort of labor which will invalidate the heifer will be pulling on the yoke.]"

[B]   He said to him, "If it had been written, 'Which had not been worked and which had not drawn . . . ,' what you say would have been so. It is written only, 'With which labor had not been done.' There is no generalization and particularization here at all.

[C]   "But the qualifying language serves to encompass, interpreting the reference to 'yoke' for purposes of establishing a linguistic analogy [with reference to yoke elsewhere, namely, with regard to the red cow burned for the purification water, Num. 19:2: '. . . a red heifer without defect, in which there is no blemish, and upon which a yoke has never come.]' "

[**IV**.A]   Just as in the case of the yoke stated with regard to the heifer, Scripture has treated all other sorts of labor as equivalent to pulling on the yoke, so in the case of the yoke stated with regard to the red cow, Scripture has treated all other sorts of labor as equivalent to pulling on the yoke.

[B]   Just as in the case of "yoke" stated with regard to the heifer, an act of labor invalidates the heifer, whether or not done with the owner's knowledge, so "yoke" stated with regard to the red cow means that an act of labor done with it invalidates it, whether this is or is not with the knowledge and consent of the owner.

[C]   Just as in the case of "yoke" stated with regard to the red cow, the yoke [itself] invalidates the cow, so "yoke" stated with regard to the heifer [means that] the yoke invalidates it.

[D]   If we then propose, "Just as 'yoke' stated with reference to the red cow means that blemishes of the cow invalidate it, so 'yoke' stated with reference to the heifer means that blemishes invalidate it," Scripture explicitly stated, "in which there is no blemish," meaning, blemishes invalidate in the case of the red cow, and blemishes do not invalidate in the case of the heifer.

[E]   [But if that is the mode of argument], then let us say, "With which labort had not been done" (Deut. 21:3) means an act of labor invalidates the heifer, but an act of labor does not invalidate the red cow.

[F]   [Indeed, there is an exclusionary meaning in the use of the language "with which." But it is not that which H has proposed. Rather it is as follows:] Here "with which labor had not been done" is stated, so indicating, work invalidates the heifer, but an act of work with the beast does not invalidate animals set aside as holy [for use on the altar]. [If they are used for labor, they remain valid for the altar.]

[G]   [With respect to the language used in description of the red cow,] do you have the possibility of saying "in which there is no blemish" to indicate, in the selection of the red cow, blemishes serve to invalidate the cow, but as regards animals set aside for consecrated purposes, blemishes do not invalidate such beasts? [That would be a self-evidently absurd proposition, but it can now be proposed in line with the reasoning at I. Scripture specifies, to the contrary, that such beasts must be without blemish.]

[**V**.A]   As to the absence of major limbs, what is the rule for such a defect's serving to invalidate the heifer?

[B]   [What sort of a foolish question is that?] Even in the case of offerings coming from the children of Noah [that is, non-Israelites], such beasts are not acceptable!

[C]   Did not R. Yosa state, "R. Eleazar explained for the associates, 'And of every living thing of all flesh [you shall bring two of every sort into the ark]' (Gen. 6:19)? [The meaning of 'all' flesh is, 'whole' of flesh, that is:] they are to be whole as to their limbs."

[D]   [No, the question is not so absurd. For] there, [in reference to the beasts selected by Noah,] some parts of them were to be used for the altar. But here [with reference to the heifer], no part of the beast is to be used on the altar [burned as an offering].

[E]   [Answering the question of A, D, with reference to Deut. 21:8, "Forgive, O Lord, thy people Israel . . . ,"] R. Huna in the name of R. Jeremiah: "Since you may note 'forgiveness' is written in regard to the heifer, it is tantamount to Holy Things [used to attain forgiveness by serving as an offering]. Accordingly, in the case of the heifer it is as if part of the beast is offered on the altar."

[F]   If the heifer suffers a blemish which would render it *terefah*, what is the law as to its being deemed invalid?

[G]   Since you have maintained that part of the beast is deemed as if it were to be offered up on the altar, a defect which would render the beast *terefah* serves to invalidate it.

[H]   For that reason it is self-evident to you that a defect which would render the beast *terefah* does invalidate it.

[I]   If its hoof is cloven like that of an ass, how do you treat it?

[J]   Is it deemed like a beast which is lacking a limb, or like one which has suffered a blemish?

[K]   If you treat it like a beast which is lacking a limb, it is invalid [Leiden MS and *editio princeps:* valid].

[L]   If you treat it like a beast which has suffered a blemish, it is valid [Leiden MS and *editio princeps:* invalid]. [This question is not answered.]

[M]   As to its blood, what is the law as to its having the capacity [as does the blood of a valid beast] to impart susceptibility to uncleanness [in line with Lev. 11:34, 37]?

[N]   Since R. Hiyya taught, "Its blood is susceptible to uncleanness," [it follows that] its blood [also] has the capacity to impart susceptibility to uncleanness.

[VI.A]   An elder asked the rabbis of Caesarea, "[In the case of a beast suffering blemishes which render it *terefah*, if one breaks the neck], what is the law as to that action's rendering the carrion clean of the uncleanness pertaining thereto? [That is, the law in general is that if one properly slaughters a beast which is *terefah*, the proper act of slaughter removes the uncleanness pertaining to the carion of a *terefah* beast. So the question is whether we deem this unusual mode of killing the beast to be tantamount to a proper act of slaughter.]"

[B]   They said to him, "And is it not an explicit statement in the Mishnah [at M. Hul. 5:3A–E]: *He who slaughters a beast and it turns out to be terefah, he who slaughters a beast for idolatrous purposes, and he who slaughters a cow to be burned for purification water, an ox to be stoned, or a heifer whose neck is to be broken [none of which is eaten at all]—R. Simeon declares exempt, and sages declare liable?* [Sages' position, then, is that it is a valid act of slaughter, and, it follows, in the case of the heifer, the uncleanness of a *terefah* heifer's carrion indeed is removed by the breaking of its neck, yet another unusual mode of slaughter.]"

[C]   He said to them, "Now how can this be? We ask you about the law covering a *terefah* beast, and you introduce evidence concerning a beast which is properly slaughtered! [Here we are talking about breaking the neck, not properly slaughtering the beast at all.]"

[D]   They said to them, "Did not R. Yannai state, 'In the opinion of R. Meir, even if the beast were a *terefah* beast [and so not suitable for eating at all, in the case at M. Hul. 5:3 cited above], one is liable.' " [Hence the fact that the heifer is not going to be eaten at all has no bearing. The main point is as is stated above.]

[E]   He said to them, "Now are you going to attempt to formulate a reply to me on the basis of what R. Yannai has said?"

[VII.A]   *Rugged ('YTN) is meant literally, hard [M. 9:5D].*

[B]   "Enduring ('YTN) is your dwelling place, and your nest is set in the rock" (Num. 24:21).

[C]   *Even if it is not rugged, it is valid.*

[D]   And along these same lines, even though it is not a valley, is it valid?

[E]   R. Simeon b. Yohai taught, " 'Bring down . . . and they shall bring down . . .'—even though it is not a valley."

[F]   As to this teaching of R. Simeon b. Yohai, we do not know who are those who taught thus [in his name].

[G]   For R. Yohanan said, "As to all these sayings of R. Simeon b. Yohai, [we do not know] who are those who taught them in this wise. They are singletons, and we do not rely upon them" [cf. Y. 9:2 II.C–D].

[VIII.A]   And is it necessary to sever two or the greater part of two [of the organs of the neck, as in the case of a valid act of slaughter]?

[B]   Let us derive the answer to that question from the following:

[C]   R. Zeira stated, "R. Judah in the name of Samuel [said], 'At the place in the neck which is valid for the act of slaughter, over against it at the back of the neck is the valid place for severing the neck of a bird.' "

[D]   And thus did he maintain in the present matter as well.

[IX.A]   There we have learned: *There is one who ploughs a single furrow and is liable on eight counts of violating a negative commandment: [he who ploughs with an ox and an ass, both of which are Holy Things, in the case of ploughing for Mixed Seeds in a vineyard, doing so in the seventh year, on a festival, who was both a priest and a Nazirite ploughing in a graveyard]* [M. Mak. 3:9A–C].

[B]   R. Hoshaiah raised the question: "And let us repeat the tradition, 'He who ploughs in a place in which a heifer's neck was broken' [thus violating M. 9:5F], lo, making nine violations."

[X.A]   Associates said before R. Yosé, "Interpret the statement [of M. 9:5F, that the place may not be sown or tilled] to apply to the prior condition [of the place, that is, it must be fallow ground]."

[B]   He said to them, "If you apply the passage to the prior condition of the place, all the more so must it be treated in the future [left fallow]."

[XI.A]   **The area in which its neck is broken and the surrounding ground—lo, these are prohibited [along the lines of M. 9:5] [T. Sot. 9:1J].**

[B]   **And how large is that area of its surrounding ground? Four [Tosefta: forty] cubits [T. Sot. 9:1K].**

[C]   Rabbi says, "I say that the surrounding area is fifty cubits."

[XII.A]   R. Samuel, son of R. Yosé b. R. Bun: "['And the elders . . . shall bring the heifer down to a valley . . . which is] neither plowed nor sown . . .' (Deut. 21:4)—'Which is not plowed' is a generalization, 'nor sown' is a particularization.

[B]   "Thus we have a generalization followed by a particularization.

[C]   "Nothing is contained in the generalization except what is made explicit by the particularization. [It follows that only sowing matters is invalidating the plot of ground.]"

[D]   He said to him, "If it were written, 'Which is not plowed . . . which is not sown,' matters would be as you have stated them.

[E]   "But it is written only, 'Which is not ploughed.'

[F]   "The proper interpretation then is in line with that which R. Zeira said: 'We do not have here a case of a generalization followed by a limiting particularization, but rather a statement meant to encompass [all sorts of conditions, here, all kinds of ploughing and working of the ground].'"

The Talmud thoroughly explains both the Mishnah's ideas and the topics introduced by the Mishnah in general. Unit **I** interprets the language of Deut. 21:3, cited in M. 9:5B. Unit **II** introduces a minor detail. Unit **III** goes over the same type of exegetical problem that interests unit **I**. Its principal contribution is to introduce unit **IV**, that is, the comparison of the language pertaining to the heifer here and to the red cow at Num. 19:11ff. Unit **V** proceeds to matters relevant to the Mishnah but outside of its discourse, namely, the character of the heifer

itself. Unit **V** further lays the foundations for the secondary conundrum presented in unit **VI**. Unit **VII** then proceeds to explain other language of the Mishnah and unit **VIII** asks about
the law governing the act of breaking the neck, thus M. 9:5D,
M. 9:5E, in sequence. Unit **IX** is a singleton. Units **X**, **XI**, and
XII proceed to M. 9:5F. So, in all, we have a systematic and
wide-ranging essay on the Mishnah's language and themes.

9:6

[A]   *The elders of that town wash their hands in the place in which
the neck of the heifer is broken, and they say,*

[B]   *"Our hands have not shed this blood, nor did our eyes see it"
(Deut. 21:7).*

[C]   *Now could it enter our minds that the elders of a court might
be shedders of blood?*

[D]   *But [they mean:] He did not come into our hands and nor did
we send him away without food.*

[E]   *And we did not see him and let him go along without an
escort.*

[F]   *And [it is] the priests [who] say, "Forgive, O Lord, your people Israel, whom you have redeemed, and do not allow innocent blood in the midst of your people, Israel" (Deut. 21:8).*

[G]   *They did not have to say, "And the blood shall be forgiven
them" (Deut. 21:8).*

[H]   *But the Holy Spirit informs them, "Whenever you do this, the
blood shall be forgiven to you."*

[I]   *[If] the murderer was found before the neck of the heifer was
broken, it [simply] goes forth and pastures in the herd.*

[J]   *[If the murderer is found] after the neck of the heifer is broken,
it is to be buried in its place.*

[K]   *For to begin with, it was brought in a matter of doubt. It has
atoned for the matter of doubt on which account it was brought
and which has gone its way.*

[L]   *[If] the neck of the heifer was broken and afterward the murderer was found, lo, this one is put to death.*

[**I**.A]   [As to the statement, "Our hands have not shed this blood,"
(Deut. 21:7),] the rabbis here interpret the passage to speak of
the murderer.

[B]   The rabbis over there [in Babylonia] interpret it to speak of the
victim.

[C]   The rabbis here interpret the passage to speak of the murderer:
"He did not come into our hands and we let him go instead of
putting him to death. We did not see him and allow him to be
and neglect to bring him to judgment."

[D]   The rabbis over there interpret it to speak of the victim: "He
did not come into our hands and nor did we let him go without
a posse. We did not see him and leave him without
sustenance."

[E]   ["The elders of that city . . . wash their hands over the heifer
whose neck was broken in the valley" (Deut. 21:6).] They
wash their hands in water at the place at which the heifer's
neck is broken.

[**II**.A]   [Following the Tosefta's version:] **The elders say, "Our hands
have not shed this blood, and our eyes did not see it" [M.
Sot. 9:6B, Deut. 21:7].**

[B]   **"And the priests say, "Forgive, O Lord, your people, Israel,
whom you have redeemed" [M. Sot. 9:6F, Deut. 21:8].**

[C]   **And the Holy Spirit says, "But let the guilt of blood be forgiven them" (Deut. 21:8) [M. Sot. 9:6H].**

[D]   **In three passages the one who said one thing did not say
another.**

[E]   **Similarly you say: "We came to the land to which you sent
us," said Joshua. Caleb said, "Let us now go up and inherit
it." The spies said, "Yet the people who dwell in the land
are strong" (Num. 13:27).**

[F]   **So you have three things side by side, and the one who said
this one did not say that one, and whoever said that one did
not say the other [T. Sot. 9:2].**

[G]   **Similarly you say: "And she said, 'Mark, I pray you, whose
these are, the signet and the cord and the staff' " (Gen.
38:25), so said Tamar.**

[H]   **Said Judah, "She is more righteous than I" (Gen. 38:26).**

[I]   And the Holy Spirit says, "And he did not lie with her again" (Gen. 38:26).

[J]   So you have three things side by side, and one who said this one did not say that one, and whoever said that one did not say the other [T. Sot. 9:3].

[K]   Similarly you say: "And they said, 'Woe to us! Who can deliver us from the power of these mighty gods?' " (1 Sam. 4:8), so said the proper ones among them.

[L]   The evil ones among them said, "These are the gods who smote the Egyptians with every sort of plague in the wilderness" (1 Sam. 4:8).

[M]   And the heroes among them said, "Take courage, and acquit yourselves like men, O Philistines" (1 Sam. 4:9).

[N]   So you have three things side by side, just as before.

[O]   Similarly you say: "Out of the window she peered, she gazed" (Judg. 5:28)—said the mother of Sisera.

[P]   "Her wisest ladies make answer. . . . Are they not finding and dividing the spoil?" (Judg. 5:29–30), so said his wife and daughters-in-law.

[Q]   "So perish all thine enemies, O Lord! But thy friends be like the sun as he rises in his might" (Judg. 5:31)—so said the Holy Spirit.

[R]   Thus you have three things, side by side, just as before [T. Sot. 9:4].

[24a/   Said R. Phineas, "This mode of atonement [namely, the break-
III.A]   ing of the heifer's neck] was suitable to make atonement [even] for those who went out of Egypt [in line with Deut. 21:8: 'Forgive . . . whom you have redeemed,' that is, from Egypt]."

[IV.A]   Said R. Ila, "Will he declare him exempt on the count of 'it and its offspring' in accord with the view of R. Simeon? [This question is explained presently.]" [In Yerushalmi, IV.A follows IV.C; in Leiden MS and *editio princeps*, IV.A follows V.A.]

[B]   Said R. Yannai, [The dispute which follows pertains to the case of one who has slaughtered the offspring of a dam which has served as a heifer in the present rite, M. Hul. 5:3A–E]. [The issue is whether or not one is liable for slaughtering the offspring on the same day on which the dam has been slaughtered for the rite of the heifer.] In the opinion of R. Meir, even if [the dam] has had its neck broken [in the rite of the heifer], one who slaughters the offspring is liable. [The breaking of the neck is tantamount to a proper act of slaughter.]"

[C]   R. Jacob bar Aha, R. Ami in the name of R. Simeon b. La-qish, "Even in accord with the view of R. Meir [who is the authority named sages at M. Hul. 5:3E], if the dam has had its neck broken in the rite of the heifer, one who slaughters the offspring is exempt. [It is different here.]"

[V.A]   [As regards the prohibition of making use of the heifer set aside for the rite,] said R. Yannai, "I have heard a time limit affecting the matter. From what point is the heifer designated for the rite deemed prohibited [for all other purposes]? 'And they will bring it down' (Deut. 21:4)—it is from the time that the heifer is brought down [but not beforehand]. [That is, once the animal is killed.]"

[B]   Said R. Samuel bar R. Isaac, "While it is still alive, it is deemed to be consecrated.

[C]   "The Mishnah's law has made that point: *It simply goes forth and pastures in the herd [M. 9:6I].*

[D]   "What is the meaning of 'goes forth'? It goes forth from its status of sanctification."

[VI.A]   [Referring to M. 9:6M,] said R. Matteniah, "And that is so. Since it is written, 'But let the guilt of blood be forgiven them' (Deut. 21:8), has [Scripture then] fallen silent? No. For even then it says, 'So you shall purge the guilt of innocent blood from your midst.' [Thus even though the rite has been carried out, the obligation to punish the murderer, when he is found, remains valid.]"

Unit **I** raises the question of the referent for the statement of the elders, Deut. 21:7. Unit **II** takes up the exegetical observation of the Mishnah and gives further examples. I have supplied the Tosefta's version, which is more fully spelled out than that in Yerushalmi. Unit **III** is truncated and does not fully express its point. Unit **IV** likewise alludes to other materials and makes no contribution to the present matter. Units **V** and **VI** briefly gloss points important to the Mishnah.

9:7

[A] *[If] one witness says, "I saw the murderer," and one witness says, "You did not see him."*

[B] *[If] one woman says, "I saw him," and one woman says, "You did not see him,"*

[C] *they would go through the rite of breaking the neck of the heifer.*

[D] *[If] one witness says, "I saw," and two say, "You did not see," they would break the neck of the heifer.*

[E] *[If] two say, "We saw," and one says to them, "You did not see," they do not break the neck of the heifer.*

[I.A] Giddul bar Benyamin in the name of Rab: "In any case in which [sages] have declared the testimony of a woman to be as valid as that of a man, the testimony of a man serves to discredit that of a woman, and the testimony of a woman serves to discredit that of a man."

[B] [If that is so, then let the Tanna of M. Sot. 9:7A–B] teach [the law as follows]: "[If] one [male] witness said, 'I saw the murderer,' and a woman said, 'You did not see him,'

[C] "[or if] a woman said, 'I saw the murderer,' and a [male] witness said, 'You did not see him,' [and that would have indicated the point made by Rab at A]."

[D] [Leiden MS and *editio princeps* omit:] Along these lines did the House of Rabbi [teach the law].

[II.A] It was taught in the name of R. Nehemiah, "They follow the greater part of the [available] testimony."

[B] What would be a practical illustration of that proposition?

[C] In the case in which two women testify [in one wise], and one woman [testifies in another], they have treated such a case as one in which there are two witnesses against one witness.

[D] That rule which you have stated applies to a case in which there was one woman against two women.

[E] But if they were a hundred women and a single male witness, all the women are deemed equivalent to a single male witness.

The Talmud to M. 6:4 is revised, B, to fit the context provided by M. 9:7.

9:8

[A]   *When murderers become many, the rite of breaking the heifer's neck was cancelled.*

[B]   *[This was] when Eleazar b. Dinai came along, and he was also called Tehinah b. Perishah. Then they went and called him, "Son of a murderer."*

[I.A]   [The Hebrew] "Son of a murderer" is [in Aramaic] "Son of a murderer."

The Talmud supplies a light gloss.

9:9

[A]   *When adulterers became many, the ordeal of the bitter water was cancelled.*

[B]   *And Rabban Yohanan b. Zakkai cancelled it, since it is said, "I will not punish your daughters when they commit whoredom, nor your daughters-in-law when they commit adultery, for they themselves go apart with whores" (Hosea 4:14).*

[I.A]   It is written, "For they themselves go apart with whores" (Hosea 4:14).

[B]   And it is written, "And the woman shall become an execration among her people" (Num. 5:27).

[C]   That applies when her people are at peace.

[D]   But when her people are licentious [it does not apply].

[E]   "The man shall be free from iniquity" (Num. 5:31).

[F]   When does "the woman bear her own sin" (Num. 5:31)?

[G]   When the man is free of iniquity.

The Talmud expands upon the Mishnah's point and applies it more explicitly to the relevant verses on the rite of the accused wife.

9:10

[A]   *When Yosé b. Yoezer of Seredah and Yosé b. Yohanan of Jerusalem died, the grape clusters were cancelled,*

[B]   *since it is said, "There is no cluster to eat, my soul desires the first ripe fig" (Mic. 7:1)*

[I.A]   And there was no grape cluster to come until R. Aqiba arose.

[B]   And were all of the pairs not grape clusters?

[C]   But these served as sustainers, while the others did not.

[II.A] It was taught: **Among all the grape clusters which arose for Israel from the death of Moses to the rise of Joseph b. Yoezer of Seredah and Joseph b. Yohanan of Jerusalem, it is not possible to find a blemish.**

[B]   **But once Joseph b. Yoezer of Seredah and Joseph b. Yohanan of Jerusalem died, until the rise of Judah b. Baba, it most certainly is possible to find a blemish among them.**

[C]   **They tell about Judah b. Baba that all of his deeds were directed for the glory of Heaven,**

[D]   **except that he raised small cattle.**

[E]   **One time he fell ill, and a physician came to examine him.**

[F]   **He said to him, "There is no remedy for you except for boiling milk."**

[G]   **He went out and got himself a goat and tied it to the leg of his bed, and he would draw hot milk from it, for he would groan [because of angina].**

[H]   **One time sages wanted to come in to him.**

[I]   **But they said, "How is it possible to come to him, when there is a robber with him in the house?"**

[J]   **And when he died, sages examined carefully all of the things he had ever done, and they found in him no sin except for this one alone.**

[K] **And he too said when he was dying, "I know that there is against my account only this sin alone,**

[L] **"which I have done in transgressing the opinion of my colleagues."**

[M] **Said R. Ishmael [Yerushalmi, Leiden MS, and editio princeps: Simeon Shezuri], "The house of my father was one of the Galilean householders.**

[N] **"On what account was it wiped out?**

[O] **"Because they gave rulings in civil cases with a single judge, and because they raised small cattle.**

[P] **"Even so, we had a thicket near the town. A field intervened between it and the town,**

[Q] **"so the cattle would come in and go out through the upper path" [T. B.Q. 8:13–14].**

The Talmud supplements the Mishnah with the Tosefta. I give the Tosefta's version, not that in Yerushalmi.

9:11

[A] *Yohanan, high priest, did away with the confession concerning tithe.*

[B] *Also: He cancelled the rite of the awakeners and the stunners.*

[C] *Until his time a hammer did strike in Jerusalem.*

[D] *And in his time no man had to ask concerning doubtfully tithed produce.*

[I.A] R. Jeremiah, R. Hiyya in the name of R. Simeon b. Laqish: "The Mishnah [at M. 9:11A, doing away with the confession concerning tithe, Deut. 26:13–15] speaks of the time after which the people were suspect of handing the [first] tithe over to the priesthood [while it should go to the Levites]. [That is why Yohanan annulled reciting the confession.]"

[B] The statement [of Simeon, A] supports the position of R. Yohanan [cited below, that whatever Yohanan did was praiseworthy, I–M], in one aspect and stands at variance with it in another:

[C]   For we have learned there: *A Levite girl betrothed to a priest, pregnant by a priest, awaiting levirate marriage with a priest, and so too, a priestly girl married to a Levite, eats neither heave offering nor tithe [M. Yeb. 9:4G–I].* [The reason is that her status is not fixed.]

[D]   Now that she should not eat heave offering makes sense, [since we are not sure that she is in the priestly caste].

[E]   But why should she not eat tithe [which goes to the Levite, for, in any event, she remains in the Levite's caste]? What difference does it make? If she is in the priestly caste, she has every right to eat it. If she is in the Levitical caste, she also has every right to eat it.

[F]   [The problem is readily solved, for] R. Ila in the name of R. Yohanan said, "This accords with the view of the one who said, 'They do not give over tithe to the priesthood at all.' "

[G]   [R. Yohanan] then accords with the view of the one who said, "They do give tithe to the priesthood [as much as to the Levites], [and this is a point of disagreement with Simeon, A–B]."

[H]   The following supports the one who said that all [of the decrees that Yohanan, high priest, made] were praiseworthy.

[I]   For R. Yohanan has said:

[J]   **[Also: he decreed concerning the confession [concerning tithes] and annulled [the rules of] doubtfully tithed produce (M. 9:1A, D).]**

[K]   **For he sent to all the towns of Israel and found that they were separating only the great heave offering alone. As to first tithe and second tithe, some of them separated these tithes, and some of them did not.**

[L]   **He said to them, "Just as the great heave offering, if neglected, is a transgression punishable by death, so tithing the heave offering, if neglected, is a transgression analogous [in regard to heave offering] to certainly untithed produce [and punishable by death].**

[M]   **"So let people designate heave offering and heave offering of the tithe and give it to the priest; as to second tithe, let them** render it unconsecrated in exchange for coins. And as to the rest of the tithes, e.g., poor man's tithe, let the one who wants to collect from his fellow produce evidence in behalf of his claim" [so now people do not have to ask, etc., as at M. 9:1D] [T. Sot. 13:10D–F].

[II.A] [As to his doing away with the confession concerning tithe, M. 9:11A,] [why should one not] confess?

[B] Said R. Ila, "It angers the Omnipresent when someone says, 'I have done . . . ,' while he has not done a thing."

[C] If so, then if there is someone who has separated the tithes, he should say the confession, and he who has not separated the tithes should not say the confession.

[D] This would be in line with the following:

[E] Up to the verse, "Look down [from thy holy habitation, from Heaven, and bless thy people Israel and the ground which thou has given us, as thou didst swear to our fathers, a land flowing with milk and honey]" (Deut. 26:15), they should say in a low voice. And from that point onward, they say in a loud voice. [So the inapplicable statements should be slurred over.]

[III.A] The awakeners [M. 9:11B]—these are the Levites who say on the platform, "Rouse yourself! Why do you sleep, O Lord?" (Ps. 44:23),

[B] [He said to them], "Now is there such a thing as sleep before him? And has it not already been said, 'Lo, the Guardian of Israel neither slumbers nor sleeps' (Ps. 121:4)? Why does Scripture say, 'Then the Lord awoke as from sleep, [like a strong man shouting because of wine]' (Ps. 78:65)?

[C] "But so long as Israel is immersed in pain and the nations of the world are immersed in prosperity, as it were, 'Rouse yourself! Why do you sleep?' " [T. Sot. 13:9].

[D] And so it says, "[Surely there are mockers about me,] and my eye dwells on their provocation" (Job 17:2).

[IV.A] The knockers [M. 9:11B]—these are those who knock the calf between its horns, just as they stun a beast to be sacrificed for idolatry.

[B] Said to them Yohanan, the high priest, "How long are you going to feed terefah meat to the altar?" [T. Sot. 13:10].

[C]   He went and set up holding rings [to keep the animals in place].

[D]   R. Ba in the name of R. Yohanan said, "He made holding rings for them, broad at the bottom and narrow at the top."

[V.A]   *Until his time a hammer did strike in Jerusalem [M. 9:11C].*

[B]   Until the beginning of his time.

[VI.A]   *And until his time no man had to ask concerning doubtfully tithed produce [M. 9:11D].*

[B]   For he set up pairs [to oversee the matter].

[VII.A]   In the view of R. Joshua b. Levi, some of the [decrees] were not praiseworthy and some of them were praiseworthy.

[B]   For R. Yosé in the name of R. Tanhum, R. Hiyya in the name of R. Joshua b. Levi, "At first tithe was divided into three parts. A third went to members of the priestly and Levitical castes, a third for storage, and a third for the poor and for associates who were in Jerusalem." [So first tithe went to priests or Levites, and Yohanan did not approve. So in this regard, it was not praiseworthy, vs. I.C–G.]

[C]   Said R. Yosé b. R. Bun, "One who went up to serve as a judge in Jerusalem—up to a third of his needs would he provide out of his own resources. From that amount onward he collected what he needed from the treasury."

[D]   When Eleazar b. Patorah and Judah b. Pakorah came along, [as powerful priests] they took them by force [that is, the first tithe for the priesthood].

[E]   [Yohanan] had the possibility of stopping them, and he did not stop them.

[F]   So he did away with the confession concerning tithe.

[24b/
VIII.A]   *The awakeners and stunners*—both of these were praiseworthy.

[IX.A]   *Until his time a hammer did strike in Jerusalem*—until the beginning of his time.

[B]   R. Hasidah asked R. Hezediah, "It is not reasonable to suppose that it was only at the end of his days [vs. V.A–B]?"

[C]   He said to him, "I too think so."

[**X**.A]   *[And in his time no man had to ask concerning] doubtfully tithed produce.*

[B]   R. Yosé in the name of R. Abbahu, R. Hezediah in the name of R. Judah b. Pazzi [said], "*Demai* means, 'Who has *(de mi)* properly dealt with his crop and who has not properly dealt with his crop.'"

While there is some disorder in the arrangement of the Talmud's materials, the demonstrated intent is to focus upon the Mishnah and to explain its items. The persistent issue is whether or not all of Yohanan the high priest's changes were praiseworthy. Unit **I** explores the problems in the view that they were, that is, R. Yohanan's position, and the focus is on doing away with the confession and dealing with doubtfully tithed produce *(demai)*. Unit **II** carries forward this same matter. Then unit **VIII** returns to it, and that is what makes the passage as a whole somewhat confusing. But, as we see, units **III, IV, V, VI, VIII,** and **IX** quite systematically gloss the Mishnah. (**V** and **IX** belong together also.) So, despite the editorial difficulties, the intent and program are clear and well executed.

9:12

[A]   *When the Sanhedrin was cancelled, singing at wedding feasts was cancelled, since it is said, "They shall not drink wine with a song" (Is. 24:9).*

[**I**.A]   Abba bar R. Jeremiah said, "The old men have quit the city gate, the young men their music" (Lam. 5:14).

[B]   Said R. Hisda, "At first, when people were afraid of the Sanhedrin, they did not sing obscene songs. But now that they are not afraid of the Sanhedrin, they sing obscene songs."

[**II**.A]   [Tosefta's version: *When the Sanhedrin was terminated, singing in wedding feasts was cancelled (M. 9:12).* **And what good was the Sanhedrin for Israel? But it was for this matter concerning which it is said, "And if the people of the land do at all hide their eyes from that man, when he gives one of his children to Molech, and do not put him to death, then I will set my face against that man and against his family" (Lev.**

20:4–5).] **At first, if a man would sin, when there was a Sanhedrin in operation, they would exact punishment from him.
Now [that there is no Sanhedrin], punishment is exacted
both from him and from his relatives, as it said, "Then I will
set my face against that man and against his family."**

[III.A] Said R. Yosé b. R. Bun in the name of R. Huna, "At first
whenever a misfortune would come upon the community, they
would declare a celebration [to commemorate their being saved
from that misfortune]."

[B] *When the Sanhedrin was cancelled, singing at wedding feasts
was cancelled.*

[C] When these and those [namely, celebrations for an occasion of
redemption and singing at wedding feasts] were cancelled,

[D] "The joy of our hearts ceased; our dancing has been turned to
mourning" (Lam. 5:15).

[E] But what good was the great Sanhedrin?

[F] But since it is said, "And if the people of the land do at all
hide their eyes from that man, when he gives one of his children to Molech, and do not put him to death, [then I will set
my face against that man]" (Lev. 20:4]—that is, if they do not
put him to death with any mode of execution they choose.

[G] [Tosefta's version:] **They made a parable. To what is the
matter comparable? They have compared the matter to one
in a town who went bad, so they gave him over to a strap-
bearer, and he strapped him.**

[H] **He was too hard for the strap-bearer.**

[I] **They gave him over to a rod officer, and he beat him.**

[J] **He was too hard for the rod officer.**

[K] **They gave him over to a centurion, and he imprisoned him.**

[L] **He was too hard for the centurion.**

[M] **They gave him over to a magistrate, and he threw him into a
furnace.**

[N] **So is Israel: the latter tribulations make them forget the former tribulations [T. Sot. 15:7D–E].**

The Talmud makes use of the Tosefta's materials, along with other sayings. Once more there is some confusion in the arrangement of the Talmud, but the main points are clear.

9:13 [Leiden MS and *editio princeps:* 9:13–14]

[A]   *When the former prophets died out, the Urim and Thummim were cancelled.*

[B]   *When the sanctuary was destroyed, the Shamir worm ceased and [so did] the honey of supim.*

[C]   *And faithful men came to an end,*

[D]   *since it is written, "Help, O Lord, for the godly man ceases" (Ps. 12:1).*

[I.A]   When the former prophets died out, the Urim and Thummim were nullified [M. 9:13A].

[B]   R. Samuel bar Nahman in the name of R. Jonathan: "This refers to Samuel and David."

[C]   R. Ba bar Kahana in the name of Rab: "This refers to Gad and Nathan."

[D]   R. Jeremiah, R. Samuel bar Isaac in the name of Rab: "This refers to Jeremiah and Baruch."

[E]   From the following saying, it is indicated that in the view of R. Joshua b. Levi, "This is Jeremiah and Baruch."

[F]   For R. Joshua b. Levi said, " 'He set himself to seek God in the days of Zechariah, who instructed him in the fear of God; [and as long as he sought the Lord, God made him prosper]' (2 Chron. 26:2).

[G]   "Who arose after him? It was Jeremiah and Baruch."

[II.A]   **When the latter prophets died, that is, Haggai, Zechariah, and Malachi, then the Holy Spirit came to an end in Israel.**

[B]   **But even so, they caused them to hear through an echo [T. Sot. 13:3].**

[C]   **MᶜSH S: Simeon the Righteous heard an echo from the house of the Holy of Holies: "Annulled is the decree which the enemy planned to bring against the sanctuary, and**

Gasqelges has been killed, and his decrees have been annulled" [T. Sot. 13:6].

[D]   M⁽SH S: Yohanan the high priest heard a word from the house of the Holy of Holies: "The young men who went to make war against Antioch have been victorious," and they wrote down the time and the day.

[E]   And they checked, and the victory was at the very hour [T. Sot. 13:5].

[F]   M⁽SH S: Sages gathered together in the upstairs room of the house of Guria in Jericho, and a heavenly echo came forth and said to them, "There is a man among you who is worthy to receive the Holy Spirit, but his generation is unworthy of such an honor." They all set their eyes upon Hillel the elder.

[G]   And when he died, they said about him, "Woe for the humble man, woe for the pious man, the disciple of Ezra" [T. Sot. 13:3].

[H]   Then another time they were in session in Yabneh and heard an echo saying "There is among you a man who is worthy to receive the Holy Spirit, but the generation is unworthy of such an honor."

[I]   They all set their eyes upon Samuel the Small.

[I]   Why was he called "the Small"? For [out of modesty] he would belittle himself. And some say that it was because he was somewhat smaller than Samuel the Ramatite.

[K]   At the time of his death what did they say? "Woe for the humble man, woe for the pious man, the disciple of Hillel the Elder!"

[L]   Also: he says [said] at the time of his death, "Simeon and Ishmael are destined to be put to death, and the rest of the associates will die by the sword, and the remainder of the people will be up for spoil. After this, great disasters will fall." This he said in Aramaic, [and they did not know what he was saying].

[M]   Also concerning R. Judah b. Baba, they ordained that they should say about him, "Woe for the humble man, woe for the pious man, disciple of Samuel the Small." But the times did not allow it [T. Sot. 13:4].

[**III**.A]   [Tosefta's version:] *When the Temple was destroyed, the Shamir worm ceased, and [so did] the honey of supim [M. 9:13B].*

[B]   **Said R. Judah, "What is the character of this Shamir worm? It is a creature from the six days of Creation.**

[C]   **"When they put it on the stones or on beams, they open up before it like the pages of a notebook. And not only so, but when they put it on iron, [the iron] splits and falls apart before it. And nothing can stand before it.**

[D]   **"How is it kept? They wrap it in tufts of wool and put it in a lead tube full of barley bran."** [Yerushalmi adds:] This is in line with that which is written, "[The Lord is his name,] who makes destruction flash forth against the strong, [so that destruction comes upon the fortress]" (Amos 5:9).

[E]   **"And with it Solomon built the Temple, as it is said, 'There was neither hammer, nor axe, nor any tool of iron heard in the house, while it was being built' "** (1 Kings 6:7), **the words of R. Judah.**

[F]   **R. Nehemiah says, "They sawed with a saw outside, as it is said, 'All these were of costly stones . . . sawed with saws in the house and outside'** (1 Kings 7:9).

[G]   **"Why does Scripture say, 'Inside the house and outside?' Inside the house they were not heard, for they prepared them outside and brought them inside."**

[H]   **Said Rabbi, "The opinion of R. Judah seems to me preferable in regard to the stones of the sanctuary, and the opinion of R. Nehemiah in regard to the stones of [Solomon's] house"** [T. Sot. 15:1].

[**IV**.A]   *The honey of supim.*

[B]   Said R. Eleazar, "It is honey which comes from the inner cells of the honeycomb."

[C]   Said R. Yosé b. R. Haninah, "It is fine flour which floats on the top of a sieve and is [like] dough kneaded with honey and oil."

[**V**.A]   [In regard to M. 9:14A:] said R. Jonathan, "Better was the overripe produce which we ate in our youth than the apricots which we eat in our old age.

[B]   "For with the passage of time the world changes."

[C]   Said R. Hiyya bar Ba, "A *seah* of Arbelit wheat would produce a *seah* of fine flour, a *seah* of flour would produce a *seah* of inferior flour, a *seah* of bran would produce a *seah* of leavings.

[D]   "And nowadays even one for one does not come up."

[VI.A]   *And faithful men came to an end.*

[B]   Said R. Zeira, "Men faithful to the Torah."

[C]   This is in line with the following: A certain rabbi would teach Scripture to his brother in Tyre, and when they came and called him to do business, he would say, "I am not going to take away from my fixed time to study. If the profit is going to come to me, let it come in due course [after my fixed time for study has ended]."

The bulk of the Talmud consists of the Tosefta's relevant materials. The Tosefta's version of unit **III** is in better sequence than Yerushalmi's. Unit **V** seems to me relevant to the following pericope of the Mishnah. Units **IV** and **VI** simply gloss the Mishnah.

9:14

[A]   *Rabban Simeon b. Gamaliel says in the name of R. Joshua, "From the day on which the Temple was destroyed, there is no day on which there is no curse, and dew has not come down as a blessing. The good taste of produce is gone."*

[B]   *R. Yosé says, "Also: the fatness of produce is gone."*

[C]   *R. Simeon b. Eleazar says, "[When] purity [ceased], it took away the taste and scent; [when] tithes [ceased], they took away the fatness of corn."*

[D]   *And sages say, "Fornication and witchcraft made an end to everything."*

[I.A]   It is written, "[God is a righteous judge,] and a God who has indignation every day" (Ps. 7:11).

[B]   Said R. Zeira, "The former [days] are [easier to] endure [since things get worse from day to day (Pené Moshe)]."

[C]   What nullifies [God's anger, so that the world is not completely wiped out]?

[D]   R. Abin in the name of R. Aha, "It is the blessing of the priests which nullifies the anger of God."

[II.A]   [Following Tosefta's order:] **Rabban Simeon b. Gamaliel said, "You should know that the dew has been cursed [M. 9:14A].**

[B]   **"In olden times, when the dew came down on straw and on stubble, it would turn white, as it is said, 'And when the dew had gone up, there was on the face of the wilderness a fine, flakelike thing, fine as hoarfrost on the ground' (Ex. 16:14).**

[C]   **"But now it turns black.**

[D]   **"In olden times, any city which got more dew than its neighbors produced a larger harvest. Now it produces less" [T. Sot. 15:2].**

[III.A]   It is taught: *R. Simeon b. Eleazar says, "[When] purity [ceased], it took away the taste and scent. [When] tithes [ceased], they took away the fatness of corn."*

[B]   From which [produce or wheat] was more removed?

[C]   Said R. Levi bar Haita, "Let us derive the answer from the following: '[Before a stone was placed upon a stone in the Temple of the Lord, how did you fare?] When one came to a heap of twenty measures, there were but ten' [Hag. 2:15–16].

[D]   "When one came to a heap of fifty measures, there were but twenty-five is not written here, but, rather, 'There were but ten.' [So the produce suffered more than wheat.]"

[IV.A]   *And sages say, "Fornication and witchcraft made an end to everything."* [Yerushalmi does not have this statement in its version of the Mishnah.]

The Talmud's gloss of the Mishnah is systematic and predictable.

9:15 [Leiden MS and *editio princeps:* 9:16]

[A]   *In the war against Vespasian they decreed against the wearing of wreaths by bridegrooms and against the wedding drum.*

[B]   *In the war against Titus they decreed against the wearing of wreaths by brides.*

[C]   *And [they decreed] that a man should not teach Greek to his son.*

[D]   *In the last war [Bar Kokhba's] they decreed that a bride should not go out in a palanquin inside the town.*

[E]   *But our rabbis [thereafter] permitted the bride to go out in a palanquin inside the town.*

[I.A]   "The crown has fallen from our head; [woe to us, for we have sinned]" (Lam. 5:16).

[B]   And what sorts of bridegroom's wreaths did they prohibit?

[24c/C]   Gold-embroidered silks.

[D]   [*Editio princeps* omits: D, E] Ba in the name of Rab: "One made of salt and brimstone."

[E]   R. Jeremiah in the name of Rab: "It is one of salt and olives."

[F]   R. Nahman bar Jacob said, "Even one of willows."

[G]   R. Jeremiah plaited and put on a crown of olive branches in honor of a bridal couple.

[H]   Samuel heard and said, "It would have been better for him had his head been removed, rather than that he should have done so."

[I]   And it was like an error which went forth from the ruler.

[II.A]   [*After the last war, they made a decree* against the marriage canopy of bridegrooms'.] **Against what sorts of marriage canopy of bridegrooms' did they make such a decree? It is against those made of gold. But he may make a framework of laths and hand on it anything he wants [T. Sot. 15:9].**

[III.A]   What is a crown worn by a bride [M. 9:15B]?

[B]   It is a golden tiara.

[C]   R. Aqiba made for his wife a golden tiara, and the wife of Rabban Gamaliel was jealous of her.

[D]   He said to her, "If you had done what she did, I would have been glad to make one for you. She sold her braids of hair and gave him the proceeds, so that he might labor in the Light [of Torah]."

[IV.A] They asked R. Joshua, "What is the law as to a man's teaching his son Greek [M. 9:15C]?"

[B] He said to them, "Let him teach it to him when it is neither day nor night,

[C] "for it has been written, '[This book of the law shall not depart out of your mouth,] but you shall meditate on it day and night, [that you may be careful to do according to all that is written in it]' " (Josh. 1:8).

[D] In that case, it should be forbidden for a man to teach his son a trade, for it is written, "You shall meditate on it day and night" (Josh. 1:8).

[E] But did not R. Ishmael teach, " '[I call heaven and earth to witness against you this day, that I have set before you life and death, blessing and curse;] therefore choose life, [that you and your descendants may live]' (Deut. 30:9)—this refers to learning a trade."

[F] R. Ba son of R. Hiyya bar Ba in the name of R. Yohanan, "It is because of traitors [who should not be able to communicate with the enemy]."

[G] R. Abbahu in the name of R. Yohanan, "It is permitted for a man to teach Greek to his daughter, because such learning is an ornament for her."

[H] Simeon bar Ba heard and said, "It is because R. Abbahu wants to teach his daughter such, that he has assigned the teaching to R. Yohanan."

[I] "May a curse come upon me, if I heard it from R. Yohanan!"

[V.A] Who releases decrees issued by the former generation [as at M. 9:15D–E]?

[B] Said R. Yosé b. R. Bun, "He who releases the decrees made by the [former ones] does the same for decrees made by the [latter ones]."

[VI.A] This [M. 9:15A] is in line with the following:

[B] The exilarch sent and asked R. Hisdai, "What is the meaning of that which is written, '[Thus says the Lord God,] 'Remove the turban, and take off thy crown; things shall not remain as they are; exalt that which is low, and abase that which is high' " (Ezek. 21:25).

[C] He said to him, "If the turban is removed, then the crown is removed. [Once the high priest is disrobed, others no longer wear their crowns either.]"

[D] R. Yohanan heard and said, "His name (Hisda) means grace, and what he says is full of grace."

The Talmud does a good job of systematically augmenting the Mishnah. Each of its items is explained in sequence, as indicated.

9:16 [Leiden MS and *editio princeps:* 9:17]

[A] *When R. Meir died, makers of parables came to an end.*

[B] *When Ben Azzai died, diligent students came to an end.*

[C] *When Ben Zoma died, exegetes came to an end.*

[D] *When R. Joshua died, goodness went away from the world.*

[E] *When Rabban Simeon b. Gamaliel died, the locust came, and troubles multiplied.*

[F] *When R. Eleazar b. Azariah died, wealth went away from the sages.*

[G] *When R. Aqiba died, the glory of the Torah came to an end.*

[H] *When R. Hanina b. Dosa died, wonder-workers came to an end.*

[I] *When R. Yosé Qatnuta died, pietists went away.*

[J] *(And why was he called Qatnuta? Because he was the least of the pietists.)*

[K] *When Rabban Yohanan b. Zakkai died, the splendor of wisdom came to an end.*

[L] *When Rabban Gamaliel the Elder died, the glory of the Torah came to an end, and cleanness and separateness perished.*

[M]   When R. Ishmael b. Phabi died, the splendor of the priesthood came to an end.

[N]   When Rabbi died, modesty and fear of sin came to an end.

[O]   R. Pinhas b. Yair says, "When the Temple was destroyed, associates became ashamed and so did free men, and they covered their heads.

[P]   "And wonder-workers became feeble. And violent men and big talkers grew strong.

[Q]   "And none expounds and none seeks [learning] and none asks.

[R]   "Upon whom shall we depend? Upon our Father in heaven."

[S]   R. Eliezer the Great says, "From the day on which the Temple was destroyed, sages began to be like scribes, and scribes like ministers, and ministers like ordinary folk.

[T]   "And the ordinary folk have become feeble.

[U]   "And none seeks.

[V]   "Upon whom shall we depend? Upon our Father in heaven."

[W]   With the footprints of the Messiah: presumption increases, and dearth increases.

[X]   The vine gives its fruit and wine at great cost.

[Y]   And the government turns to heresy.

[Z]   And there is no reproof.

[AA]   The gathering place will be for prostitution.

[BB]   And Galilee will be laid waste.

[CC]   And the Gablan will be made desolate.

[DD]   And the men of the frontier will go about from town to town, and none will take pity on them.

[EE]   And the wisdom of scribes will putrefy.

[FF]   And those who fear sin will be rejected.

[GG]   And the truth will be locked away.

[HH]   Children will shame elders, and elders will stand up before children.

[II] *"For the son dishonors the father and the daughter rises up against her mother, the daughter-in-law against her mother-in-law; a man's enemies are the men of his own house" (Mic. 7:6).*

[JJ] *The face of the generation in the face of a dog.*

[KK] *A son is not ashamed before his father.*

[LL] *Upon whom shall we depend? Upon our Father in heaven.*

[MM] *[R. Pinhas b. Yair says, "Heedfulness leads to cleanliness, cleanliness leads to cleanness, cleanness leads to abstinence, abstinence leads to holiness, holiness leads to modesty, modesty leads to the fear of sin, the fear of sin leads to piety, piety leads to the Holy Spirit, the Holy Spirit leads to the resurrection of the dead, and the resurrection of the dead comes through Elijah, blessed be his memory, Amen."]*

[I.A] **When R. Eliezer died, the glory of the Torah ceased.**

[B] **When R. Joshua died, men of counsel ceased, and reflection ended in Israel [M. 9:16D].**

[C] **When R. Aqiba died, the [strong] arms of Torah were taken away, and the springs of wisdom ceased [cf. M. 9:16G].**

[D] **When R. Eleazar b. Azariah died, the crown of wisdom ceased, for "The crown of the wise is their riches" (Prov. 14:24) [cf. M. 9:16F] [T. Sot. 15:3].**

[E] **When Ben Azzai died, the diligent students came to an end [M. 9:16B] [T. Sot. 15:4].**

[F] **When Ben Zoma died, the exegetes came to an end [M. 9:16C].**

[G] **When R. Haninah b. Dosa died, wonder-workers came to an end in Israel [M. 9:16H].**

[H] **When Abba Yosé B. Qitnit of Qatanta died, piety became small in Israel.**

[I] **Why was he called a man of Qatanta? Because he was the very essence of piety.**

[J] **When Rabban Simeon b. Gamaliel died, locusts came and troubles multiplied [M. 9:16E].**

[K] **When Rabbi died, troubles were doubled [T. Sot. 15:5].**

[II.A]   R. Jacob bar Idi in the name of R. Joshua b. Levi: "When Rabban Yohanan b. Zakkai lay dying, he commanded, saying, 'Clear the courtyard [of articles susceptible to uncleanness] because of uncleanness [consequent upon my death, since the corpse produces heavy contamination], and prepare a throne for Hezekiah, king of Judah.'

[B]   "R. Eliezer, his disciple, when he lay dying, gave orders, saying, 'Clear out the courtyard because of uncleanness, and prepare a throne for Rabban Yohanan ben Zakkai.' "

[C]   And there are those who say, "The one whom his master envisioned is the one whom he envisioned."

[D]   The patriarchate wanted to marry into the house of Pazzi, and he did not agree.

[E]   He told them that they should not be ashamed.

[F]   When he lay dying, he gave orders and said, "Clear out the courtyard because of uncleanness, and prepare a throne for Jehoshaphat, king of Judah."

[G]   Thab said, "Let this one, who pursued honor, come after that one, who fled from honor."

[H]   R. Jacob bar Idi in the name of R. Joshua b. Levi: "M'SH S: Elders assembled in the upstairs room in the house of Gedaya in Jericho, and an echo went out and said to them, 'There are among you two who are worthy of receiving the Holy Spirit, and Hillel the elder is one of them.'

[I]   "They all gazed upon Samuel the Small.

[J]   "Again: The elders got together in the upstairs room in Yavneh, and an echo went forth and said to them, 'There are among you two who are worthy of receiving the Holy Spirit, and Samuel the Small is one of them,' and they all gazed at R. Eliezer b. Hyrcanus.

[K]   "And they were all happy that their opinion was the same as the opinion of the Omnipresent."

The bulk of the Talmud's materials are drawn from the Tosefta. The secondary stories at the end are relevant to the Mishnah's themes, so the whole has clearly been composed as an anthological supplement to the Mishnah.

Abbreviations

Ar.: Arakhin.

A.Z.: Abodah Zarah.

b.: *Babli*, Babylonian Talmud; *ben*, "son of."

B.B.: Baba Batra.

Bek.: Bekhorot.

Ber.: Berakhot.

Bes.: Besah.

Bik.: Bikkurim.

B.M.: Baba Mesia.

B.Q.: Baba Qamma.

Chron.: Chronicles.

Comm.: Commentary.

Dan.: Daniel.

Dem.: Demai.

Deut.: Deuteronomy.

Ed.: Eduyyot.

Editio princeps: Talmud Yerushalmi . . . Venezia. Reprinted without place or date. Originally printed by Daniel Bomberg, 1523–24.

Erub.: Erubin.

Ex.: Exodus.

Ezek.: Ezekiel.

Gen.: Genesis.

Git.: Gittin.

Hag.: Hagigah.

Hal.: Hallah.

Hor.: Horayot.

Hul.: Hullin.

Is.: Isaiah.

Jer.: Jeremiah.

Josh.: Joshua.

Judg.: Judges.

Kel.: Kelim.

Ker.: Keritot.

Ket.: Ketubot.

Kil.: Kilayim.

Lam.: Lamentations.

Leiden MS: *The Palestinian Talmud. Leiden MS. Cod. Scal. 3. A facsimile of the original manuscript.* 4 vols. Jerusalem: Kedem Publishing, 1970.

Lev.: Leviticus.

Lit.: Literally.

M.: Mishnah.

Ma.: Maaserot.

This appendix was prepared by Professor Alan J. Avery-Peck.

Mak.: Makkot.

Makh.: Makhshirin.

Mal.: Malachi.

Me.: Meilah.

Meg.: Megillah.

Men.: Menahot.

Mic.: Micah.

Mid.: Middot.

Miq.: Miqvaot.

M.Q.: Moed Qatan.

M.S.: Maaser Sheni.

Naz.: Nazir.

Ned.: Nedarim.

Neg.: Negaim.

Neh.: Nehemiah.

Nid.: Niddah.

Num.: Numbers.

Oh.: Ohalot.

Or.: Orlah.

Par.: Parah.

Pe.: Peah.

Pené Moshe: Moses Margolies (d. 1780). *Pene Moshé*. Amsterdam: 1754; Leghorn: 1770. Reprinted in the Yerushalmi Talmud.

Pes.: Pesahim.

Prov.: Proverbs.

Ps.: Psalms.

QH: *Qorban ha'edah*. Elijah of Fulda, *Qorban Ha'edah*. Dessau: 1743; Berlin: 1757, 1760–62. Reprinted in the Yerushalmi Talmud.

Qid.: Qiddushin.

Qin.: Qinnim.

Qoh.: Qoheleth (Ecclesiastes).

R.: Rabbi.

R.H.: Rosh Hashshanah.

Sam.: Samuel.

San.: Sanhedrin.

Shab.: Shabbat.

Shabu.: Shabuot.

Sheq.: Sheqalim.

Sot.: Sotah.

Suk.: Sukkuh.

T.: Tosefta.

Ta.: Taanit.

Tam.: Tamid.

Tem.: Temurah.

Ter.: Terumot.

Toh.: Tohorot.

T.Y.: Tebul Yom..

Uqs.: Uqsin.

Y.: Yerushalmi, Talmud of the land of Israel.

Yad.: Yadayyim.

Yeb.: Yebamot.

Yom.: Yoma.

Y.T.: Yom Tob.

Zab.: Zabim.

Zeb.: Zebahim.

Zech.: Zechariah.

Index of Biblical and Talmudic References

25:21, 212
28:21, 188
30:23–24, 205
30:24, 206
30:25, 206
30:31, 207
30:37, 206
35:25, 95

Ezekiel
21:25, 266
23:48, 35–36
39:14, 233
39:14–15, 231
44:15, 184

Genesis
3:16, 175
6:19, 242
12:6, 180
18:15, 176
22:20–21, 158
24:50, 179
25:23, 175
26:12–13, 161
30:16, 97
31:47, 179
34:7, 158
38:13–14, 41
38:14, 32
38:25, 247
38:26, 247–48
46:4, 50
49:10, 207
49:19, 226
50:7, 47
50:9, 47
50:11, 47–48

Haggai
2:11–14, 141
2:15–16, 263

Hosea
2:1, 159
4:14, 251

Isaiah
3:9, 237
9:5, 37
11:9, 47

24:9, 257
27:8, 37
33:12, 190
46:6, 76
48:1, 188
57:2, 52
58:8, 47
60:12, 190
63:11, 153

Jeremiah
10:11, 179
11:5, 72
31:3, 47
45:3, 29

Job
1:1, 158, 161
1:8, 157, 159
1:15, 159
1:17, 159
1:20, 160
2:10, 158
13:15, 155
13:16, 155
15:17–18, 158
15:18, 32
15:19, 32
16:11, 158
17:2, 255
27:2, 155
27:5, 155
27:12, 159
32:2, 160
42:15, 159

Joshua
1:8, 265
3:12, 191
3:16, 192
4:3, 189
4:5, 191
4:8, 189
5:1, 193
8:33, 182–83
8:34, 184
11:33, 187

Judges
5:1–2, 154
5:28, 248

5:29–30, 248
5:31, 248
13:24, 42
13:25, 42
14:1, 41
14:4, 42
14:5, 41
16:21, 40
16:28, 42
16:31, 43

1 Kings
1:33–34, 207
1:36–37, 72
6:7, 261
7:9, 261
15:22, 226

2 Kings
20:14, 192
22:1, 92
24:17, 208

Lamentations
5:14, 257
5:15, 258
5:16, 264

Leviticus
2:2, 86
2:3, 85
2:8, 84, 86
2:9, 84, 86
2:10, 86
2:15, 128
2:16, 86
4:15, 232
5:13, 103
6:14, 83
6:22, 109
6:23, 104, 106, 108
6:25, 224
7:6, 110
7:10, 85–86
7:19, 146
9:22, 194
11:33, 132, 134, 136, 140, 145–46
11:34, 145, 243

11:37, 243
12:8, 56
13:44, 111
13:44–45, 110
13:45, 230
Ch. 14, 214
14:1, 57, 65
14:5, 60
14:6, 56, 67
Ch. 15, 143–44
16:1ff., 194
18:20, 131
19:18, 35
19:20, 21, 65
19:23–25, 218
19:24, 218
20:4, 258
20:4–5, 257–58
21:1, 110
21:4, 117
21:15, 109
22:11, 108
22:12–13
23:17, 58

Micah
7:1, 252
7:6, 268

Nehemiah
9:8, 156

Numbers
5:1–31, 1
5:11–13, 10
5:11–14, 125
5:12, 11, 78–79
5:13, 21, 23, 77, 79, 123, 164, 168
5:14, 9, 23, 75, 115
5:15, 30, 53–54, 58, 79, 84, 88, 93, 114, 125–26
5:16, 34–35
5:17, 60, 66–67
5:18, 34, 53, 62
5:19, 67–68, 72, 115, 175

General Index

Abba Bar Jeremiah: celebrations, ending of rites, 257; Sanhedrin canceled, 257

Abba Bar Kahana: bitter water ordeal, 95; execution of orders for ordeal, 95; exemptions from orders for ordeal, 143; rites in Hebrew language, 190

Abba b. R. Papi, execution of orders for ordeal, 40, 64

Abbahu: bitter water ordeal, 97; celebrations, ending of rites, 257, 265; execution of orders for ordeal, 48, 77, 97, 108; exemptions from orders for ordeal, 139, 145, 151, 154, 163; rites in Hebrew language, 198; Sanhedrin canceled, 257

Abba Mari: anointed for battle and draft exemptions, 226; exemptions from order for ordeal, 139, 163; witnesses to infidelity, 172

Abin: allegations of infidelity, 19, 23, 28–29; celebrations, ending of rites, 263; execution of orders for ordeal, 38, 42, 55, 66–67; exemptions from orders for ordeal, 149; meal-offering, ordeal for infidelity, 55; prohibitions imposed, 28–29

Abina, execution of orders for ordeal, 66

Ada Bar Ahvah, witnesses to infidelity, 171

Aha: anointed for battle and draft exemptions, 201; celebrations, ending of rites, 263; court trial for infidelity, 32; execution of orders for ordeal, 32, 42–43, 45, 66, 110;

exemptions from orders for ordeal, 138, 143, 156; meal-offering, ordeal for infidelity, 110; rites in Hebrew language, 201

Aibu Bar Nigri: execution of orders for ordeal, 41; rites in Hebrew language, 197

Allegations of infidelity, 4, 18–30

Ami: exemptions from orders of ordeal, 128; red heifer rite, 249; rites in Hebrew language, 197, 249

Anointing for battle and draft exemptions, 6–7, 199–221

Aqabiah b. Mehallel, execution of orders for ordeal, 64, 78

Aqiba, 266, 268; allegations of infidelity, 22, 25; anointed for battle and draft exemptions, 200, 226; bitter water ordeal, 91, 93; celebrations, ending of rites, 264; confessions abolished, 252; execution of orders for ordeal, 75–79, 85, 91, 93; exemptions from orders for ordeal, 5, 127–28, 132–34, 136–38, 140–41, 145–46, 148, 150, 156–57, 160, 165, 167–68; meal-offering, ordeal for infidelity, 58, 85; red heifer rite, 191–92, 200, 237–38; rites in Hebrew language, 237–38; witnesses to infidelity, 165, 167–68

Ba: allegations of infidelity, 15, 17; bitter water ordeal, 15, 17; celebrations, ending of rites, 256, 264; exemptions from orders for ordeal, 135, 150; Sanhedrin canceled, 256; witnesses to infidelity, 15, 17